WESLEY

AND

MEN WHO FOLLOWED

Engraved by G. Cook.

John Wesley

WESLEY

AND

MEN WHO FOLLOWED

Iain H. Murray

THE BANNER OF TRUTH TRUST

THE BANNER OF TRUTH TRUST
3 Murrayfield Road, Edinburgh EH12 6EL, UK
P O Box 621, Carlisle, PA 17013, USA

*

© Iain H. Murray 2003
ISBN 0 85151 835 4

*

Typeset in 12/14 pt Galliard by
Initial Typesetting Services, Dalkeith
Printed in Great Britain by
The Bath Press,
Bath

To
J. GRAHAM AND FLORA MILLER
ESTEEMED FRIENDS,
ENCOURAGERS AND
EXAMPLES

Contents

Illustrations

Preface

While preparing the following pages I have often thought of how our lives are changed by events that took place before we were born. In my own life I think often of the Rev. James Shiphardson who died in Durham City in 1929, after forty years in the Methodist ministry. His study and splendid library, contained in a separate brick building in his back garden, was then well kept but shut up for twenty-three years. Then Mr Shiphardson's daughter, now advanced in years, passed on a message to some of us students in the university that she had books for disposal and the old building was re-opened. At very modest prices we were allowed to take our pick from rows of the best books I ever saw in Durham, some of which have been with me ever since. I owe a great debt to the man who died before I was born.

Another event which affected me was more remote. About the year 1850, Robert Roberts, a Methodist minister, preached on a Whit Sunday evening in Abergavenny, South Wales. One of the lives permanently changed that night was that of a man named George Morgan. A Christian home of Morgans came into being after that conversion and out of that home came another preacher, G. Campbell Morgan, who became minister of Westminster Chapel, London. In the 1930s, when Morgan was in his second period at that church, he changed the future direction of the congregation by calling D. Martyn Lloyd-Jones as his colleague. Two decades later, in 1956, the present writer was called to assist Lloyd-Jones. It was all linked to that one sermon in Abergavenny.

In 1956 I had little acquaintance with Methodism, apart from Wesley's sermons, but although Westminster Chapel was Congregational and, at that date, Calvinistic, the name of John Wesley was held in high regard. My own regard deepened in 1958 when Wesley was my subject for three mid-week meetings, and I was living in the excitement of a first reading of Luke Tyerman's three-volume *Life and Times of John Wesley.*

I owe much to men who either were Methodist or had been so in times past. The Rev. J. D. Blinco, when minister of the Methodist Central Hall, Southampton, was one of the first men from whom I heard clear gospel preaching. Later, in the mid-1950s, it was a mark of Joe Blinco's catholicity, when minister at Highgate in London, that he sent Jack Cullum, a businessman who had been recently converted, to Westminster Chapel. Mr Cullum, whose family background was Methodist, was among the listeners when I spoke on Wesley. It was he who provided the means for reprinting the older evangelical classics. Such was the origin of the publishers of this present volume. Other early helpers in the work of the Banner of Truth Trust were Mr S. M. Houghton and Mr John Raynar, the former from Lancashire and the latter from Yorkshire Methodist stock. When, from 1982 to 1991, I was in Australia, with my wife and most of our family, it was John and Elspeth Raynar who made their home at Lolworth a haven for us on visits to the United Kingdom. There, in the bedroom we used so often, was the fourteen-volume edition of Wesley's *Works* which I have used again in the preparation of these pages.

I had to go to Australia to have my interest in Methodism awakened in a new way. Prior to living there, I had no conception of what the Methodists had achieved so remarkably both in that land and among the islands of the Pacific. It is a story worthy of a volume on its own and it fills me with admiration to this day. On the same subject I owe much to what I learned from the Reeve family of Gowrie, Campbelltown; from Rex and Joan Burns of Kingsgrove; and from Robert and Elaine Evans, of Hazelbrook – all places in New South Wales. Nor was the knowledge gained only of Australian Christian history: it was in Australia that I first heard of such men as Thomas Collins and Gideon Ouseley.

This book took shape in connection with an invitation to speak on John Wesley at a conference at the Epworth Centre, on St Simon's Island, Georgia, in June 2002. It was sponsored by Pastor Steve Martin and Heritage Church, of Fayetteville, Georgia. Only a mile from where we met, John and Charles Wesley had ministered at Frederica in 1736. Today the old settlement of Frederica is no more but the research facility at the Epworth Centre contains a library of 6,000 books relating to all aspects of Methodist history. The memory of those shelves is a constant reminder to me of how very much remains unsaid in these few pages.

Thanks are also due to Phil Roberts whose work with Tentmaker Publications has brought old Methodist treasures to light;[1] to Ian Barter and John R. de Witt for reading the manuscript; to my colleagues in the Banner of Truth Trust; and, as ever, to my wife, without whom neither this nor so many other things could be done.

Due to many factors my thinking on Wesley has matured over the years. I am not an uncritical admirer, but in the continuing struggle which divides those 'born

[1] Tentmaker Publications, 121 Hartshill Road, Stoke-on-Trent, Staffs, UK ST4 7LU.

after the flesh' and those 'born after the Spirit' (*Gal.* 4:29), and also divides formal religion from supernatural Christianity, there is much to be re-learned from the Methodist leader who was born three hundred years ago.

IAIN H. MURRAY
Edinburgh,
March 2003

Principal Abbreviations

Works   Thomas Jackson (ed.), *The Works of John Wesley*, 14 volumes, 1829–1831, London, Wesleyan-Methodist Bookroom.

Reprinted and bound as 7 vols, Grand Rapids, Baker, 1998.

Works (Abingdon), Frank Baker (ed. and others), *The Works of John Wesley*, 26 volumes, 1975–2003 and in progress, Oxford and Nashville, TN, OUP and Abingdon.

Journal   Nehemiah Curnock (ed.), *The Journal of the Rev. John Wesley*, 8 vols., London, Robert Culley, 1909.

Letters   John Telford, *The Letters of the Rev. John Wesley*, 8 vols., London, Epworth, 1931.

Tyerman, *Wesley*   Luke Tyerman, *The Life and Times of the Rev. John Wesley*, sixth edition, 8 vols., London, Hodder and Stoughton, 1890.

Part One

Wesley

I should rejoice (so little ambitious am I to be at the head of any sect or party) if the very name [Methodist] might never be mentioned more, but buried in eternal oblivion. But if that cannot be, at least let those who will use it, know the meaning of the word they use. Let us not always be fighting in the dark. Come, and let us look one another in the face. And perhaps some of you who hate what I am *called*, may love what I *am* by the grace of God; or rather, what 'I follow after, if that I may apprehend that for which also I am apprehended of Christ Jesus.'

John Wesley
The Character of a Methodist,
1742

The Foundery, Moorfields.
The first buildings owned by Wesley in London. The main part was
adapted to seat fifteen hundred people, other rooms were used for
bands and living accommodation for preachers, including Wesley.
Susanna Wesley died here in 1742.

Chapter 1

From Oxford Don to Open-Air Preacher

John Wesley left behind him a family of churches among which his reputation was to be revered across the earth. Twenty-six years after his death, William Carvosso spoke for thousands when he wrote of Wesley in the year 1817, 'I often think I shall praise God to all eternity for His raising him up, and sending him into Cornwall.'[1] Ten years later, as missionaries established an outpost in one of the darkest corners of the Pacific – Bay of Islands, New Zealand – affection led them to name it 'Wesleydale'. A century and a half later Wesley's 'Twelve Rules' for preachers were still being used in Papua New Guinea. Summing up a life-long study of Wesley, Frank Baker wrote in 1974: 'In all sincerity, and with all the weight I can muster, I claim that whatever his errors of memory, in judgment, in tact, throughout his long adult life until his death at the age of 87 in 1791, John Wesley consistently and courageously lived to the glory of God.'[2]

---

[1] *Memoir of William Carvosso*, written by himself (London: Wesleyan-Methodist Book-Room, 1835), pp. 87–8.

[2] 'The Real John Wesley', in *Methodist History*, News Bulletin, Quarterly Review, July 1974 (Philadelphia: World Methodist Historical Society), p. 197.

These quotations are from Methodists, but it would be a great mistake to suppose that Wesley's reputation as a Christian leader depends on that source. Charles Hodge, the Presbyterian Princetonian, placed him among the very few whom he called 'world controllers', men whose power affected not only the faith and character of their own time but coming generations.[1] The Baptist C. H. Spurgeon said that his own ministry compared with that of Wesley was like a 'farthing candle' beside the sun.[2] Bishop J. C. Ryle called him 'a mighty instrument in God's hand for good',[3] and believed that the Church of England would have fared better if Wesley had become Archbishop of Canterbury.[4]

In recent years it has been customary in some circles to represent George Whitefield to the disadvantage of John Wesley, almost as though Wesley is a figure we can ignore. But that is certainly not a judgment which Whitefield himself would have owned. In the year Whitefield was converted he called Wesley 'my spiritual father in Christ'.[5] In later years he concluded a letter to Wesley with the words, 'your most affectionate, younger brother, in the gospel of our common Lord';[6] and at the end of his life it was Wesley that he designated to preach his funeral sermon.

John Wesley was born on 17 June 1703, at Epworth in Lincolnshire where his father was rector of the parish church. His parents, Samuel and Susanna Wesley had

---

[1] C. Hodge, *Systematic Theology* (London: Nelson, 1874), vol. 3, p. 485.
[2] 'John Wesley' (a lecture given in 1861), *Banner of Truth* magazine, July–August, 1969, p. 58.
[3] J. C. Ryle, *The Christian Leaders of the Eighteenth Century* (Edinburgh: Banner of Truth, 1978), p. 105.
[4] Marcus L. Loane, *John Charles Ryle 1816–1900* (London: Hodder and Stoughton, 1983), p. 64.
[5] *George Whitefield's Letters: 1734–1742* (Edinburgh: Banner of Truth, 1976), p. 484.
[6] *Works of George Whitefield*, vol. 3 (London: Dilly, 1771), p. 45.

nineteen children. Only ten, seven girls and three boys, survived infancy. Of these the eldest son, Samuel, left home when John was only one year old. Closest to John throughout life, and born four years after him, was his brother Charles. Their able mother schooled all her offspring at home until the boys were old enough to go to boarding schools. From the age of ten to sixteen John was at Charterhouse; the following year, 1720, he went on to Christ Church, Oxford. At that date the university was pre-eminently designed to prepare men for the ministry of the Church of England, and into this ministry John Wesley was ordained as a deacon in 1725. For the next ten years much of his life was spent at Oxford, tutoring students as a Fellow of Lincoln College, and enjoying a social as well as an increasingly religious life. He preached at various times and places, including on two occasions in the university pulpit of St Mary's. There were also lengthy visits to Epworth, where he helped, but he declined to leave Oxford and take up the work there when his father died in 1735.

Up to this point it might be said that Wesley's career was predictable and similar to that of many other ambitious young men. In 1735, however, came a surprising change of direction. The Oxford scholar, now thirty-two years old, decided to become a missionary to the Indians of North America. Accordingly, he sailed for Savannah, Georgia, along with his brother Charles and two other Oxford graduates. His *Journal* for Friday, 6 February 1736 records, 'About eight in the morning I first set my foot on American ground.' A week later he first met Tomo-chachi, 'King of the Savannah nation' – Wesley dressed in his black clergyman's gown, and the chief with face stained red, a feather in his ear and covered by one large blanket.

Why did Wesley choose to go to Savannah? The reputation of its weather was hardly an attraction,[1] and it certainly was not the prospect of bodily comfort. Georgia, as Britain's latest colony, was one of the most newsworthy places of the 1730s. 'Savannah Town' had won attention and stirred the public imagination as soon as it came into existence in 1733. When Wesley, with over 200 others arrived three years later, it had no church building, probably only one store, and so few houses for the population of around 300 that there were nights when he slept in the open air and on the ground. The British had established Savannah to defend the southern frontier of their American colonies against the French and Spaniards. In addition, advantages for trade were anticipated, and the provision of land for poor immigrants. None of this explains Wesley's decision to join the settlement. From childhood he had been made to think of the need for missionary outreach, and when he was asked by the Society for the Propagation of the Gospel (SPG) to be a missionary to the Indians in Georgia he saw the invitation as an opportunity not to be set aside. Further, because no church traditions were yet established in Georgia, he had a vision for the introduction of a form of Christianity much closer, as he believed, to the original apostolic pattern.

But as well as this public reason for going to America Wesley also had more private ones. Despite his high ambitions for work among the Indians, he was inwardly a dissatisfied man. From the time of his ordination, and

---

[1] On 10 June 1738 Whitefield was to write from Savannah: 'All things have happened better than expectation. America is not so horrid a place as it is represented to be. The heat of the weather, lying on the ground, etc. are mere painted lions in the way.' *Whitefield's Letters*, p. 44.

more seriously since 1729, he had sought inward holiness of life and not found it. His hope was that going to Savannah would be good for his own soul: 'My chief motive, to which all the rest are subordinate, is the hope of saving my own soul. I hope to learn the true sense of the gospel of Christ by preaching it to the heathen.'[1]

There was one particular hindrance to 'the spiritual life' which he hoped would be solved by the trans-Atlantic location. At Oxford he had found that some of the charming female company which he at times enjoyed was unsettling to his religious commitment, particularly since he had been impressed by early-century arguments for celibacy in the Christian ministry: 'I was then persuaded', he later wrote to his brother, '"it was unlawful for a priest to marry," grounding that persuasion on the (supposed) sense of the primitive church.'[2] In Georgia, he anticipated, there would be no such attractive company to divert him from his calling.

Once settled in Savannah, things turned out very differently from his expectations. He found himself so tied down by duties among the British settlers that he had little time for Indian contacts; and the more he learned of the Indians the less expectation he had for success among them. Only a fraction of Savannah's inhabitants belonged to the Church of England and of those who did there were soon a number who did not agree at all with his view of 'primitive Christianity'. He insisted, for instance, that the only orthodox baptism for babies was by triple immersion and if parents declined this treatment

---

[1] Letter of 10 October 1735, *Works of John Wesley*, vol. 25, Letters 1721–1739, ed. Frank Baker (Oxford: Clarendon Press, 1975), p. 439. Hereafter this edition of Wesley's writings I will identify as *Works* (Abingdon).

[2] 25 September 1749, *Works 9* (Abingdon), vol. 26, p. 381. It was a subsequent reading of Bishop Beveridge that disabused him of this opinion.

there would be no baptism. But his main problem turned out to be the one that he thought he had left behind in England. Sophy Hopkey was the teenage niece of one of Savannah's chief citizens. Wesley fell for her and was soon in a turmoil as great as anything he had known before. The attractions of marriage collided with resolutions to remain single. For a time the former prevailed and he even seems to have gone as far as an informal proposal of marriage to Sophy. But his hesitancies re-asserted themselves and in the end, Sophy, confused by her half-hearted suitor, decided to marry someone else. Wesley was mortified.

Although no longer her suitor, as her pastor he meant to remain the overseer of her conduct and in this role he declined to admit her to the Lord's Table in August 1737. From that point on his continuance in the town became untenable. He was cited to appear before the magistrates for defaming Sophy's character along with other charges. The community was divided over him and in December he thought it best to take ship before the formal trial commenced. Thus his two years away from home ended in no small controversy and failure.

In February 1738 Wesley was back in England, and a few months later came the great crisis. On 24 May 1738, the best-known incident of his life, he became, as he believed, a real Christian. It happened in a small gathering in Aldersgate Street, London, when someone was reading Luther's Preface to the Epistle to the Romans:

'About a quarter before nine, while he was describing the change which God works in the heart through faith in Christ, I felt my heart strangely warmed. I felt I did trust in Christ, Christ alone for salvation; and an assurance was given me, that He had taken away *my* sins, even *mine*, and saved *me* from the law of sin and death.'[1]

From this point Wesley was a changed man. Had he died before 24 May 1738, his name would have been unknown to history. He would certainly never have become, in Hodge's phrase, a 'world controller'. It was what happened to him in the year of his thirty-fifth birthday that made the difference and the effects of the change in him were immediate. Previously he had learned the art of sermon writing, and had written many, now he could *preach*. This he proceeded to do. On 11 June, eighteen days after Aldersgate Street, he was in the pulpit of St Mary's, Oxford, when his text was, 'By grace are ye saved through faith' (*Eph.* 2:8). Salvation, he told his hearers, meant,

'a deliverance from guilt and punishment, by the atonement of Christ actually applied to the soul of the sinner now believing on Him, and a deliverance from the power of sin, through Christ *formed in his heart*. So that he who is thus justified, or saved by faith, is indeed *born again*. He is *born again of the Spirit* unto a new life.'

If this teaching was new to many of the churchmen who heard him, newer still was the preacher's evident belief that many of them were not Christians at all. 'None can trust in the merits of Christ', he told them, 'until they have renounced their own.' Those who trust in their own obedience to God's law were 'as far from life and salvation as the depth of hell from the height of heaven.' 'Never', he declared, 'was the maintaining of this doctrine more

---

[1] *Journal of the Rev. John Wesley*, edited by Nehemiah Curnock (London: Culley, 1909), vol. 1, pp. 475–6. Hereafter, *Journal*. The *Journal* was originally published by Wesley at intervals in twenty-one duodecimo volumes.

seasonable than it is at this day . . . It was this doctrine, which our Church justly calls *the strong rock and foundation of the Christian religion*, that first drove Popery out of these kingdoms; and it is this alone can keep it out. Nothing but this can give a check to that immorality which hath "overspread the land as a flood".[1]

Wesley was excluded from some Church of England pulpits before the end of 1738. George Whitefield, who had begun to preach the same truth earlier, was also being excluded and this led first him, then Wesley, to preach in the open air. When, later, Wesley returned to the scene of his childhood at Epworth, and found he was not allowed to speak in the church, he preached standing on top of his father's flat grave stone to 'such a congregation as I believe Epworth never saw before . . . I am well assured that I did far more good to my Lincolnshire parishioners by preaching three days on my father's tomb, than I did by preaching three years in his pulpit.'[2]

If Wesley was now a different preacher, the change in his private life was no less. Prayer took on new meaning. 'I began', he says, 'to pray with all my might.' The end of the year 1738 was marked by unforgettable prayer

---

[1] *Works of John Wesley* (*London: Wesleyan-Methodist Book-Room*, n.d.), vol. 1, p. 15. Future references to *Works*, refer to this, the fourteen-volume edition edited by Thomas Jackson, unless otherwise stated. Although Wesley's first recorded sermon is from January 1727, it is significant that Wesley placed the sermon quoted above first in the edition of his *Works* published in 1771–74. In another sermon on 'Justification by Faith' he writes that God '"made Christ to be sin for us" that is, treated him as a sinner, punishing him for our sins; so he counteth us righteous, from the time we believe in him' (Ibid., p. 62). The truth he was preaching was the same for which Thomas Cranmer, in the same Oxford church, was condemned to martyrdom on 21 March 1556.

[2] *Journal*, vol. 3, p. 19, and *Works*, vol. 12, p. 84. The 'three years' refers to the period August 1727–November 1729 when he served as his father's curate at Epworth and Wroote (a curacy within the parish). I will discuss later whether Wesley's change was quite a sudden as it seemed to be in the common representation that I have give above.

meetings. One meeting on 31 December lasted until three in the morning of the first day of the New Year, 1739. After another such meeting on 5 January, Whitefield, who was present, said, 'We parted with full conviction that God was going to do great things among us.'

With this praying there was a new spirit of praise. For several years Wesley had been interested in hymnody and had even published a small hymn book while in Savannah. But writing of the pre-1738 period, Nehemiah Curnock, editor of Wesley's diaries and *Journal*, observed that before May 1738, 'There is little joy in his religion. His sacred song is set in a minor key. It is a wail of distress and disappointment. In his first Diary there is no rejoicing.'[1] What a change was to follow in this regard! In 1739 and 1740 new books of vibrant hymns came from Wesley, together with many written by his brother Charles that were soon to be on the lips of thousands. Curnock says that Wesley now carried about with him a manuscript hymn-book and the page more stained by frequent use than any other has on it the words

> Oh for a thousand tongues to sing
> My great Redeemer's praise.

Charles Wesley had entered into the same experience as his brother. Joseph Williams, a stranger who attended a meeting led by Charles, has left us a description which conveys some idea of the spirit which now possessed these men. He writes:

'We found them singing a hymn; he then prayed; and proceeded to expound the twelfth chapter of the Gospel of John, in a sweet, savoury, spiritual manner. This was followed by singing another hymn; and he then prayed

[1] Introductory, *Journal*, vol. 1, p. 35.

. . . Never did I see or hear such evident marks of fervency in the service of God. At the close of every petition a serious Amen, like a gentle, rushing sound of waters, ran through the whole audience. Such evident marks of a lively devotion I was never witness to before. If there be such a thing as heavenly music upon earth, I heard it there. I do not remember my heart to have been so elevated in Divine love and praise, as it was there and then, for many years past, if ever.'[1]

* * * * *

We have seen the great change in Wesley which occurred in 1738, but to understand the man it is necessary to go back some years earlier and to ask what were the influences which explain his previous religious views.

Among those influences the first place belongs to the ethos of his home. His parents, Samuel and Susanna, had both been born into distinguished Puritan families, his father in 1662 and his mother in 1669. It was the decade which saw the ultimate failure of the Puritans to reform the Church of England. When some two thousand ministers and teachers were ejected from positions in that Church in 1662, Wesley's grandparents – John Wesley and Samuel Annesley – were among that number. Those thus ejected, and their followers, were given the name of 'Dissenters', and the government took care to weaken their testimony further by various penalties, including the exclusion of all Dissenting students from the universities.

---

[1] Quoted by Luke Tyerman, *Life and Times of John Wesley* (London: Hodder and Stoughton, 1890), vol. 1, pp. 253–4. Hereafter, Tyerman, *Wesley.*

Children do not necessarily follow parents; by the time John Wesley's parents married in 1688 they had both transferred their loyalty away from the Dissenting cause and become decided members of the Church of England. Samuel Wesley was ordained in that Church in the same year. No sure explanation for this parental change has survived.[1] Samuel can barely have known his father for he was still a child when the latter died, about seven years after his separation from his congregation in Dorset. His mother, daughter of John White, one of the leading Westminster divines, was left in poverty. The friends of these Wesley grandparents included such men as Joseph Alleine.

We would have had more light on the reason for Susanna Annesley's defection if it had not been for a fire which destroyed the Epworth rectory when John was six years old. Among the possessions lost at that time was an account by her of how she came to attach herself to the Church of England. In that document, she later noted, 'I had included the main of the controversy between Dissenters and the Established Church, as far as it had come to my knowledge.'[2] Her father was one of the leading London Puritans. After his ejection from St Giles, Cripplegate, and ten years of enforced silence, the Declaration of Indulgence of 1672 permitted Dr Annesley to take up ministry in a Dissenting congregation in Little

---

[1] See L. Tyerman, *The Life and Times of the Rev. Samuel Wesley* (London: Simpkin, Marshall, 1866), pp. 77–9. Samuel Wesley had met John Owen and, curiously, on the latter's death, it was £10 from his estate which first enabled the former Dissenter to go up to Oxford.

[2] Quoted in Richard Green, *John Wesley, Evangelist* (London: Religious Tract Society, 1905), p. 22. In Wesley's *Journal* (Sept. 3, 1739), he records comment from his mother on her father's ministry. It would appear this record is coloured by the anti-Puritan feeling that had long prevailed in the family.

St Helens, Bishopsgate Street, London. His worth is evident in the *Morning Exercises*, a series of Puritan sermons continued in the city from 1659 to 1689, and in which he took a major share.[1] 'Nothing abated his cheerfulness', wrote one who knew him. 'He had uninterrupted peace in his spirit, and assurance of God's love, for the last thirty years of his life.'[2] As this committed Puritan lived until 1696 it must have been with mixed feelings that he viewed his youngest daughter's marriage to Samuel Wesley, and their subsequent settlement in a Church of England parish in Lincolnshire in 1692. But he had known greater reasons for concern for his youngest daughter. While still a teenager Susanna had been influenced by the Socinian form of unbelief that led her away from all true Christianity; it was from this state, it is said, that she was rescued by her future husband.

As a young man Samuel Wesley did not lack contact with his father's tradition. He heard such preachers as Stephen Charnock and John Bunyan, and, for a time, attended a Dissenting academy. But at this date the prospects for serving in the Dissenting ministry were bleak,[3] and, being ambitious to study at Oxford, the loss of influence and opportunities involved in an attachment to the Dissenters may well have had a bearing on his decision. Later he was engaged in a fiery public disagreement with Dissenters on what he alleged was the

---

[1] *The Morning Exercises* were published in six volumes between 1660 and 1690. Two of the volumes contain Prefaces by Annesley and there are six of his sermons. The six volumes were reprinted in 1844, which edition was republished as *Puritan Sermons 1659–1689* (Wheaton: Richard Owen Roberts, 1981).

[2] Edmund Calamy, *An Abridgement of Mr Baxter's History of his Life and Times* (London, 1702), p. 214.

[3] Not until June 1694 were any men ordained for the Dissenting ministry. The first occasion occurred in Annesley's meeting-house.

poor state of education among them, and vowed he would 'never drop the controversy'.[1]

It is true there could be other reasons for dissatisfaction with Dissent at the time when Samuel Wesley and his future wife were growing up. The Puritan tradition was less attractive than it had been earlier in the century. Controversies over details of doctrine, an over-scrupulous regard for points of church government, the fragmentation into Presbyterians, Independents and Baptists, too much engagement in politics (Puritans would long be blamed for the overthrow of the monarchy in the days of Charles I) – all these factors contributed to the weakness of Dissent. 'Alas!' wrote Oliver Heywood in 1682, 'what divisions, what decays, deadness, unprofitableness! The old Puritan spirit is gone; we are woefully degenerated.'[2]

Such conditions could well induce a younger generation to listen to the able divines of the Restoration period who were now directing the thought of the Church of England. Yet to be attracted that way was to turn from settled evangelical convictions. Upholding the beliefs of the Reformation was not the priority of the late seventeenth-century divines of the Church of England, several of whom were ambitious to find a way between Roman Catholicism and Protestantism. As a result evangelical beliefs went into eclipse. They were certainly not preached at Epworth in Samuel Wesley's day. The ministry of the

---

[1] For documentation, see *John Wesley*, edited by Albert C. Outler (New York: OUP, 1964), pp. 5–7. Outler says that in 1705 Samuel Wesley 'was jailed in Lincoln Castle, ostensibly for debt but actually because of the offence which he had given by his violent attacks upon the Dissenters.' The offence must have been considerable to provoke such action for it was not a time when Dissent was in favour.

[2] *Whole Works of Oliver Heywood*, vol. 3 (Idle: Vint, 1825), p. 426.

Church of England had come to be marked by high views of the efficacy of the sacraments, and clergy praised Christian virtues on the assumption that their baptized hearers were all already Christians. It was an Anglican of a later generation who summarized the position after 1662 with the words: 'When the Puritans were expelled, they carried with them the spiritual light of the Church of England; and yet even amongst themselves the light had become dim and the glory had departed.'[1]

Thus John Wesley was born into a rectory where 'High Church' beliefs prevailed. 'I believed, till I was about ten years old I had not sinned away that "washing of the Holy Ghost" which was given me in baptism.'[2] 'I am an High Churchman, the son of an High Churchman.'[3] The authors he heard praised were certainly not those whom his grandparents had esteemed. And while religion was taken seriously, it was not a religion that interfered with such things as card playing, dancing and the theatre.

The correspondence between Wesley and his mother, when he became a student at Oxford confirms that it was not Puritan theology that was embraced in the Epworth rectory. Among the letters of Susannah to 'Jacky' are ones dealing with such questions as assurance of salvation and

---

[1] J. B. Marsden, *History of the Later Puritans* (London: Hamilton, Adams & Co., 1852), p. 473.

[2] *Journal,* vol. 1, p. 465. Curiously, Tyerman wanted to deny that John's father was High Church and yet he provides testimony that he was (*Samuel Wesley*, pp. 439,458). Samuel wrote to John in 1734 of 'austerity and mortification' as 'a means of promoting holiness' (Ibid., p. 433). 'My father did not die unacquainted with the faith of the gospel,' John wrote in 1748. 'What he experienced before I know not; but I know that during his last illness, which continued eight months, he enjoyed a clear sense of acceptance with God' (*Samuel Wesley*, p. 444).

[3] *Letters of John Wesley.* ed. John Telford, vol. 6 (London: Epworth, 1931), p. 156. The context of the quotation has to do with 'notions of passive resistance and non-resistance' in which, he says, he 'was bred up' from childhood. Hereafter, *Letters.*

predestination. She believed that there is a 'reasonable persuasion of the forgiveness of sins, which a true penitent feels when he reflects on the evidences of his own sincerity'. In his reply John wrote, 'I am not satisfied what evidence there can be of our final perseverance, till we have finished our course.' He proceeded to comment on how the predestination of part only of mankind to salvation, with others 'only born to eternal death', contradicts 'the clearest ideas we have of the Divine nature'. His mother agreed and did not want him to stumble over Article 17 of the 39 Articles on 'Predestination and Election.' She assured him that 'election is founded upon foreknowledge . . . God saw who would make a right use of their powers, and accept offered mercy.' 'John Wesley', commented Luke Tyerman, 'substantially adopted his mother's predestinarian views.'[1] In fact they were common among most Church people who were against Dissent.

For confirmation in High Church belief John Wesley could not have gone anywhere better than Oxford. One of his favourite early authors was Bishop Jeremy Taylor who, along with others, taught him to believe, 'Whether God has forgiven us or not we know not; therefore still be sorrowful for ever having sinned.'[2] The writings of this same mentor encouraged clergy to assess their hearers in the following manner:

'They are the smallest number of Christian men, who can be divided by the character of a certain holiness, or an open villany: and between these there are many degrees

---

[1] For this correspondence see Tyerman, *Wesley*, vol. 1, pp. 38–40, and more fully in *Works* (Abingdon), vol. 25, pp. 175–6, 180.
[2] Quoted by Wesley in 1725, *Works* (Abingdon), vol. 25, p. 169. The benefit of keeping a diary was something Wesley learned from Taylor.

of latitude, and most are of a middle sort, concerning which we are tied to make the judgments of charity, and possibly God may too.'[1]

Of this 'middle sort' Wesley certainly was when he was ordained in 1725. It was not until 1729, he later wrote, that 'I began not only to read, but to study the Bible, as the one, the only standard of truth.' By that date he had become concerned about his soul and particularly how he was to find inward holiness, as we have already noted. The quest had led him to broaden his reading and to turn to such mystic writers as Thomas à Kempis, William Law and others who depicted the experience he sought to attain and directed him to find it along a pathway of solitude and asceticism. The Christian life meant, primarily, self-effort, self-denial, and self-discipline in the imitation of Christ. Such was the ethos which John and his brother Charles encouraged in the 'Holy Club' they established at Oxford before they went to Georgia in 1735. Referring to those university years, Wesley was to write, 'When I was at Oxford, and lived like an hermit, I saw not how any busy man could be saved. I scarce thought it possible to retain the Christian spirit amidst the noise and bustle of the world.'[2]

The writings of the mystics were thus a second powerful influence on Wesley's thinking and undoubtedly influenced his decision to go to America in 1735. 'Cannot you save your own soul in England as well as in Georgia?' was a question he put in the mouth of a supporter of the Georgia mission to whom he wrote on 10 October 1735. To which

---

[1] Jeremy Taylor, *The Rule and Exercises of Holy Dying* (1650, repr., London: Rivington, 1833), p. xvi.
[2] *Letters*, vol. 6, p. 292.

he answered: 'No; neither can I hope to attain the same degree of holiness here which I may there.'[1]

What Wesley began to discover in Georgia was not at all what he had imagined and it brings us to the third and the most decisive influence upon his thinking. This time it was not through books but people. Other passengers on his voyage out were Moravians, devout emigrants and missionaries from the evangelical settlements led by Count Zinzendorf and others in Germany. Once at Savannah he met the Moravian leader, August Spangenberg, and he recorded their conversation as follows:

'I asked Mr Spangenberg's advice with regard to myself – to my conduct. He told me he could say nothing till he had asked me two or three questions. "Do you know yourself? Have you the witness within yourself? Does the Spirit of God bear witness with your spirit that you are a child of God?" I was surprised and knew not what to answer. He observed it, and asked, "Do you know Jesus Christ?" I paused, and said, "I know He is the Saviour of the world." "True," replied he: "but do you know He has saved you?" I answered, "I hope He has died to save me." He only added, "Do you know yourself?" I said, "I do." But I fear they were vain words.'[2]

Wesley's esteem for the Moravians deepened in the months that followed. When a house was finally provided for him in Savannah it was to be shared with some of these surprising people who, he noted, were 'always employed, always cheerful themselves, and in good humour with one another . . . they adorned the gospel of our Lord in all things.'

---

[1] *Letters*, vol. 1, p. 190.   [2] *Journal*, vol. 1, p. 151.

By these testimonies Wesley came gradually into the light of evangelical belief.[1] On his return journey from Georgia, he could write in his Journal that he has learned 'what I least suspected, that I, who went to America to convert others, was never myself converted to God.'[2] It is true he had always believed in the atonement but not as the very centre of belief and not as the meritorious cause of all grace, received by personal faith in Christ alone. Once back in London it was among other Moravians that he found new congenial friends and it was in their company at Aldersgate Street that the truth was confirmed to him that changed his life – 'absolutely renouncing all dependence, in whole or in part, upon my own works of righteousness; on which I had really grounded my hope of salvation, though I knew it not, from my youth up.'[3]

Thereafter preaching faith in Christ crucified was at the heart of his message. In 1745 he could write: 'About seven years since we began preaching *inward, present* salvation, as attainable by *faith alone.* For preaching *this doctrine* we were forbidden to preach in the churches.'[4] Wesley understood well the teaching of the clergy who opposed him for he had once believed it himself. It was put to him on one occasion by a Dr Robertson who wrote, 'The immediate, essential, necessary means of reuniting men to God are prayer, mortification, and self-denial.' To which he answered: 'No, the immediate, essential, necessary means of reuniting me to God is living

---

[1] Although his experience of 24 May 1738 was sudden, the change in Wesley's thought was gradual, witness the fact that he had started to preach justification by faith some weeks *before* that date.

[2] *Journal*, vol. 1, p. 422.

[3] Ibid., p. 472.

[4] *Works* (Abingdon), vol. 26, p. 125.

faith, and that alone. Without this I cannot be reunited to God. With this I cannot but be reunited.'[1]

But the message was not that God is reconciled to sinners by accepting their faith, as though there was salvation *in* faith. Wesley responded to another critic that

'There was no merit at all in good works. Most true. No, nor in *faith* neither (which you may think more unaccountable still), but only in "the blood of the everlasting covenant." We assuredly hold that "there is no justification" – in *your* sense – either by faith or works, or both together; i.e., that we are not pardoned and accepted with God for the *merit* of either, or both, but only by the *grace*, or free love, of God, for the alone merits of his Son, Jesus Christ.'[2]

So all were to be directed to the person of Christ and his redeeming love. What Wesley believed in this regard in 1738 he was still affirming in 1778 when he wrote in a letter, 'Nothing in the Christian system is of greater importance than the doctrine of the Atonement.' When a critic described those who 'represent the expiatory sacrifice of Christ as destined to appease vindictive justice' as believing 'frivolous and blasphemous notions', Wesley replied: 'These "frivolous and blasphemous notions" do I receive as the precious truth of God.'[3] To those who saw no need for propitiation he said, 'I know He was angry with me till I believed in the Son of His love.'[4]

We have already noted that in 1738 Wesley saw the Aldersgate experience as his conversion to real Christianity. Just four days later, on 28 May, he told a startled gathering that five days before he was not a Christian. Two

---

[1] Ibid., p. 523.
[2] Ibid., p. 150.
[3] Ibid., p. 523.
[4] *Letters*, vol. 6, p. 299.

consequences were to follow so great a change. The first
was private, the second public.

The first was the turmoil produced among his family
and friends. Reporting 'Mr John's' words of 28 May, just
quoted, to his elder brother, Samuel, Mrs Hutton believed, 'Your brother John seems to be turned a wild
enthusiast, or fanatic.'[1] Samuel Wesley, Jr., himself a High
Church clergyman, was ready to agree. Great was his
astonishment and annoyance when, the next year, John
published an abridgement of the *Life and Death of the
Reverend Learned and Pious Mr Thomas Halyburton*. The
offence was that Halyburton was a Scots divine in the
Puritan tradition and Wesley praised the book as one that
was second only to Scripture in its value. Such an opinion
could surely never be consistent with adherence to the
Church of England. Samuel wrote to his brother: 'My
mother tells me she fears a formal schism is already begun
among you, though you and Charles are ignorant of it
. . . your eyes are so fixed on one point that you overlook
everything else.'[2]

The pain of Samuel Wesley, Jr. was still greater shortly
when their mother stopped opposing the 'new notions'
of her two younger sons. A later biographer of Wesley,
Robert Southey, who was no supporter of evangelical
religion, suspected, 'her powers of mind must have been
impaired', when she told John, 'till lately she had scarce
heard of a present forgiveness of sins, or of God's Spirit
witnessing with our spirit; much less had she imagined it
was the common privilege of all true believers.'[3] When
Susanna Wesley died in 1742 the inscription on her

[1] *Journal*, vol. 1, p. 480n.
[2] Robert Southey, *Life of Wesley and the Rise and Progress of Methodism*
(London: Bohn, 1864), pp. 155–6.
[3] Southey, *Wesley*, p. 175.

gravestone, authorized by John and Charles, carried verses which included the lines,

> Mourn'd a long night of griefs and fears,
> A legal night of seventy years.[1]

The family consequences of John Wesley's changed life passed; it was the second, the public consequence, which became the stuff of history. Thereafter Wesley's ministry was to be close to the centre of the Evangelical Revival in England. Some have written as though he was the organizer of the revival, and hence the existence of such titles as *England Before and After Wesley*.[2] That view underestimates the significance of the fact that an awakening had begun in England the year *before* Wesley's experience at Aldersgate Street: George Whitefield was preaching the new birth to crowded congregations, and had taken to the open-air, before Wesley followed in the same path. It was not a follower of Whitefield but a Moravian who wrote of a 'general awakening' in 1737 and of Whitefield as the instrument in London.[3] But an examination of the comparative influence of the two men is not a theme I mean to follow. 'My view in writing history', Wesley once said, 'is to bring God into it.'[4] And once that is done the advance of the gospel in the eighteenth century is not to

[1] Southey, *Wesley*, p. 260. Tyerman (*Samuel Wesley*, p. 125) treats the words as asserting she was not a Christian until she was seventy and calls them 'monstrous'. But the real issue was assurance, not regeneration, although, as we shall see, John and Charles confused the two things at this date. In a letter of 2 October 1740, Susanna Wesley wrote of herself as a backslider who had been recovered. *Susanna Wesley, The Complete Writings*, ed. Charles Wallace Jr. (New York: OUP, 1997), p. 186.

[2] J. Wesley Bready, *England Before and After Wesley* (London: Hodder & Stoughton, 1938).

[3] See W. Batty, *Church History* (1779), p. 4, quoted by Henry D. Rack *Reasonable Enthusiast; John Wesley and the Rise of Methodism* (London: Epworth, 1989), p. 177.

[4] *Letters*, vol. 6, p. 67.

be seen as a matter of personalities. The truth is that the revival was a mystery in a real sense even to its leading participants. Thus Wesley could write in later years:

'We do not throughly understand the meaning of that word, "The times and seasons God hath reserved in His own power." Undoubtedly He has wise reasons for pouring out His Spirit at one time rather than another; but they lie abundantly too deep for human understanding to fathom.'[1]

[1] *Letters*, vol. 6, p. 331.

Chapter 2

'Kingdoms on a Blaze'

Numbers are in themselves no proof of an outpouring of the Holy Spirit, and it has to be said that the numbers reported at the beginning of the Evangelical Revival by its supporters were sometimes wildly, though not deliberately, inaccurate. Yet what is certain is that the year 1739 saw crowds gathering to hear preaching in numbers that had no comparison in living memory. In London one open-air congregation was estimated at fifty thousand. At Blackheath, it was said that Wesley preached to 12 or 13,000 people. At Kingswood, Bristol, 'a hell upon earth', in the bleak months of February and March 1739, numbers grew from hundreds to an estimated 10,000.[1] Opponents had their explanations. Dr Joseph Trapp, a leading London cleric, believed that 'Methodism was nothing but a revival of the old fanaticism of the last century; when all manner of madness was practised.' Through different eyes, Wesley affirmed: 'The word of the Lord again runs and is glorified. Great multitudes are everywhere awakened, and cry out, "What must we do to be saved?"' And Wesley was certain of the message which was bringing this upheaval:

'Being convinced of that important truth, which is the foundation of all real religion, that "by grace we are saved

---

[1] Such a non-Methodist source as the *Gentleman's Magazine* also attested the very high numbers that gathered.

through faith," we immediately began declaring it to others. Indeed, we could hardly speak of anything else, either in public or private. It shone upon our minds with so strong a light, that it was our constant theme.'[1]

Although the Evangelical Revival of the eighteenth century was a turning point in English history, that was by no means known to Wesley in 1740. As yet he had no evidence that what they had seen in parts of London and Bristol would be repeated elsewhere, nor had he any clear idea of what his future work was to be: ought he to take a curacy, or return to Lincoln College and prepare students? Commenting in later years on their thoughts at this date, Wesley was later to say that he and the few others similarly engaged 'had no plan at all. They only went hither and thither, wherever they had a prospect of saving souls from death.'[2]

The principle on which Wesley acted was 'to follow providence', and by that means, in 1742, he took a step which was to lead to a life-time of itinerant ministry. At the suggestion of the Countess of Huntingdon, and without any anticipation of the consequences, Wesley went to the North of England. At Newcastle upon Tyne, on Sunday 30 May, at seven o'clock in the morning, he preached by the river in the poorest part of the town. His text was: 'He was wounded for our transgressions, he was bruised for our iniquities: the chastisement of our peace was upon him; and by his stripes we are healed.' By the time he concluded a large crowd had gathered and 'stood gaping, with the most profound astonishment'. He told them: 'If you desire to know who I am, my name is

---

[1] Tyerman, *Wesley*, vol. 1, p. 238.
[2] *Works*, vol. 7, p. 207.

John Wesley. At five in the evening, with God's help, I design to preach here again.'[1]

On his way to Newcastle, Wesley had preached in Yorkshire (where others were already evangelizing). On returning to the south he preached in the open-air at Epworth on the occasion already mentioned. Such was the response to this unorthodox manner of proceeding that from this date Wesley knew what his future work was to be. He was now thirty-nine and itinerant preaching was to be the main work of his life. The Oxford scholar had become the horseback rider.

To judge Wesley's sermons from the calmness of the written form in which they were later published would be a mistake. Especially in the early years of the revival, he was vehement, convicting and constantly evangelistic. There was an authority in his preaching that nothing could deter. Twice he was seriously mobbed. Nor could weather hinder him; we read of him preaching in the North of England 'amid wind, sleet and snow till he was encased in ice'.[2] His brother Charles commented, 'You build, as Caesar fights, in all weathers.'

When Wesley went to preach at Bath, the fashion centre of the day, he was interrupted by its 'King', the dissolute gambler Richard Nash. 'Beau Nash', as he was commonly known, complained that Wesley's preaching 'frightens people out of their wits'. When this rake of a man claimed to know this 'by common report', Wesley silenced him with, 'Sir, I dare not judge you by common report.'[3] One listener in 1740 thought that Wesley's peculiar gift was

---

[1] The place where this happened remains marked by a monument on the riverside in Newcastle.
[2] Tyerman, *Wesley*, vol. 1, p. 404.
[3] Ibid., p. 238.

'to awaken souls in preaching'.[1] He was plain, pungent and direct; perhaps too direct at Epworth when in the course of preaching he challenged a gentleman with the question, 'Sir, are you a sinner?' 'Sinner enough', was the reply.

John Nelson has left an account of how he and others came to faith under Wesley's preaching. He was present the first time Wesley preached in the open-air at Moorfields in London and writes:

'O that was a blessed morning to my soul! As soon as he got upon the stand, he stroked back his hair, and turned his face towards where I stood, and I thought fixed his eyes upon me. His countenance struck such an awful dread upon me, before I heard him speak, that it made my heart beat like the pendulum of a clock; and, when he did speak, I thought his whole discourse was aimed at me.'[2]

Nelson's friends did their best to dissuade him from hearing Wesley again, telling him that 'to go too far in religion' would ruin his business prospects, and that they would not hear Wesley preach for fifty pounds. A little while later, however, when Nelson was 'going out of the Park into Westminster', he overheard a very different assessment of Wesley from a soldier who was telling some women how he had become a Christian. The man reported:

'As I was coming out of the country by Kennington Common, Mr John Wesley was going to preach, and I

---

[1] Ibid., p. 299, the words of James Hutton, one of the Moravian Brethren. The Moravians seemed to share this view, another of them said, 'Mr Wesley was only a John Baptist, to go before and prepare them for the Brethren to build up.' [2] *The Journal of John Nelson* (London: Mason, 1846), p. 35.

thought I would hear what he had to say; for I had heard
many learned and wise men say, he was beside himself.
But when he began to speak, his words made me tremble.
I thought he spoke to no one but me, and durst not look
up, for I imagined all the people were looking at me.'

This unexpected testimony re-awakened all that Nelson
himself had felt. He resumed hearing Wesley and later,
he says, 'I found power to believe that Jesus Christ has
shed his blood for me, and that God, for his sake, had
forgiven my offences. Then was my heart filled with love
to God and man.' He adds that when he spoke of this at
his former lodging house, the owner and his wife 'both
went to hear Mr Wesley, when the woman was made a
partaker of the same grace; and I hope to meet them both
in heaven'.[1]

John Nelson became one of Wesley's first assistant
preachers and in 1743 the two men were together,
preaching in the open-air in Cornwall. Both men were
unknown to the local people and no comfortable lodgings
were available for them during their weeks there:

'All that time, Mr Wesley and I lay on the floor: he had a
great coat for his pillow, and I had Burkitt's *Notes on the
New Testament* for mine. After being here near three
weeks, one morning, about three o'clock, Mr Wesley
turned over, and finding me awake, clapped me on the
side, saying, "Brother Nelson, be of good cheer: I have
one whole side yet, for the skin is off but on one side."
We usually preached on the commons, going from one
common to another, and it was but seldom any one asked
us to eat and drink.'[2]

---

[1] *Journal of Nelson*, pp. 13–21.
[2] Ibid., p. 87.

Tyerman says that in the early years of the revival Wesley's favourite text was Ephesians 2:8: 'For by grace are ye saved through faith; and that not of yourselves: it is the gift of God.' The evidence is that his texts were carefully chosen for the occasion, and certainly not chosen to please his hearers. With the opportunity to preach on one occasion before the Mayor of Bristol, his subject was the rich man and Lazarus. Another time, before what was described as 'a genteel audience', his text was, 'Ye serpents, ye generation of vipers, how can ye escape the damnation of hell.' After that sermon one of his listeners remonstrated with him that such a verse was suitable for Billingsgate (one of the worst areas of London) but not for these hearers. Wesley replied that if he had been in Billingsgate his text would have been, 'Behold the Lamb of God, which taketh away the sin of the world.'

The text which abruptly ended any further preaching in Oxford sounded inoffensive enough when he announced it in the university church of St Mary's on 24 August 1744, being the words of Acts 4:31: 'And when they had prayed, the place was shaken where they were assembled together; and they were all filled with the Holy Ghost, and they spake the word of God with boldness.' But as he proceeded to make a comparison between the apostolic church and the existing one, many of his distinguished hearers felt themselves insulted. One hearer reported:

'The assertion that Oxford was not a Christian city, and that this country not a Christian nation, were the most offensive parts of the sermon, except when he accused the whole body (and confessed himself to be one of the number) of the sin of perjury . . . Had these things been omitted, and his censures moderated, I think his discourse, as to style and delivery, would have been un-commonly pleasing to others as well as to myself.'[1]

Wesley's 'failure' among the type of hearers he had at Oxford was matched elsewhere. The 'wise' and the 'learned' were seldom in sympathy, yet the numbers in 'Mr Wesley's Connexion' increased continually. By 1743 there were about 700 in the Bristol society, 800 at Newcastle, and 2,020 in London where his society met in three different locations. He wrote from Cornwall on 18 July 1747: 'A great door and effectual is opened now, almost in every corner of this country. Here is such a change within two years as has hardly been seen in any other part of England. Wherever we went we used to carry our lives in our hands; and now there is not a dog to wag his tongue.'[2] That same year came the first of Wesley's societies in Manchester and Dublin. On 2 February 1748, Wesley wrote to a friend: 'Both in Ireland, and in many parts of England, the work of our Lord increases daily. At Leeds, only, the society, from an hundred and four score, is increased to above five hundred persons.'[3]

Such events were not going on quietly unnoticed by the world at large. The cynical Horace Walpole, in a letter of 3 May 1749, advised a friend: 'If you ever think of returning to England, you must prepare yourself with Methodism. This sect increases as fast as any religious nonsense ever did.'[4]

---

[1] Quoted by V. H. H. Green, *Young Mr Wesley: A Study of John Wesley* (London: Epworth, 1963), pp. 283–4. As to 'perjury', the reference was to the subscription to the 39 Articles required of all clergy.

[2] *Works* (Abingdon), vol. 26, p. 253.

[3] Ibid., p. 277. A beginning was made in Scotland in 1751.

[4] Tyerman, *Wesley*, vol. 2, p. 32. Earlier in the year Walpole remarked: 'Methodism in the metropolis is more fashionable than anything but brag' [a popular card game].

How was growth of this kind, and Wesley's influence in it, to be explained? There was no lack of critics among the clergy who knew the answer. One of them, with the pseudonym of 'John Smith', was confident the explanation was Wesley's 'natural knack of persuasion' plus the sheer novelty of a clergyman, in 'canonical dress', preaching in the open-air. Such conduct, he suggested to Wesley, was bound to impress the ignorant and the credulous. If he preached standing on his head it would have the same effect.[1]

Wesley was in Newcastle when he replied to this letter and used his experience there as an argument against his opponent's case:

'When I had preached more than sixscore times at this town I found scarce any effect, only that abundance of people heard and gaped and stared, and went away much as they came. And it was one evening while I was in doubt if I had laboured in vain that such a blessing of God was given as has continued ever since, and I trust will be remembered unto many generations.'[2]

The real difference in this discussion was over the place of faith in salvation, and over God as the immediate author of that faith. 'You seem to me', wrote 'Smith', 'to contend with great earnestness for the following system, viz., that faith (instead of being a rational assent and a moral virtue for the attainment of which men ought to yield the utmost attention and industry) is altogether a divine and supernatural illapse from heaven, the immediate gift of God, the mere work of omnipotence.'[3] With

---

[1] *Works* (Abingdon), vol. 26, p. 213. It has been conjectured that 'Smith' was Thomas Secker, who was Dean of St Paul's and became Archbishop of Canterbury in 1758, but his true identity remains uncertain.
[2] Ibid., p. 237.   [3] Ibid., p. 139.

obvious qualification, this was what Wesley believed; faith is supernatural, 'wrought in us (be it swiftly or slowly) by the Spirit of God'.[1] He replied to 'Smith':

'Supposing a man be now void of faith and hope and love, he cannot effect any degree of them in himself by any possible exertion of his understanding, and of any or all of his other natural faculties, though he should enjoy them to the utmost perfection. A distinct power from God, not implied in any of these, is indispensably necessary before it is possible he should arrive at the very least degree of Christian faith, or hope, or love. In order to his having any of these (which on this very consideration I suppose St Paul terms "the fruits of the Spirit") he must be created anew, throughly and inwardly changed by the operation of the Spirit of God, by a power equivalent to that which raises the dead, and which calls the things which are not as though they were.'[2]

In accordance with this belief Wesley preached in the conviction that saving results depended upon the power of the Holy Spirit through the instrumentality of the Word of God. Thus through his *Journals* are such sentences as the following:

At Berwick the Word of God was 'as a fire and a hammer'.

At Stanley, near Gloucester, 'I was strengthened to speak as never before; and continued speaking near two hours, the darkness of the night and a little lightning not lessening the number, but increasing the seriousness of the hearers.'

---

[1] Ibid., p. 179.

[2] Ibid., p. 199–200. This remained Wesley's conviction on conversion. Writing to an Assistant who he believed was in danger of Pelagianism, he said of the 'marks of a Christian', 'No power can give me these but that which made the world.' Ibid., p. 108.

At York, 'I began preaching at seven, and God applied it to the hearts of the hearers. Tears and groans were on every side, among high and low. God, as it were, bowed the heavens and came down.'

At Castlebar, 'I spoke with such closeness and pungency, as I cannot do but at some peculiar seasons. It is indeed the gift of God, and cannot be attained by all the efforts of nature and art united.'

I take these examples from John Telford's *Life of Wesley.* Telford also noted in Wesley such phrases as, 'God himself made the application', and, 'Truly God preached to their hearts.'[1] The way in which Wesley attributed the efficacy of preaching to the Holy Spirit led to the charge that he and Whitefield were claiming a gift which belonged only to the apostolic age; it was an accusation they repeatedly disclaimed.

But I turn now to another charge levelled against Wesley, namely, that it was pride and concern for prominence which motivated his conduct. Why else would he ignore good Church order and roam the country without regard for bishops, clergy and parish boundaries? Wesley's reply to this goes to the heart of the controversy occasioned by the revival: it was that a saving gospel was not being heard by the majority of the people, and that *love* demanded the course that he took. Replying to 'Smith' on this point, he said:

'What is the end of all *ecclesiastical order*? Is it not to bring souls from the power of Satan unto God? And to build them up in his fear and love? *Order*, then is so far valuable as it answers these ends; and if it answers them not it is

---

[1] John Telford, *Life of John Wesley* (London: Hodder and Stoughton, 1886), pp. 318–20.

worth nothing. Now I would fain know, Where has *order* answered these ends? Not in any place where I have been: not among the tinners in Cornwall, the keelmen at Newcastle, the colliers in Kingswood and Staffordshire; not among the drunkards, swearers, sabbath-breakers of Moorfields, or the harlots of Drury Lane. They could not be built up in the fear and love of God while they were open, bare-faced servants of the devil.'[1]

Faultless Wesley was not; nor was all that his critics said ungrounded. He was no more fully delivered from pride than any other man. But the record of his life and labours leads us to see him as a man largely prompted by a different motivation: love to God was his chief source of action, the consequence of God's love to him. 'And from this principle of grateful love to God arises love to our brother also.' In the words of his brother, Charles,

> Jesus' love the nations fires
> Set the kingdoms on a blaze.

Love is the key to Wesley; and the key also to the tenderness of his preaching. There were occasions, as can be seen in his *Journal*, when he had to break off preaching because 'our hearts were so filled with a sense of God's love, and our mouths with prayer and thanksgiving'. This same spirit explains the fearlessness and zeal of his whole ministry. In the words of another evangelist:

'The love of God breeds an enthusiasm, and a sacred fervour within the soul, which lifts men out of themselves, and bestows upon them a sort of celestial other-life, a divine *furore*, by which the soul is up-borne as on eagle's wings, and triumphs in joy unspeakable. This makes men

---

[1] *Works* (Abingdon), vol. 26, p. 206.

ten times stronger, braver, grander, happier than they were before.'[1]

But to be a loving preacher did not mean to be always speaking of love. Love will make men bold in challenging men; Wesley spared none in rebuking sin. On the theme of love he says, 'There is a peculiar blessing . . . But yet it would be utterly wrong and unscriptural to preach of *nothing else*.'[2] 'May not *love* itself constrain us to lay before men "the terrors of the Lord"?'[3]

The two issues most in controversy at the beginning of the Evangelical Revival were, first, how one becomes a Christian, and, second, what is the evidence that a Christian profession is real. On the second of these lay the increasing emphasis of Wesley's ministry. A sound definition of salvation by faith was only the starting point and accurate definitions were not his main concern; the great need, as he conceived it, was for the recovery of *experimental* Christianity, or, as he put it, 'to bring all the world to solid, inward, vital religion'.[4]

This could not be unless love was seen as the true end. 'I regard not even faith itself as an *end*, but a *means* only. The end of the commandment is love – of every commandment, of the whole Christian dispensation.'[5] 'Faith is seeing God; love is feeling God.'[6] 'There is nothing better in heaven or earth than love! There

---

[1] C. H. Spurgeon, preaching on 'Keep yourselves in the love of God', in *Metropolitan Tabernacle Pulpit* (London: Passmore and Alabaster, 1877), p. 188.
[2] *Works* (Abingdon), vol. 26, p. 418.
[3] Ibid., p. 197.　　　　　　[4] Ibid., p. 138.
[5] Ibid., p. 203. This should not be confused with the mystic teaching he had renounced and which he described in the words, 'Love is all; all the commands beside are only means of love; you must choose those which you feel are means to you and use them as long as they are so.' *Journal*, vol. 1, p. 420. For Wesley, love and obedience were never separable.
[6] *Works* (Abingdon), vol. 26, p. 108.

cannot be, unless there were something higher than the God of love! So that we see distinctly what we have to aim at.'[2]

* * * * *

Where a movement of the Holy Spirit is conceived as a means for the removal of all problems and errors the Evangelical Revival can be little understood. The very years which were so promising in England were also years of many and continued troubles. God works through human means and even in a revival – sometimes more so in revival – 'to err is human'.

Trouble emerged in the area of relationships. The society at Aldersgate Street, London, in May 1738, has already been mentioned. Religious societies of various kinds were a feature of the early eighteenth century. They provided a meeting place for the like-minded in various enterprises without the members being required to break their church commitment. Such a society Wesley had formed with Peter Böhler, the Moravian, and others in London on 1 May 1738. Two days later, writes Wesley in his *Journal*, 'it pleased God' to open the eyes of his brother Charles 'so that he also saw clearly what was the nature of that one true living faith, whereby alone, "through grace we are saved".' This was the society where Wesley had his memorable experience on 24 May 1738. About three months later the meeting moved to a room in Fetter Lane and when Whitefield returned from America in November he also joined.

Within two years the members of this society had split three ways. The first break was with the Moravians. Böhler was out of the country and by 1740 Philip Molther had

---

[1] *Letters*, vol. 6, p. 136.

become the society's favourite teacher. But Wesley was now disturbed by aspects of Moravian teaching and was no longer welcome to preach at Fetter Lane. Accordingly, he met separately with twenty-five men and fifty women for the first time on 23 July 1740. Thereafter the Moravian wing of the Evangelical Revival had little to do with the Methodist mainstream.[1]

The mainstream itself, however, was in the process of division. In 1739 Wesley had preached a sermon against the Calvinistic understanding of predestination, and, though Whitefield pleaded that he should not do so, he published it, with the title *Free Grace*. By the time of its publication Whitefield had again left England for America. Correspondence ensued between the two friends, only to widen the difference, and on Whitefield's return to England in March 1741, he published a strong reply to Wesley's sermon.[2] Before that date, the society in Bristol (to which Whitefield had introduced Wesley in 1739) had split after Wesley expounded Romans chapter nine, intent (his brother is reported to have said) 'to drive John Calvin out of Bristol'.

The Kingswood society, near Bristol, also divided for the same reason in February 1741. John Cennick left with others, and about 100 adhered to Wesley. Thus on his return Whitefield found it necessary to start a new work in London, independently of his former colleague. Before the end of 1741, Wesley had 'purged' the three societies

---

[1] The name 'Methodist', first coined in derision against the members of the Holy Club at Oxford, was thereafter applied to all serious evangelicals, to Whitefield equally with Wesley. It was only in the process of time that the Wesleyan wing of the revival adopted the name more particularly for themselves, hence the later denominational connotation. In these pages I will commonly use the term in the Wesleyan sense.

[2] *A Letter to the Rev. Mr John Wesley*, reprinted in *George Whitefield's Journals* (London: Banner of Truth, 1960), pp. 569–88.

in London, Bristol and Kingswood so that they were, in Tyerman's phrase, 'purely and properly his own'.[1]

Discussion on the break between Wesley and Whitefield was not dispassionate at the time nor has it always been so since. On one side, the public criticism of Wesley by a man eleven years his junior, and formerly his 'son' in the faith, gave offence. For those closer to Whitefield it looked as though work that owed so much to him had been commandeered. Setting aside the doctrinal difference for the moment, it is clear that Wesley possesed gifts of organization and management that Whitefield did not, and so, if a new and common structure was going to emerge it would be dependent on Wesley: 'I know this is the peculiar talent which God has given me.'[2] Hence the development of 'Mr Wesley's Connexion', or as he called it, 'The United Societies', which spread across the country in the way already mentioned. This structure need not be attributed to aggrandizement on Wesley's part. Given the state of the Church, as Tyerman said, without societies 'the preacher would not be able to give proper instruction to them that were convinced of sin; nor the people to watch over one another in love, bear one another's burden, and build up each other in faith and holiness.' Further, as we shall see, there were reasons in the divine providence why a common structure should survive after Wesley's death to fulfil a world-wide mission.

Wesley's societies brought problems with them. It was one thing for the Church of England to tolerate the quiet and inconspicuous societies of the earlier years of the century, quite another to allow the growth of an organization that appeared to challenge the Church of

---

[1] Tyerman, *Wesley*, vol. 1, p. 352.
[2] *Works* (Abingdon), vol. 26, p. 91.

England while professing loyalty to it. Wesley denied any such challenge. He meant to augment the work of the Church, not supplant it. Society membership was not intended as an alternative to church attendance; society meetings were not held in church hours; no sacraments were administered; rather, for these, members should go to their local churches (commonly the Church of England). Wesley intended to be loyal to the Church of England and as late as 1784 could write, 'I believe I shall not separate from the Church of England till my soul separates from my body.'[1]

Yet despite such often-repeated words there was too much that *looked like* a church in Wesleyan Methodism to allay the criticism, and nothing fuelled that criticism more than the step Wesley took to minister to the spiritual needs of the people in his societies. How the numbers had grown to thousands by 1748 has already been mentioned. Neither he, his brother Charles, nor the few clergymen who were sympathetic, could provide ministry on the scale that was now required. When he saw that God had given preaching gifts to non-ordained men, such as John Nelson, he believed this was the answer to the problem. A breach of Church order it might be but that was no longer his first principle, rather, 'Church or no Church, we must attend to the work of saving souls.' And when challenged he would reply, 'Soul-damning clergy-men lay me under more difficulties than soul-saving laymen.'[2]

These lay-preachers Wesley named his 'Assistants' or 'helpers'. At an annual conference, instituted in 1744, their movements were discussed and decided by him.

---

[1] *Letters*, vol. 7, p. 321.
[2] Tyerman, *Wesley*, vol. 2, p. 211.

Within a few years the country came to be divided into 'circuits' or 'rounds', with so many societies in each. In turn the societies were divided into classes, with class leaders, and these met weekly. Membership tickets were to be given to none till they were recommended by a leader with whom they had met for three months on trial. One or more Assistants were appointed to each circuit for one or two (rarely three) years, with duties which could require a few hundred miles travel on horseback every month. In time these men came to be known as the 'travelling preachers', as distinct from 'local preachers', who lived by their several occupations and were permanent in the same locality. In Wesley's day, however, the distinction between 'travelling' and 'local preachers' was not always hard and fast. Only the travelling preachers attended the annual conference and obtained financial help from Wesley or the societies. There were seven circuits in 1746, nine by 1748.

How Wesley could hold a high view of the Church of England and at the same time develop this connexion is explicable only by recognizing that his priority was not ecclesiology. He would not break with Church order wilfully, only when it stood in the way of evangelism, and then he did not hesitate. It was expediency based on the concern to reach men and women in both Church and Dissent. 'The Methodists are to spread life in all denominations; which they will do till they form a separate sect.'[1] 'Let us all be men of *one business.* We live only for this, to save our own souls, and them that hear us.' Whatever his deficiencies, this was the spirit of John Wesley, and of the other leaders of the Evangelical Revival.

[1] *Letters,* vol. 8, p. 211.

Chapter 3

Understanding Wesley's Thought

From 1729, Wesley said, he became 'a man of one book'. The Bible was his authority and to it he made his final appeal: 'I receive the written Word as the whole and the sole rule of my faith.'[1] Those who do not share that judgment are unlikely to be appreciative readers of his sermons. Yet it would be true to say that he popularized a school of Christian thought which in some respects is distinct from any previous tradition of teaching that claimed Scripture as it source. While there is a common evangelicalism at the bedrock of Wesleyan Methodism, original aspects were also present in the amalgam of beliefs that made up the Wesleyan tradition. Given the fact that Wesley never saw himself as a theologian this fact is the more surprising. How is it to be explained?

In the first place it is relevant to understand that Wesley had grown up impatient with any theological thinking that was merely theoretical or over-dogmatic. He was convinced that Christianity is pre-eminently intended to be *practical*, it is meant to change lives. The influence of his mother – whom he resembled more closely than his

[1] *Works* (Abingdon), vol. 26, p. 155.

father – is discernible here. In 1725 Susanna Wesley wrote
to him urging 'greater application in the study of practical
divinity . . . I earnestly pray God to avert that great evil
from you of engaging in trifling studies to the neglect of
such as are absolutely necessary.'[1] Wesley increasingly
understood the warning. He saw that Christianity may exist
in forms of critical learning, and in precise theological
formulations, yet make no impact upon the world. Its
sphere is only that of intellect and theory. Oxford
illustrated this for him. For all its religion there was little
or no living knowledge of God. This propensity to reduce
Christianity to words, instead of power, was not confined
to High Churchmen. As I have already mentioned, some
branches of Puritanism had given too high a profile to
exactness of belief on issues not fundamental to the faith.
Wesley cannot be understood without recognizing that
his life was a reaction to all such tendencies. The Bible,
he would insist, is given us for our salvation and for our
holiness. And the remedy, he thought, for the avoidance
of profitless discussion was to hold to the fundamental
beliefs – 'Christ dying for us and Christ reigning in us' –
and to regard all else as 'opinions'; that is to say, as matters
not warranting controversy or division among Christians.[2]

---

[1] Tyerman, *Wesley*, vol. 1, p. 32. See also Wesley's 'Demonstration of the
Divine Inspiration of the Holy Scriptures,' in *Works*, vol. 11, p. 484.

[2] The later Puritans had also seen the need to distinguish between truths
necessary for salvation and subjects upon which differences should not
prevent brotherly love. For instance, John Collinges: 'It is matter of
amazement to consider, what feuds, what alienations of affection, are the
products of *differences in opinion*: as if heaven were entailed to understandings
of one complexion. There always were in the Church of God, and there
always will be, different apprehensions in some matters of truth; and generally
they have brought forth disorders (great disorders) in men's practice; each
one hugging his particular opinion, as if he judged himself, and none but
himself, *infallible*.' *Several Discourses Concerning the Actual Providence of
God* (Parkhurst: London: 1678), p. 731.

But the problem with Wesley's distinction between fundamental beliefs and 'opinions' was that a considerable number of so-called opinions remained so influential in his thinking that they coloured his outlook and led to the distinctive Wesleyan theology. I have already mentioned the three main sources, next to the Bible, which moulded his thought – High Church divinity, Christian mysticism and Moravian evangelicalism. It would be a mistake to suppose that the influence of the first two ended when he embraced the third.

High Church thinking remained with him in more than one area. On baptism, for instance, he continued to believe that a decisive change occurs when a child receives the sacrament. Before that event original sin operates in its full power in all the sons of Adam, but in baptism the merit of Christ's death begins to be applied to all and there is a general giving of the Holy Spirit sufficient to enable a response to the gospel. This was his teaching on 'prevenient grace'.[1] He also believed that the Lord's Supper could be viewed as a means of conversion. His 'High' beliefs about the sacraments likewise may have entered into his readiness to allow unordained preachers to expound Scripture, whereas they were not to baptize or to administer the Lord's Supper.[2]

---

[1] *Works*, vol. 10, p. 191. This 'grace', however, he did not necessarily link to baptism: 'No man living is without some preventing grace, and every degree of grace is a degree of life. That, "by the offence of one, judgement came upon all men"(all born into the world) "unto condemnation," is an undoubted truth, and affects every infant as well as every adult person. But it is equally true that, "by the righteousness of one, the free gift came upon all men" (all born into the world, infant or adult) "unto justification." *Letters*, vol. 6, p. 239.

[2] But to be fair to Wesley, when he was later challenged on this inconsistency, he replied that while he was willing to break his Church's rules in order for men to hear the gospel, it was not necessary to do so over the sacraments for these did not involve salvation. Probably the practice of the Salvation Army , at a later date, was a follow-on from this thinking.

From this same High Church background came what can only be called a form of 'asceticism' which remained in Wesley's thinking. High Church and mystical writers majored on self-denial. Certainly, self-denial is a Christian duty and it was to contribute largely to the spirituality and vigour which would characterize Methodists. In Wesley, however, it could pass into asceticism, not simply in such things as early rising and abstinence from tea-drinking but, more seriously, in his whole view of marriage. To a young preacher who nearly fell into matrimony he could write, 'I congratulate you on your deliverance . . . remember the wise direction of à Kempis, "Avoid *good women*, and commend them to God."'[1] His own problem in this regard we have already noticed. After the Sophy Hopkey affair there was another lapse of resolution in 1749 when he would have married Grace Murray had his brother Charles not prevented it by hastening her into marriage with someone else. Charles had no second opportunity to intervene when John suddenly married Molly Vazeille, widow of a banker, in 1751. The marriage was a disaster. This might well have been the case whoever he had married, given his estimation that celibacy remained a higher state, and that marrying for happiness was somehow beneath a Christian: 'I married because I needed a home', he tells a correspondent, 'in order to recover my health; and I did recover it. But I did not seek happiness thereby, and I did not find it.'[2] Who can be surprised?

---

[1] *Letters*, vol. 8, p. 116. He did not follow this advice himself. As has been said: 'While he was well-liked by his fellow men, he seems always to be more at home in female company. The influence of the sisterhood was without doubt pervasive.' Green, *Young Mr Wesley*, p. 56.

[2] *Letters*, vol. 8, p. 223.

With some justification Molly Wesley came to think that her husband did not need a wife. They were too often apart and were finally to be so alienated and separated that it was to be days after her funeral that he even heard of her death. It is not an overstatement on the part of Robert Southey when he says that the kind of life which Wesley prescribed for his preachers 'left them little opportunity for the enjoyment of domestic life. Home could scarcely be regarded as a resting-place for men who were never allowed to be at rest.'[1] In this Wesley too largely made his own practice the model for others, and the fact that so many of the marriages of his preachers survived was because they rested on a love which had eluded their leader. Whatever Molly Wesley's faults (and we know little of her) there is more than enough in Wesley's letters to her to explain why she also did not find the relationship a happy one.

Asceticism is not a charge which Wesley would have recognized, but there was another strand in his thinking that he willingly attributed to his early reading of High Church authors and the mystics. This was his teaching on 'Christian perfection' and this became in some ways the most distinctive of all his 'opinions' (using the word in his sense of the term). Far from 'perfection' being a later development in his thought, he was corresponding with his mother on the subject in 1725 when she was pressing 'after greater degrees of Christian perfection'. She recommended to 'Jacky' a volume on the subject by Richard Lucas,[2] and a few years later he read William Law on the same subject. By 1733 Wesley was ready to make it the subject of a sermon preached in the university church. In its final form his teaching, in brief, was that

---

[1] Southey, *Wesley*, p. 379.

[2] Richard Lucas (1648–1715), *Religious Perfection. Or, a Third part of the Enquiry after Happiness*, 2nd ed. (London: Smith and Walford, 1697).

the mature or 'perfect' Christian (the word in New Testament Greek may mean 'full grown', 'mature') can attain to loving God with heart and soul and strength before death, and so overcome all inbred sin that sinning may be said to have ceased. To describe this attainment he used several terms, 'full sanctification', 'pure love', 'Christian perfection', and less commonly, the 'second blessing'. This condition might be received by faith in an instant. 'Full deliverance from sin, I believe, is always instantaneous.'[1] 'This doctrine is the grand *depositum* which God has lodged with the people called Methodists; and for the sake of propagating this chiefly He appeared to have raised us up.'[2] 'Everywhere exhort the believers to expect full salvation now by simple faith.'[3]

The scriptural basis he advanced for this teaching may be read in *A Plain Account of Christian Perfection As Believed and Taught By the Rev. Mr John Wesley From the Year 1725 to 1777*. But it is no conjecture to believe that Wesley's 'evidence' for the opinion rested quite as much upon alleged experiences as upon any interpretation of Scripture, and the point of controversy is whether the experiences were rightly correlated with biblical teaching. There is no lack of testimony from church history that full assurance is *sometimes* given to Christians in an instant and, as Wesley more or less identified his 'Christian perfection' with full assurance, his people could easily confuse the former with the latter in speaking of their experience.[4] Although Wesley criticized the mystic writers with the

---

[1] *Letters*, vol. 8, p. 190.
[2] Ibid., p. 238.   [3] Ibid., vol. 6, p. 378.
[4] 'Many of our brethren and sisters in London, during that great outpouring of the Spirit, spoke of several *new* blessings which they had attained. But after all, they could find nothing higher than *pure love*, on which the full assurance of hope generally attends.' Ibid., vol. 7, p. 57. I discuss this more full below in chapter 10.

words, 'each of them makes his own experience the standard of religion',[1] a propensity to depend on experience
as a guide to truth also remained with him. For example,
to support his assertion, given above, that 'full deliverance
from sin, I believe, is always instantaneous', he adds, 'at
least, I never yet knew an exception.'

It is true that Wesley's readiness to argue from experience was sometimes sound. He asserts, for instance,
that we know from experience that we cannot believe just
when *we like*. But that same truth is clearly authenticated
by Scripture. On the subject of perfection it was the lack
of such authentication which produced both trouble and
controversy.

How much Wesley was led by the experience, and the
example of others, brings us to the question how far
Moravian evangelicalism permanently affected his whole
thinking. That it brought grace, the cross and justification
by faith to the forefront of his consciousness is beyond
question. And from the same source he had, he believed,
confirmation of the possibility of Christian perfection. On
a visit to Moravians in Germany in August 1738 he was
so impressed with the experience of Arvin Gradin that he
asked for the latter's definition of assurance in writing.
Gradin's statement read:

'Repose in the blood of Christ: a firm confidence in God
and persuasion of his favour: the highest tranquillity,
serenity and peace of mind, with a deliverance from every
fleshly desire, and a cessation of all, even inward sins.'[2]

---

[1] Ibid., p. 44. Among the Roman Catholic mystics his references are to
such people as Madame Guyon.

[2] Wesley quotes Zinzendorf as saying that the believer, 'In the moment he
is justified, he is sanctified wholly . . . Our whole justification and
sanctification are in the same instant. From the moment anyone is justified,
his heart is as pure as it ever will be.' Tyerman, *Wesley*, vol. 1, p. 340.

Wesley accepted the whole statement as what he had 'before myself learned from the oracles of God'. But confusion followed his supposed discovery. Some Moravians, at least, identified this assurance and perfection with justification. Philip Molther, the leading Moravian in the Fetter Lane society in London, taught that 'no one has any faith while he has any doubt; and that none are justified till they are sanctified'.[1] So conversion entailed instant assurance and, along with assurance, as Wesley had heard in Germany, a 'cessation of all sins'. At first Wesley went along with this identification of justification with assurance and the cessation of sin. His Preface to the *Hymns and Poems*, published in 1740, described the believer as freed from pride, self-will, evil thoughts, doubts and fears. Given such a definition it is very understandable that, eight months *after* his Aldersgate experience, Wesley could affirm in January 1739 that he was not yet a Christian at all. His statement of the latter date began:

'My friends affirm I am mad, because I said I was not a Christian a year ago. I affirm I am not a Christian now . . . For a Christian is one who has the fruits of the Spirit of Christ, which (to mention no more) are love, peace, joy . . . And I *feel* this moment I do not love God . . . joy in the Holy Ghost I have not . . . Though I have constantly used all the means of grace for twenty years, I am not a Christian.'[2]

There is no distinction here between faith and feeling, or between justification and assurance. For several years after 1738 Wesley held to the conviction that faith

[1] Ibid., p. 303.
[2] *Journal*, vol. 2, pp. 125–6.

(justification) and assurance were always together, and that if there is no assurance there can be no true conversion. Thus he believed in 1744 that 'No man can be justified and not know it.' But within three years of that date he appears, privately at least, to have abandoned the Moravian insistence that assurance *always* accompanies justification. He wrote to Charles on 31 July 1747:

'Some years ago we heard nothing about either justifying faith or a sense of pardon: so that, when we did hear of them, the theme was quite new to us; and we might easily, especially in the heat and hurry of controversy, lean too much either to the one hand or to the other.

'By justifying faith I mean that faith which whosoever hath not is under the wrath and curse of God. By a sense of pardon I mean a distinct, explicit assurance that my sins are forgiven . . . I allow it is the common privilege of *real* Christians . . . But I cannot allow that justifying faith is such an assurance, or necessarily connected therewith.'[1]

In other words, the lack of assurance of acceptance with

---

[1] *Letters*, vol. 2, p. 108. I say that 'privately' Wesley accepted this change because, strangely, in 1753, when his Conference asked Whitefield not to reflect critically on Wesley's doctrines if he was to preach in their midst, Whitefield's saying that, 'a man may be justified and not know it,' was given as an example of what offended them (Ibid., vol. 3, p. 101). In 1757 Wesley avoided giving the Rev. Samuel Walker a definite answer on the subject (Ibid., p. 222), yet unquestionably he had come to believe that 'a man may be a real Christian without being "assured of his salvation"' (Ibid., vol. 4, p. 144). 'I have not for many years thought a consciousness of acceptance to be essential to justifying faith' (Ibid., vol. 5, p. 359). But he was very sensitive about exposing himself to the charge of inconsistency. Similarly, he did not persist in the idea that Christian perfection is a necessary accompaniment of conversion. He wrote in 1748: 'I no more imagine that I have already attained, that I already love God with all my heart, soul and strength, than that I am in the third heavens.' Ibid., vol. 2, p. 140.

God is not *proof* that a person remains an unbeliever. The slow recognition of this fact brought a crucial change to Wesley's thinking. The truth was that in treating as non-Christians all who lacked the certainty that their sins were forgiven, they had set the definition of Christian too high. In his old age Wesley wrote to Melville Horne:

'When fifty years ago my brother Charles and I, in the simplicity of our hearts, told the good people of England, that unless they *knew* their sins were forgiven, they were under the wrath and curse of God, I marvel, Melville, they did not stone us! The Methodists, I hope, know better now: we preach assurance as we always did, as a common privilege of the children of God; but we do not enforce it, under the pain of damnation, denounced on all who enjoy it not.'[1]

Yet it was not only aspects of Wesley's preaching between 1738 and the mid-1740s which required re-evaluation in view of this change in his thinking. What about the Aldersgate experience itself? Was it, as he said at the time, the day he became a Christian or was it rather an assurance resulting from a clearer sight given to him of Christ and his work? Once what happened to him on 24 May 1738 is re-examined in the light of that question, the once-popular assumption that Wesley was 'converted' at Aldersgate Street begins to fall apart. A great change there was, as I have already said, but that would not have been the first or the last time that a believer suddenly gaining strong assurance becomes almost a different person. In point of fact, Wesley himself was to revise his early statements. Against the *Journal* words written in February

---

[1] Quoted in Southey, *Wesley*, p. 177. This letter, undated, does not appear in Telford's definitive edition of Wesley's *Letters*.

1738 (and first published in 1740), where he spoke of himself as unconverted, he was later to add the words, 'I am not sure of this', and to say, 'I had even then the faith of a *servant*, though not that of a *son*.'[1] By 'servant' he meant a Christian without assurance as reference to his words elsewhere clearly show.[2] And in another later footnote to his words of February 1738, 'I am "a child of wrath," an heir of hell', there is his correction, 'I believe not.'

Frequently, in later years, Wesley makes autobiographical references that clearly show he had come to think of himself as a Christian before 1738,[3] and there is no lack of evidence from other individuals, Whitefield among them, who clearly thought the same.

It may well have been Wesley's reading of the Puritans that helped him to see that conversion and assurance are not necessarily the same thing. Certainly when he began a first extensive reading of the Puritans after the mid-1740's,[4] it led him to a very considerable revision of his earlier estimates. In 1747 when a clerical opponent likened the Methodists' work to the 'irregularities' prac-

---

[1] *Journal*, vol. 1, p. 422–3. The additions to the text of his *Journal* are said to have first appeared in the editions of his *Works* of 1774 and 1797.

[2] See 'On Faith,' *Works*, vol. 7, p. 199, where again he criticises the mistake made 'nearly fifty years ago.'

[3] In his *Plain Account of Christian Perfection* (1777), in which he speaks at length on his spiritual experience, there is not so much as a mention of the Aldersgate Street experience. In 1772, writing to Charles of his pre-1738 days at Oxford, he says: 'I did then walk closely with God' (*Letters*, vol. 6, p. 6).

[4] In 1739 he was, as noted above, familiar with Thomas Halyburton; he was also reading Daniel Neal's *History of the Puritans*, and some of John Bunyan but, these and some other items, did not amount to any real acquaintance. Whitefield knew this when he says that Wesley told him 'in a letter you wrote me not long since,' that 'no Baptist or Presbyterian writer whom you have read, knew anything of the liberties of Christ.' 'A Letter to the Rev. John Wesley' (Dec. 24, 1740) in *Whitefield's Journals* (London: Banner of Truth, 1960), p. 583.

tised by Thomas Cartwright and the Puritans, Wesley responded:

'I look upon him and the body of the Puritans in that age (to whom the German Anabaptists bore small resemblance) to have been both the most learned and most pious men that were then in the English nation. Nor did they separate from the Church, but were driven out, whether they would or no.'[1]

Just how much Wesley had been reading the Puritans was to become apparent in 1749 when he launched his 'Christian Library'. From that date to 1755, he was to publish fifty small (duodecimo) volumes that would contain the 'choicest pieces of Practical Divinity'. 'My purpose', he wrote to a friend, 'was to select whatever I had seen most valuable in the English language, and either abridge or take the whole tracts, only a little corrected or explained, as occasion should require.'[2] So many Puritans appeared in this Christian Library that one Church of England critic put it down as an 'odd collection of mutilated writings of dissenters of all sorts'.[3] Wesley disagreed but the number was considerable and included such names as those of Robert Bolton, John Preston, Richard Sibbes, Thomas Goodwin, John Owen, John Flavel, Joseph Alleine, and John Howe. Also included in Volume XLIV of the Library were two sermons by Samuel

---

[1] *Letters*, vol. 2, p. 94. It was not always commendation, however. In his *Journal* for 13 March 1747, when he was again reading Daniel Neal, he noted 'the weakness of those holy confessors, many of whom spent so much of their time and strength in disputing about surplices and hoods, or kneeling at the Lord's Supper.' From this criticism he elsewhere exempted Philip Henry and 'those that were of his spirit.' *Works*, vol. 8, p. 243.

[2] *Letters*, vol. 2, p. 152.

[3] *The London Magazine*, November 1760, quoted by Robert C. Monk, *John Wesley: His Puritan Heritage* (London: Epworth, 1966), p. 37.

Annesley. It is probable that his grandfather's writings had not been brought before him by his parents.[1]

In reading John Bunyan's masterpiece, *The Pilgrim's Progress*, Wesley may have come to recognize in 'Christian' something similar to his own experience. Christian, writes Bunyan, left the City of Destruction for Mount Zion with a burden on his back. Immediately he is in the company of Mr Worldly Wiseman who tells him to go to a town called Morality where a certain man named Legality, the son of the Bondwoman, was a great remover of burdens. Instead of deliverance the pilgrim finds himself in the Slough of Despond (conviction of sin) about which Bunyan says, this Slough has 'swallowed up at least twenty thousand cart loads; yea, Millions of wholesome Instructions . . . but it is the Slough of Despond still; and so will be when they have done what they can.'

The picture is very like that of Wesley in the 1720s and 1730s, leaving the world but entangled with authors who could provide him with no sure remedy. Thus Wesley endured long conviction of sin, an experience not uncommon among men whom God prepares to be eminent evangelists. Bunyan has been criticized for the way he describes the next stage in Christian's experience: he passed through the Strait Gate (regeneration), on to the narrow way, where he ran with difficulty and with no deliverance from his burden

'till he came at a place somewhat ascending, and upon that place stood a Cross, and a little below, in the bottom a Sepulchre. So I saw in my dream, That just as Christian

---

[1] Monk, *Puritan Heritage*, p. 39. This author, after examining the whole of Wesley's Christian Library, estimated that, taking the word 'Puritan' in a broad sense, Puritan authors numbered thirty-two, while twenty-eight might be said to be Church of England. But ambiguities of terminology make such enumerations very uncertain.

came up with the Cross, his Burden loosed from off his shoulders, and fell off his back, and began to tumble, and so continued to do, till it came to the mouth of the Sepulchre, where it fell in, and I saw it no more . . . Then he stood still a while to look and wonder; for it was very surprising to him, that the sight of the Cross should thus ease him of his Burden . . . Then Christian gave three leaps for joy, and went on singing.'[1]

For Bunyan's Christian there was a clear interval between passing through the Strait Gate (regeneration) and having such assurance as comes from a clear sight of Christ crucified. What Christian experienced at the cross, Wesley found on 24 May 1738 in Aldersgate Street. But when, then, was the eighteenth-century pilgrim regenerated? We do not know and nor did he himself; it is enough to say that there are signs in the 1730s that he was on the narrow way, before he and brother Charles could sing,

> No condemnation now I dread;
> Jesus, and all in him, is mine.

---

[1] John Bunyan, *The Pilgrim's Progress* (1678, 1685; reprint ed., Edinburgh: Banner of Truth, 1977), pp. 35–6.

Chapter 4

The Collision with Calvinism

In addition to High Church theology, mysticism and Moravianism, Wesley's life was related to another school of belief – the one which, as already noted, led to the division of the Evangelical Revival leadership in 1740–41. The reason for the breach with Whitefield is essential to any understanding of John Wesley. The Gloucestershire youth who had joined the Holy Club in the early 1730s, and called Wesley 'my spiritual father in Christ', had become his public critic. Thereafter the two men were seldom able to work long together. The difference involved personality factors, and failures on both sides, but the real collision was not between the individuals; it was between differing theologies. Whitefield had been far less exposed to the thinking of the High Church writers, the mystics, and the Moravians, and comparatively soon after his entrance into the ministry he was an enthusiastic reader of the Puritan authors from whom Wesley's parents had early departed. And in 1739–40 Whitefield met prominent evangelicals on the other side of the Atlantic whose ministries demonstrated to him the relevance of the Reformed and Puritan writers.

Wesley disagreed with his former disciple but what has to be recognized is that from the outset the two men meant different things by 'Calvinism'.[1] For Whitefield – if he used the word at all – it meant the evangelical theology of the Reformation; for Wesley it meant the imposition on Christianity of a form of belief that had brought decadence on the churches. 'The polemical and systematical writers of the last century', 'John Smith' reminded Wesley, had been exploded 'to the satisfaction of most men of learning and piety'.[2] Wesley, taught to regard the Puritans in that light from his youth, did not need the reminder. His sister, Mrs Emilia Harper, spoke for the whole family when she wrote to John, 17 June 1741, 'I am glad at heart you oppose Whitefield and his horrid doctrines of predestination.'[3]

Their mother went further and took up her pen to write against Whitefield in an anonymous publication of 1741. In doing so she drew on her own Dissenting background:

'I have been well acquainted with many predestinarians and have observed two sorts of people amongst them. The one were serious and, I believe, sincerely desirous of salvation, and striving to enter by the strait gate into the kingdom of heaven. These were generally much dejected and (excepting a few) always seeking after marks of grace, being doubtful of their own election, often upon the point of despair, being ignorant of that true gospel liberty which is attainable in this life and which many who hold universal redemption do actually enjoy.

'Others, and they the far greater number, were very confident of their own election, thought it a great sin to make any doubt of it, and could not patiently hear it

---

[1] Whitefield spoke of 'free grace' and professed he had never read a line of Calvin when the controversy began. Once the label of Calvinism was introduced it was impossible to avoid its continuance as a party term.

[2] *Works* (Abingdon). vol. 26, p. 169.

[3] Ibid., p. 63.

questioned. These were commonly sunk in carnal security and without scruple gave in to all manner of self-indulgence, fancying that what would be sin in a reprobate would be none in them'.[1]

When allowance is made for prejudice, the fact remains that Susanna Wesley's perception of the consequences of Calvinistic belief was common to her generation, and it gained credibility from existing conditions in many Dissenting 'meeting houses' (as the churches of the lineal descendants of the Puritans were called). Too often there was little zeal shown for evangelism among them. As Henry Rack writes, Dissent 'became a static, ingrown, hereditary (though also declining) creed'; and, 'It is not surprising that Wesley, a High Churchman . . . should have had a lifelong distaste for what he saw as a hole-in-the-corner, static, localized form of religion.'[2]

Some of Wesley's reading at the Bodleian Library in Oxford in 1741 also confirmed his worst fears about Calvinism, particularly the wrangling at the Synod of Dort, and Calvin's treatment of Michael Servetus.

There was another reason why, as early as April 1739, Wesley opposed Calvinistic teaching. Tyerman says, 'It is a curious fact, that Whitefield was more violently attacked than the Wesleys were.'[3] But one of the reasons for this is clear: Whitefield spoke of the Evangelical Revival as a recovery of the beliefs of the previous century, in other words, it was said, of 'Calvinism'. In Wesley's view this was playing into the hands of such critics as Dr Trapp

---

[1] *Some Remarks on a Letter from the Reverend Mr Whitefield to the Reverend Mr Wesley, In a Letter from a Gentlewoman to her Friend* (London, 1741), quoted from *Susanna Wesley*, p. 470. Frank Baker has proved that Mrs Wesley was the author.

[2] Rack *Reasonable Enthusiast*, pp. 35,38.

[3] Tyerman, *Wesley*, vol. 1, p. 326.

who sought to smear the Methodists by identifying them with the Puritans. Wesley wanted to avoid that identification and the resultant criticism. His motivation was not any concern for popularity; that was not his make-up. It was rather that he saw no reason why he should accept opprobrium for teaching which he rejected. A *Journal* entry for 9 October 1739 makes the point plain. At that time both he and his brother, Charles, had been cautioned by a local public figure at Buryfield not to preach there again. The reason given was that a previous sermon by Charles had given great offence: 'It [is] everywhere reported that I am a strong Predestinarian. Much pain had been taken to represent me as such. We judged this a call for me to declare myself.' So, despite the advice to the contrary, the two brothers went and took a service in the open-air at which Charles, John writes, 'was constrained to explain himself on that head, and to show, in plain and strong words, that God "willeth all men to be saved"'.

The last quotation brings us to the main theological reason why Wesley opposed Calvinism. How could a belief that God has elected some to salvation, and decreed the reprobation of all others, be consistent with the love that has commanded the good news to be proclaimed to every creature? If only the salvation of the elect is certain, then God must have predestinated all others to damnation. 'Predestinarian' belief therefore had to be a threat to evangelical Christianity; he was sure it would imperil the work of evangelizing the masses so wonderfully begun. For how could a passion to bring the gospel to all be maintained if it were not true that God 'is not willing that any should perish'(*2 Pet.* 3:11)? And how could such texts as, 'Why will ye die, O house of Israel?' (*Ezek.* 33:11) be preached if predestination was accepted? With an aside meant for Calvinists to digest, Wesley noted in his *Journal* for 31 May 1741:

'In the evening I published the great decree of God, eternal, unchangeable (so miserably misunderstood and misrepresented by vain men that would be wise): "He that believeth shall be saved; he that believeth not shall be damned."'

So Calvinism, as Wesley misunderstood it, meant *no* proclamation of the love of God for all men. Yet John Calvin himself had preached, 'Jesus Christ offers himself generally to all men without exception to be their redeemer', and that 'love . . . extends to all men, inasmuch as Jesus Christ reaches out his arms to call and allure all men both great and small, to win them to him'.[1]

Wesley had made up his mind that the Calvinistic belief of Reformers and Puritans was contrary to evangelism, and that there was no way they could have sung:

> O that the world might taste and see
> The riches of his grace;
> The arms of love that compass me
> Would all mankind embrace.

But he was wrong. The Puritans had no problem in speaking of 'God's unspeakable love to mankind', or in asserting that 'God hath a general love to all the creatures'.[2]

---

[1] See, John Calvin, *Sermons on Deuteronomy* (1583; reprint ed., Edinburgh: Banner of Truth, 1987), p. 167; and his *Commentary* on John 3:16.

[2] See, for instance, Thomas Manton on John 3:16 in *Works of Thomas Manton*, vol. 2 (London: Nisbet, 1871), p. 340; *Works of Hugh Binning*, vol. 3 (Edinburgh: Whyte, 1840), p. 411. The Westminster divines were agreed that 'the gospel, where it cometh, doth tender salvation by Christ to all', and, in the words of Edmund Calamy, 'It is most certain that God is not the cause of any man's damnation. He found us in Adam, but made none sinners.' *Minutes of the Sessions of the Westminster Assembly of Divines*, edited by A. F. Mitchell and J. Struthers (Edinburgh: Blackwood, 1874), pp. lx–lxi.

For Wesley it was impossible to hold the beliefs of Calvinists about salvation and still write, as Whitefield wrote to him in 1740, 'God is loving to every man'.[1] Whitefield's Calvinism, observed Curnock, 'Wesley apparently never understood'.[2] Wesley saw his friend as an inconsistent Calvinist,[3] and that because he did not fit his perception of what a Calvinist had to be. He was to say of Whitefield:

'How few have we known of so kind a temper, of such large and flowing affections? Was it not principally by this, that the hearts of others were so strangely drawn and knit to him? Can any thing but love beget love? This shone in his very countenance, and continually breathed in all his words'.[4]

There is however something to be said in defence of Wesley's misconception. The Reformers and Puritans had never had to deal with Hyper-Calvinism; that is to say, with an outlook which allows for no divine compassion for the non-elect, no universal duty to believe on Christ for salvation, and no need on the part of preachers to desire the salvation of all their hearers. The opinion of W. H. Goold, editor of the *Works of John Owen*, on the seventeenth century generally, carries weight:

'To counteract the tendency of the religious mind when it proceeded in the direction of Arminianism, Calvinistic divines, naturally engrossed with the points in dispute, dwelt greatly on the workings of efficacious grace in election, regeneration, and conversion, if not to the

---

[1] 'Letter to John Wesley,' *Whitefield's Journals*, p. 585. The issue between Calvinism and Arminianism is not whether God loves all men, it is whether God loves all men equally.

[2] Wesley, *Journal*, vol. 5, p. 386.

[3] *Letters*, vol. 3, p. 230.

[4] *Works*, vol. 2, pp. 175–6.

exclusion of the free offer of the gospel, at least so as to cast somewhat into the shade the free justification offered in it.'[1]

But if evangelical 'guns' had been facing one direction in the seventeenth century, by the eighteenth there was danger from another direction, from Hyper-Calvinism with its denial of a love of God for all men and of the free offer of the gospel to all. The meaning of Scripture texts that did not fit this scheme was strained away.[2] That there were Dissenting ministers with such convictions, and opposed to the Wesleyan Methodists on that account, is clear enough. John Nelson gives several instances of such pastors who would not accept that God 'is loving to every man'. To one such he spoke as follows:

'Tell me, Sir, did you ever feel the love of God in your own soul? If you did, I appeal to your conscience, whether at that time you did not find love to every soul of man. Now, this was not your nature, but the nature of God; and if one drop of the bucket could so swell your soul, what must that ocean be from which it came?'[3]

If ministers professing strict orthodoxy thought this way, is it any wonder that their hearers had trouble? Thomas Collins, a Methodist itinerant whom we shall meet in later pages, gives an instance of a woman who had long been accustomed to a certain type of Calvinistic teaching. She

---

[1] Prefatory Note, *Works of John Owen* (London: Banner of Truth, 1967), vol. 5, p. 2.

[2] For example, Wesley's opponent, John Gill, argued that when God said, 'Why will ye die?', we are to understand that 'the death expostulated about is not eternal, but a temporal one, or what concerns their temporal affairs.' See my *Spurgeon v. Hyper-Calvinism* (Edinburgh: Banner of Truth, 1997), p. 128. On this and similar texts Gill was followed by A. M. Toplady.

[3] *Journal of Nelson*, pp. 182–3.

first heard Collins preaching in the open-air. On the evangelist's speaking with her he found her to be 'much conscience-smitten'. He visited her in her home for further conversation. When he was about to leave,

'Seeing that she had seven children, he prayed for them, blessed them, and besought her to "bring them up in the nurture and admonition of the Lord;" for, said he, all their immortal souls are precious in His sight. That 'all' was fatal. It broke the spell thrown over her. All precious to God? Not one, out of so many, reprobated? What heresy! To whom had she been listening? What terrible falsehood had well-nigh beguiled her? From that day she held him to be a deceiver, and would never see or hear him more'.[1]

By the recovery of Puritan literature, by Whitefield's preaching, and other influences, the Dissenting churches had to be brought from Hyper-Calvinism, and no doubt at times the Wesleyan Methodists helped in that deliverance.[2] While the recognition of the existence of such teaching in Wesley's day does not excuse the persistence of his misconception, it may help us to understand it.

There was another reason why Wesley was so opposed to Calvinism, as he conceived it. Under the shadow of orthodox Puritan belief Antinomianism had too often sprung up. Testimonies more weighty than that of Susanna Wesley's childhood memories endorsed that fact. John Owen had written:

'It cannot be denied but that some men may, and it is justly to be feared that some men do, abuse the doctrine

---

[1] Samuel Coley, *Life of Thomas Collins* (London: Hamilton, Adams and Co., 1868), pp. 131–2.
[2] It was when this happened among the circle of William Carey, John Ryland Jr. and Andrew Fuller, in the 1780s, that the Baptists became a vital missionary force.

of the gospel to countenance themselves in a vain expectation of mercy and pardon, whilst they willingly live in a course of sin.'[1]

Antinomians, making a Christian profession yet living careless or immoral lives, persisted in the eighteenth century. Wesley found them in his own societies and a painful example was the disgraceful conduct of his own brother-in-law, the Rev. Westly Hall. But Wesley was convinced that this blight was more common in professedly Calvinistic circles and before the end of the eighteenth century that might have been true. An unbalanced form of doctrinal preaching, with emphasis on unconditional election and final perseverance, and faith constantly treated as though it was the only Christian duty, is bound to lead to moral casualties. In emphasizing the danger of Antinomianism Wesley was not dreaming. Before the end of the century the warnings on the same subject were to be common among the Calvinists who followed in the tradition of Whitefield. Henry Venn, for instance, warned his son of it in these words:

'The sovereign and electing grace of God, by which alone we are brought to Him, bears no proportion in the Scripture to the continual mention that is made of the absolute necessity, beauty, and excellency of a holy life and conversation, in the sight of God and man – bears no proportion, I say, to the practical part of our holy religion . . . St Paul had no sooner finished his triumphant account of grace reigning through righteousness, than he leaves the subject; and writes a whole chapter, by way of

---

[1] John Owen, *Exposition of Hebrews* (Edinburgh: Banner of Truth, 1991) vol. 5, p. 27.

guarding against Antinomian interpretation of his doctrine'.[1]

But for Wesley, Antinomianism was not a question of wrong balance, or the mishandling of certain scriptures, it was a direct consequence of Calvinistic belief. Teach men to believe in election, and in their future security, and he feared it would be bound to induce carelessness. If the Calvinistic tenets were true, he asked, why the need of such warnings in Scripture as, 'We are made partakers of Christ, if we hold the beginning of our confidence steadfast unto the end', and, 'Beware lest ye also, being led away with the error of the wicked, fall from your own steadfastness' (*Heb.* 3:14; *2 Pet.* 3:17)? So Wesley's solution to Antinomianism was to oppose election. In doing so he denied that he was speaking against the grace of God in salvation. To the Calvinists who said, 'We ascribe to God alone the whole glory of our salvation', he would reply, 'So do we too.'[2] His concern was to uphold the truth that where the work of salvation is real there will always be the ethical, moral dimension. Thus it

---

[1] *The Life and Selection from the Letters of Henry Venn*, ed. Henry Venn, Jr. (1836; reprint ed., Edinburgh: Banner of Truth, 1993), p. 531. Another non-Wesleyan witnesses to the danger of Antinomianism in the later eighteenth century was the Rev. Thomas Scott who believed, 'Gradually a view of the gospel rather tending to antinomianism was introduced by the successors of the ministers that have been mentioned – that is Mr Whitefield and Co. . . . By carrying certain parts of religion to an extreme . . . a most subtile, pernicious, and disgraceful bias to *practical*, and in some sense to *doctrinal*, antinomianism has become very general.' *Letters and Papers of Thomas Scott*, edited by John Scott (London: Seeley, 1824), pp. 181, 21. An Anglican colleague of Scott's did not have quite the same assessment. Writing in 1803, Isaac Milner believed: 'The danger of Antinomianism, though dreadful, is not extensive. I have rarely, if ever, met a single instance of the kind; whereas I meet with thousands of Pharisees . . . it is natural to man, whereas salvation by grace is not natural.' Mary Milner, *The Life of Isaac Milner* (London: Parker, 1842), p. 277.

[2] *Works*, vol. 10, p. 230.

was quite within the intention of Wesley's teaching when one of his preachers responded to the question of a Calvinist, 'Do you believe in the perseverance of saints?' with the answer, 'Certainly'. When the questioner registered his surprise and said, 'I thought you did not', the Methodist preacher explained, 'O, Sir, you have been misinformed; it is the perseverance of *sinners* we doubt'.[1]

Yet sincere though he was, the standpoint Wesley adopted encouraged him, in my opinion, into two errors. First, it led him to weaken the finality of justification, as I shall discuss more fully below.[2] He feared that a justification once-and-for-all came too close to the Calvinistic scheme; it could induce false confidence by removing any possibility of a believer falling away. Taken as a whole, his teaching on justification made the gospel of salvation by faith in Christ clear, but at times under the pressure of controversy he wavered, most seriously in a controversy of 1770.

Second, in his fear that Calvinism was allied to Antinomianism, Wesley committed himself to the beliefs of his earlier years on Christian perfection, as already noted. This belief, he was convinced, would provide the antidote to the idea that the believer can stop and rest at conversion, treating it as the goal instead of the starting point. He saw a denial of teaching on perfection as taking away the incentive to seek for full deliverance from sin and perfect love to God. Every believer needs to be taught to press on to perfection. So stated, the teaching might be unexceptionable; where it became so controversial and problematical was in Wesley's insistence that the attainment of the goal was promised in this life and that

[1] Coley, *Collins*, p. 132.
[2] I discuss this more fully below, pp. 217–31.

the promise could be received instantaneously by faith. This, also, I will consider more fully later on.

As I have said earlier, Wesley believed that his Christian-perfection teaching rested on the twin pillars of Scripture and experience. But it was the experience to which others witnessed that bore the main weight. By far the majority of those who testified to perfection were women belonging to his societies and they occupied an important place in his correspondence. But there were severe disappointments; it was not without reason that Charles Wesley used to charge his brother with 'credulity'.[1] One of John's great favourites as an outstanding Christian in the 1750s was Sarah Ryan, 'one whose equal I have not yet found in England'.[2] Wesley would often write to her in the highest terms of Christian esteem and affection, but in 1766 it was in a different tone:

'For some time I have been convinced it was my duty to tell you what was on my mind . . . You appear to be above instruction – I mean instruction from man . . . You appear to think (I will not affirm you do), that none understands the doctrine of Sanctification like you . . . You appear to undervalue the experience of almost everyone in comparison of your own'.[3]

There were a number of other cases similar to Ryan's. Jeannie Keith, one of the women leaders in the Newcastle society, was known as 'holy Mary'. But then we find Wesley writing of her to his brother, 'Alas, from what a height she has fallen'.[4] Wesley never seems to have suspected that his encouragement to some of these

[1] Works (Abingdon), vol. 26, pp. 17, 41,479n.
[2] *Letters*, vol. 4, p. 14.
[3] *Letters*, vol. 5, p. 17.
[4] *Works* (Abingdon), p. 479.

women may have contributed to their mistake. It is also true that his correspondence with some of these favourites upset his wife and contributed to the disharmony of their marriage.

* * * * *

There were factors in the Evangelical Revival which, it might have been thought, would have moderated Wesley's opposition to Calvinism. As conversions multiplied, for example, and as he himself believed they all demonstrated the immediate intervention of God, he might have had cause for second thoughts. As Henry Rack has written:

'It is not surprising that many evangelicals should have developed Calvinistic and predestinarian views as a result of their conversions: revivals of a strong doctrine of sin and of grace always produce this result. The surprising thing is that, exceptionally within the Revival as a whole, Wesley did not.'[1]

Again, Wesley's growing acquaintance with Puritan authors after the mid-1740s, might have prompted a re-evaluation of his understanding of Calvinism. Instead he usually 'corrected' and edited out of the Puritan reprints that he supervised those passages which conflicted with his position.[2] The truth is that Wesley's opposition to Calvinism stiffened rather than weakened.

---

[1] Rack, *Reasonable Enthusiast*, p. 388.

[2] How he 'revised' the Westminster *Shorter Catechism* can be seen in *Wesley's Revision of the Shorter Catechism* (Edinburgh: Morton, 1906). Whatever we think of Wesley's practice in this regard, he was hardly acting according to the rule he required of others when it came to hymns: 'Many gentlemen have done my brother and me . . . the honour to reprint many of our Hymns. Now they are perfectly welcome to do so, provided they reprint them just as they are.' *Works*, vol. 14, p. 341.

As I have said above, I believe the main reason for this was his sincere belief that the teaching he opposed did not do justice to Scripture. But an element of natural stubbornness and confidence in his own judgment cannot be ruled out. One of his own preachers once spoke of Wesley's 'excessive attachment to particular opinions'.[1] Luke Tyerman, a warm admirer of Wesley, believed that he had a teachable spirit in 1739, he was 'docile and eager to be taught'.[2] But not, Tyerman adds, by Whitefield, because, 'While at college, he [Wesley] had thoroughly sifted the subject for himself . . . Whitefield, on the contrary was no theologian'.[3]

When a whole succession of men took the same position as Whitefield on the doctrines of grace, Wesley was unmoved. Richard Hutchins and James Hervey, former members of the Holy Club under Wesley, moved away from their former leader on the points of difference.[4] So did such a promising young preacher as John Cennick and, later, a number of his own itinerants, headed by John Bennet, John Whitford and John Edwards. Still more painful to Wesley was the succession of Church of England clergy, initially close to him, with whom co-operation failed after they 'turned to Calvinism'. The number included, John Newton, John Berridge, Henry Venn, and Augustus Toplady. For Wesley, as Henry Rack has said,

---

[1] John Hampson, quoted by Rack, *Reasonable Enthusiast*, p. 540. Charles Wesley, writing to his brother in 1746, said, 'I find it is utterly in vain to write to you upon anything whereon we are not already agreed . . . you take no notice of my reasons'. *Works* (Abingdon), vol. 26, pp. 207–8.

[2] Tyerman, *Wesley*, vol. 1, p. 230.

[3] Ibid., p. 312.

[4] When Wesley, in his *Preservative against Unsettled Notions in Religion* (1758), answered Hervey's Calvinistic teaching, his concluding remonstrance with his old friend reveals his sense of hurt: '"And is this thy voice, my son David?" Is this thy tender, loving, grateful spirit?'

'The growing number of Calvinistic Evangelical clergy
was a particularly sore point.'[1] Even the Countess of
Huntingdon, whom Wesley had nurtured as a young
Christian, and who once wrote to him, 'Whatever you
think best will soon be my choice',[2] joined the other side.
Speaking of the evangelical clergy, and the teaching of
Christian Perfection, Tyerman comments that in the year
1766, 'Wesley stood almost alone, with the exception of
his friend Fletcher.'[3]

Writing to the Countess of Huntingdon in 1771,
Wesley defended his spiritual consistency over the previous
thirty years. 'But', he continued, 'during this time, well
nigh all the religious world hath set themselves in array
against me, and among the rest many of my own children,
following the example of one of my eldest sons, Mr
Whitefield'.[4] So near paranoid did Wesley become on the
extent of the defection of others from what he believed
to be true that when for a short time he heard nothing
from his close associate, John Fletcher, whose parish was
at Madeley, the worst possibility at least crossed his mind.
To his brother Charles he confides: 'I wonder why it is
that we hear nothing from Madeley. Surely, prejudice has
not stepped in, or Calvinism!'[5]

Wesley never seems to have questioned that his opposition was due to anything other than duty in the midst
of spiritual warfare, 'Satan threw Calvinism in our way',
he told his conference of 1765.

* * * * *

[1] Rack, *Reasonable Enthusiast*, p. 500.
[2] *Works* (Abingdon), vol. 26, p. 76.
[3] Tyerman, *Wesley*, vol. 2, p. 563.
[4] *Letters*, vol. 5, p. 259.
[5] *Letters*, vol. 7, p. 70. The truth may be that it was romance that somewhat
occupied Fletcher: he was shortly to marry Mary Bosanquet!

What did the Calvinists think of Wesley? Whitefield wrote: 'Mr Wesley I think is wrong in some things; yet I believe . . . Mr Wesley, and others, with whom we do not agree in all things, will shine bright in glory'.[1] And at another time Whitefield wrote to Wesley himself, 'The regard I have always had for you is still great, if not greater than ever; and I trust we shall give this and future ages an example of true Christian love abiding, notwithstanding differences in judgment'.[2] William Grimshaw, referring to Wesley and Whitefield, affirmed that his heart was 'indivisible knit to both', and went on, 'I doubt not but yt. notwithstanding their Differences in Judgment in some even material points of Religion, they are both undoubtedly taught by the Holy Spirit. Luther, Zwingli and Calvin widely differ'd, but no doubt were Spiritual Ministers of Christ'.[3] John Newton, while young, said of Wesley, 'I know of no one to whom I owe more as an instrument of divine grace.' Cornelius Winter wrote to the older man, 'Give me leave to differ and to love. God bless you to your latest period, and make your last days your best days.' More fully Henry Venn expressed himself to Wesley in these words:

'I have often experienced your words as thunder to my drowsy soul . . . It is the request of one who, though he differs from you, and possibly ever may, on some points, yet must ever acknowledge the benefit and light he has received from your work and preaching; and, therefore, is bound to thank the Lord of the harvest for sending a labourer among us so endowed with the spirit and power

---

[1] Whitefield, *Works*, vol. 1, p. 438.
[2] *Works* (Abingdon), vol. 26, p. 220.
[3] *William Grimshaw 1708–1768*, Frank Baker (London: Epworth Press, 1963), p. 233.

of Elias; and to pray for your long continuance among us, to encourage me and my brethren by your example, while you edify us by your writings.'[1]

It has to be added that not all Calvinists had this esteem for Wesley. In the 1770s younger men such as Richard and Rowland Hill, who had never met him, were to attack him in a way that would have shocked Whitefield, and which they later regretted. Augustus Toplady (who was particularly provoked) was to go so far as doubting whether Wesley was a Christian at all.[2] Doubt on that point turned to the certainty that Wesley was lost in a sermon of the voluble Antinomian, William Huntington, *The Funeral of Arminianism* (1791). In Huntington's blindness there is a moral which is worth noting. William Hone was a child brought up in the home of parents who followed Huntington and who taught their son to regard Wesley – then still alive – as a 'child of the devil'. Strangely enough the boy was sent to a school run by a Wesleyan woman. Pupil and teacher were much attached and when she became ill he was permitted to visit her. On one such visit, as he was sitting by her bedside, he was alarmed to hear a maid announce another visitor, none other than John Wesley himself. We read:

'There entered a venerable old man, his silvered hair hanging down his shoulders, his complexion fresh and placid, his smile sweet. To the boy's amazement he seemed to have the countenance of an angel. He

---

[1] The words of Newton, Winter and Venn are taken from *The Wesley Memorial Volume*, edited by J. O. A. Clark (New York: Phillips and Hunt, 1880), p. 655. Other testimonies given are from Berridge, Hervey and Haweis.

[2] *Complete Works of Augustus M. Toplady* (London: Cornish, 1861), p. 732.

ministered to the lady, spoke comforting words, knelt down, prayed, and took his departure, saying to the awe-struck lad as he did so, "God bless you, my child, and make you a good man." In later years, Hone passed his comment: "I never saw Mr Wesley again; my dame died; but from that hour I never believed anything my father said, or anything I heard at chapel."[1]

* * * * *

That the older Calvinistic leaders in the Evangelical Revival commended Wesley does not mean that they ignored his inconsistencies. They noted one in particular. Wesley urged, as already noted, that the essence of bigotry was to contend for 'opinions' instead of fundamentals. 'Warm Calvinists' he treated as among the worst offenders in this regard.

But if the matters dividing the evangelicals were only 'opinions', why did Wesley continue to contend for them so persistently? This was the question which John Newton pointedly put to him and in his reply Wesley summarizes the point in these words:

'You have admirably well expressed what I mean by *an opinion* contra-distinguished from an *essential* doctrine. Whatever is "compatible with a love to Christ and a work of grace," I term an opinion. And certainly the holding "particular election" and "final perseverance" is compatible with these. "Yet what fundamental error (you ask) have you opposed with half *that frequency and vehemence* as you have these opinions?"'[2]

---

[1] Quoted in S. M. Houghton, *My Life and Books* (Edinburgh: Banner of Truth, 1988), p. 79.
[2] *Letters*, vol. 4, p. 297.

The only option open to Wesley in answering this was to deny the sustained opposition which Newton alleged. This he did, and no doubt sincerely, but the denial is hard to sustain from the facts. There is not only the number of his publications attacking Calvinism, culminating in *The Arminian Magazine* (launched in 1788 to uphold General Redemption); there were many practical directions to his people along the same lines. His preachers in the 1750s were directed not to attend Dissenting congregations and later the same counsel was given to all his society members, and this, he said, because of 'danger from imbibing the grand error – Calvinism – from the Dissenting ministers. Perhaps thousands have done it already, most of whom have drawn back to perdition'.[1] 'Is not Calvinism', he says elsewhere, 'the most deadly and successful enemy?'[2] So the difference was scarcely one of 'opinions'! Perhaps, as I have said before, under the common label of 'Calvinism' different things were being described or imagined.

It is very noticeable in Wesley's correspondence to his own people that his references to Calvinism differ markedly from the irenical language he used when speaking to those on the other side. To the Rev. Samuel Walker, another of the Calvinistic clergy, he defends the strong words used in counselling his people not to hear 'predestinarian preachers' by the shift, 'We find by long experience that this is "deadly poison," not *in itself* but to *the members of our Societies*.'[3]

---

[1] Ibid., vol. 6, p. 326. Compare this language with the way he insists to John Newton that the difference between them 'is only an *opinion*; it is not subversive "of the very foundations of Christian experience".' Ibid., vol. 4, p. 298. To other correspondents he speaks of 'vile bigotry! The exact spirit of Calvinism!' Again: 'Nothing can more effectually stop the work of God than the breaking in of Calvinism' (Ibid., vol. 7, pp. 206, 136).

[2] Ibid., vol. 8, p. 95. [3] Ibid., vol. 3, p. 144.

Another thing which troubled Wesley's Calvinistic brethren, and especially after the death of Whitefield in 1770, was the way the Methodist leader allowed Whitefield's name to drop out of the record when he was describing the beginnings of the Evangelical Revival. The subject is, 'My brother and I'. 'Two young men without a name, without friends, without either power or fortune "set out from College with principles totally different from those of the common people", to oppose all the world, learned and unlearned.'[1] God's 'great work in our land . . . has never been intermitted one year, or one month, since the year 1738 in which my brother and I began to preach that strange doctrine of salvation by faith.'[2] Statements of this kind were intended to show that the awakening had proceeded on the basis of *his* distinctive beliefs. But defending this proposition involved him in contradictions, when, for instance, he asserted in 1777 that he had been first to preach in the open-air, 'I preached in the open air in October, 1735. Mr Whitefield was not then ordained.'[3] Long before, however, he had admitted that it was Whitefield's example that had moved him to that practice. 'Mr Whitefield's *public preaching*', he wrote in 1748, 'was not the *consequence* but the cause of mine.'[4]

* * * * *

[1] Ibid., vol. 6, p. 61.

[2] *Journal*, vol. 6, p. 135.

[3] *An Answer to Mr Rowland Hill's Tract, Entitled, 'Imposture Detected,'* in *Works* vol. 10, p. 447. But the reference is to his first voyage to America and it was normal practice for services to be held on the quarter deck of ships at sea.

[4] *Works* (Abingdon), vol. 26, p. 287. See also Wesley's *Journal* for March 31, 1739. On this and on kindred points Arnold Dallimore worked to set the record straight – perhaps too straight – in his masterful work, *George Whitefield: The Life and Times of the Great Evangelist of the 18th Century Revival*, vol. 1 (London: Banner of Truth, 1970), vol. 2 (Edinburgh: Banner of Truth, 1980).

Summarizing Wesley's theology it can be said that it underwent a number of changes and variations. For example, he early abandoned the idea he held in 1738–40 that conversion meant an end to all sin in the believer; he gave up identifying assurance as a necessary part of justification, yet what it was, and how it related to other parts of the believer's experience, was never lucid;[1] his teaching on Christian perfection he had to modify; the supposed instantaneous possession of full sanctification also needed qualification; and from his unwise words suggesting different degrees of justification in 1770 he had to withdraw. These things are reminders that his beliefs in their totality made up a loose synthesis, an amalgam, rather than a coherent system. Taken as a whole there was an absence of consistency, and it is arguable that this affected his spiritual life. For while insisting on Christian perfection he admitted that he had not attained to it himself. As J. Ernest Rattenbury, a Methodist of more recent times has said, some of his doctrines 'would not fit his experience'.[2] The fault lay not in his life but in the teaching. His instincts were right, his formulation was wrong. His eagerness to hear the experiences of others, especially on Christian perfection, looks like an attempt to bolster an attainment which he was too honest to pretend to have reached.

[1] 'It is difficult to know what Wesley meant at different times by the Witness of the Spirit. I have wondered when I have read his three sermons whether he ever quite arrived at a final conclusion as to its meaning himself.' J. Ernest Rattenbury, *The Conversion of the Wesleys: A Critical Study* (London: Epworth,1938), p. 130.

[2] Rattenbury, *Conversion of the Wesleys*, p. 130. The same writer is surely perceptive when he says that Wesley's problem was that the 'new doctrines' of the evangelical revival 'were held in England only by the Calvinists. Assurance and Justification by Faith, though embedded in the Articles, were not living truths, except among the Calvinists' (p. 189). Thus Wesley, rather than be a Calvinist, sought to modify the meaning of some of these terms.

Yet the foundation of Wesley's theology was sound. On the objective facts of the salvation revealed in Scripture – Paul's 'first of all' of 1 Corinthians 15:3 – Wesley was clear. On what happens to the sinner *in the sight of God* on his reception of that salvation, he was definite, Christ stands for us.[1] It was on the subjective side salvation, on the nature of Christian experience – Christ in us – that there was sometimes incoherence, and particularly on the issue of what is an 'act' (an event not needing to be repeated), and what is rather a 'process' or a matter of degrees. From quotations I have given earlier regarding conversion and rebirth as a divine work – a creation – one would suppose Wesley held that regeneration was an act, introducing a new and an eternal life in union with Christ. But the contents of Wesley's amalgam required him to question this, to think that regeneration could be repeated and that it might involve a process. Yet when it came to sanctification, Wesley wanted to depart from the traditional Christian belief that this was a process, incomplete in this life, and rather introduce the idea of the instantaneous, although the gradual could go before and follow after.

Of course, I do not mean to deny that Wesley said many good things on the Christian life, and his fear of Antinomianism was not misplaced. But he could not accept the Calvinists' response to that danger, namely, that a person who lacks holiness of life has never known the regenerating power of God, no matter how orthodox their profession. Thus he disagreed with Jonathan Edwards definitive book on the subject, *The Religious Affections.* Wesley thought that when Edwards argued that those who fell away after the Great Awakening had

---

[1] I will add some qualification to this statement in chapter 9 below.

never been truly converted, he was simply defending his Calvinism.

At the conclusion of their lives, let it be said, these Christians of differing persuasion all finished their course in the same manner, that is, in evangelical humility. When Wesley thought he was dying in 1753 he ordered the wording for his gravestone to read:

'John Wesley, A Brand plucked from the burning; Who died of consumption in the fifty-first Year of his Age, not leaving, after his Debts are paid, ten pounds behind him: Praying, God be merciful to me, an unprofitable servant'.

When Rowland Hill, Wesley's fervent young antagonist in the 1770s, came to die many years later, his testimony was: 'I can see more of my Saviour's glory than of my interest in him. God is letting me down gently into the grave, and I shall creep into heaven under some crevice of the door'.[1]

Perhaps Wesley's mistakes were allowed so that the church would not make too much of him. The injunction to call no man 'teacher, for one is your teacher, even Christ', has never been easy for Christians to learn. In his lifetime, some of his friends, brought to recognize his fallibility, reached the 'determination to call no man "Rabbi", *as a pattern or teacher*'.[2] Others failed to reach that conclusion. We are prone to suppose that a man of Wesley's stature could not be wrong. How he could have failed to recognize the biblical nature of some of the truths he opposed remains a mystery. Perhaps the opposition his failure incurred was needful for him, and a clue to the mystery may come from Wesley himself when he wrote in 1774:

[1] The words are quoted with approval by William Garner in *The Life of Mr John Garner, One of the Early Ministers of the Primitive Methodist Connexion* (London: King, 1856), pp. 109–10.
[2] *Works* (Abingdon), pp. 407, 413.

'For nearly fifty years I have been called to go through evil and good report; and, indeed, the latter without the former would be "a test for human frailty too severe". But when one balances the other all is well. The north wind prevents the ill effects of the sunshine, and the providence of God has in this respect been highly remarkable'.[1]

If Wesley's theology was confused, why, some might ask, should we value his memory today? The answer is that it is not in his theology that his real legacy lies. Christian leaders are raised up for different purposes. The eighteenth-century evangelicals were primarily men of action, and, in that role, John Wesley did and said much which was to the lasting benefit of many thousands. It is to him in that role that we need to turn. The words of J. C. Ryle are a fitting conclusion to this chapter:

'That Wesley would have done better if he could have thrown off his Arminianism, I have not the least doubt; but that he preached the gospel, honoured Christ, and did extensive good, I no more doubt than I doubt my own existence'.[2]

All Christians in one degree or another are confused and ignorant, and the verse of Charles Wesley applies to all:

> Yet when the work is done,
> The work is but begun:
> Partaker of Thy grace,
> I long to see Thy face;
> The first I prove below,
> The last I die to know.

[1] *Letters*, vol. 6, p. 107.
[2] Ryle, *Christian Leaders*, p. 86.

Chapter 5

The Leader

John Wesley was a small man, just five feet two inches tall and weighing little over eight stone for much of his life. His stature as a person was on a different scale and fits no one type. Frank Baker, an eminent Methodist historian of the twentieth century, believed that his biographers have portrayed Wesley's character in as many as twenty different versions, and that, confronted with the extent of his gifts, and his psychological contradictions, 'the real John Wesley has escaped them all'.[1]

By concentrating as much as I have done on Wesley's thought in the last two chapters, my own version is probably already out of balance, and it is time that the more controversial issues were laid aside. In any remotely authentic account of his life one thing should stand out: the unifying principle was his commitment to the Bible. What he wrote in 1745 on Scripture as the 'sole rule' of his faith he maintained to the end. In 1768 he said: 'I am, at this day, hardly sure of anything but what I learn from the Bible.'[2] In 1789 it was still the same: 'Keep close to the Bible', he exhorted a preacher, 'Enjoin nothing that the Bible does not clearly enjoin. Forbid nothing that

[1] 'The Real John Wesley', in *Methodist History*, Quarterly Review, July 1974, pp. 184–5.
[2] *Works*, vol. 6, p. 142.

it does not clearly forbid.'[1] From Scripture he learned his own position: 'I desire to have both heaven and hell ever before in my eye while I stand on this isthmus of life, between these two boundless oceans.'[2] This led to his lifelong endeavour to make Christ known as the only way to heaven. 'Wherever I see one or a thousand men running into hell, I will stop them if I can – as a minister of Christ I will beseech them in his name to turn back . . . I am not satisfied God would accept my plea, "Lord, he was not of my parish."'[3]

Countless other names in church history have shared in this same endeavour; what stands out in Wesley is the way the endeavour was maintained and never seemed to flag. The earnestness of his early years did not become the easy-going pace of an old moderate. Let his *Journal* be opened at almost any point in the fifty years from the early 1740s to his death, and the life-style will be seen to be essentially the same. In a fairly typical week in his life in September 1748, we read of a Friday spent in the Midlands of England when he rode to Wednesbury and preached at about four in the afternoon. He then got back on his horse and, 'with some difficulty', reached Meriden (still in the Midlands) at about nine that night. The next day was Saturday but he needed to be back in London for the Sunday, so he was on horseback at four a.m. and rode seventy-eight miles. This still left him well short of London, so on the Sunday he was again in the saddle at four, in order to reach the Foundery – his London headquarters – 'between seven and eight' that morning. He proceeded to preach there that morning, and in the

---

[1] *Letters*, vol. 8, p. 192.
[2] *Works* (Abingdon), vol. 26, pp. 244–5.
[3] Ibid., p. 291.

open-air at Moorfields at five p.m. 'to a larger congregation than I have seen there for some years'.[1]

This was not abnormal for him at the age of forty-five years, and over twenty years later there was still little difference in his routine. In 1771 John Fletcher could report, 'He has generally blown the gospel trumpet, and rode twenty miles, before most of the professors, who despise his labours, have left their downy pillows.'[2] When almost seventy-three he was capable of riding a hundred miles on horseback.[3] By that time a chaise had become his normal conveyance, but when it failed him, as it did in the north of Scotland when he was eighty-one, he had no problem trudging twelve and a half miles through heavy rain.

Apart from the change from horse to chaise, Wesley's itinerating and preaching schedule continued. On Sunday 18 June 1786, for instance, when he was eighty-three years of age, he preached twice in Hull and then the next day he journeyed seventy-six miles to Swinefleet. En route he preached two sermons, and a third in the open air at Swinefleet the same evening. Even at the age of eighty-six he could still say, 'I travel three or four thousand miles a year.'[4] His final sermon in the open-air was on 6 October 1790,[5]

---

[1] Ibid., p. 329. By Sunday night, he confessed, he was 'much out of order' and yet preached at Wapping the following day.

[2] Quoted by Tyerman, *Wesley*, vol. 3, p. 102.

[3] *Letters*, vol. 6, p. 223.

[4] Ibid., vol. 8, p. 142,

[5] A hearer present believed 'The word was attended with mighty power.' It was, however, inevitable that his preaching in latter years could not be what it had been. He seems to have used anecdote a good deal more. Sir Walter Scott wrote in 1819: 'When I was about twelve years old, I heard Wesley preach more than once, standing on a chair in Kelso churchyard. He was a venerable figure, but his sermons were vastly too colloquial for the taste of Saunders. He told many excellent stories.' Tyerman, *Wesley*, vol. 3, pp. 371–2. See also T. S. Jones, *Life of Willielma, Viscountess Glenorchy* (Edinburgh: Whyte, 1822), pp. 152,156; and *Autobiography of William Jay* (1854; reprint ed., Edinburgh: Banner of Truth, 1974), p. 413.

and his last sermon – of 40,000 to 50,000 – was in a house at Leatherhead on 23 February 1791, when his text was, 'Seek ye the Lord while he may be found; call upon him while he is near.' His prayer was granted, 'Lord, let me never live to be useless.'

Through all these years the growth and spread of Wesley's societies continued. From the nine circuits of 1748, there were fifty in Britain and Ireland by 1770. In 1767, when national figures of his society members were first kept, there were 25,911 in England, and 2,801 in Ireland. In 1770 the figures stood at 29,406 members. Ten years later fourteen more circuits had been added, with membership at 43,830, an increase of 14,424. By 1790, the year before Wesley's death, the number of circuits had risen to 115 and there were 71,568 members.

Assistant preachers on every circuit were responsible to provide Wesley regularly with a 'circuit plan'. When one of his helpers was late in this duty Wesley reminded him of the information he wanted:

'A Plan of a Circuit should contain (1) the several Societies, (2) the number of members in each, (3) the new members, (4) the backsliders, (5) the persons in band. Then the conversions, deaths, marriages, removes, with the total number at the foot of each column. Let me have such a plan next quarter'.[1]

Attempts have been made to find a pattern of the growth of the Wesleyan Methodists but with doubtful accuracy. It was, after all, Wesley himself who said, 'God is Sovereign, in sanctifying as well as justifying.'[2] 'Chance

---

[1] Ibid., vol. 6, p. 374.
[2] Ibid., vol. 4, p. 97. We have already seen a similar comment from Wesley. This was very different from nineteenth-century 'revivalism'.

has no share in the government of the world. "The Lord reigneth."[1] It is apparent that sometimes success was rapid and concentrated in particular areas, as happened in Yorkshire and Cornwall. In the latter county there were between thirty-to-forty 'little societies' by 1756.[2] At other times the increase was slow and more general. To the letter of a critical lady, Wesley responded in 1756:

'That Methodism (so called) should seem to you, sitting snug at London or Bristol, to be "very much in its decline" is no wonder. But I, who see things in every place with my own eyes, know it is very much in its increase. Many are daily added to them that believe; many more are continually awakened: so that the Societies from east to west, from north to south, in both kingdoms, increase in grace as well as in number.'[3]

It is clear that throughout Wesley's ministry there was no constant 'revival', if that is to be understood in terms of Pentecostal success. But remarkable times of unusual power continued to occur. At Weardale, in 1772, Wesley thought 'such a work of God has not been seen before in any part of the three kingdoms'.[4] In Huddersfield, in April 1779, he found 'a great revival of the work of God. Many have found peace with God; sometimes sixteen, eighteen, yea, twenty in one day'.[5] At Burslem, in March 1787, he witnessed 'an outpouring of the Spirit . . . particularly in the meetings for prayer'. As the meeting place at Burslem was full half an hour before the appointed time, and people still 'flocking together', Wesley began the service,

---

[1] Ibid., vol. 6, p. 371.   [2] Ibid., vol. 3, p. 194.
[3] Ibid, vol. 3, p. 191.
[4] *Journals*, vol. 5, p. 469. But see Tyerman's qualifying words on this, *Wesley*, vol. 3, p. 125.
[5] *Letters*, vol. 6, p. 232.

while in the yard outside another preacher addressed those who could not get in.[1]

Just how this kind of preaching affected the moral life of communities is illustrated by the Isle of Man. In the 1770s it was anticipated that the Wesleyans had little chance of succeeding in that place. For one reason, the island was 'a nest of smugglers', and smuggling was conduct forbidden to all who would join a Methodist society. When a converted soldier, John Crook, became a travelling preacher and went there in 1775, he was to face persecution. Yet within three years there was a flourishing Methodist circuit with 1,051 society members. In 1781 Wesley visited the Isle of Man and found 'above two thousand Methodists' in a population of thirty thousand.

The case of John Crook is a reminder that much of the Methodist growth was not due to Wesley personally. As already indicated, the care of his societies and circuits depended on the full-time commitment of suitable men, his 'Assistants'. In 1760 there were ninety of them; by 1780 the number had grown to 171, and by 1790 to 294. Their lifestyle was expected to be the same as their leader's whose rule was, 'The Methodists are not called to continue in any one place under heaven. We are all called to be itinerants.'[2] 'I know, were I myself to preach one whole year in one place, I should preach both myself and most of my congregation to sleep.'[3] So Wesley's Assistants were moved every one or two years, from circuit to circuit, and there was to be constant travelling within a circuit: 'No preacher ought to stay either at Portsmouth, or Sarum, or any other place, a whole week together. That is not the Methodist plan at all.'[4] 'I wish we had no circuit

---

[1] Ibid., vol. 7, p. 255.   [2] Ibid., vol. 6, p. 131.
[3] Ibid., vol. 3, p. 195.   [4] Ibid., vol. 8, p. 104.

with fewer than three preachers on it, or less than four hundred miles' riding in four weeks. If we do not take care we shall all degenerate into milksops. Soldiers of Christ, arise!'[1]

No evangelical ever took Paul's military metaphor for the Christian worker more seriously than John Wesley. They were to 'endure hardness' (*2 Tim.* 2:3). Yet while he believed that fresh air and much exercise were good for 'soldiers' this was not the explanation for the regimen he meant to see maintained. He had a higher reason. Given the paucity of gospel preachers he knew no other way to reach the multitudes. It was not settled pastors that were needed so much as itinerant evangelists. That was the gift that he looked for in his Assistants, and in numbers of them he found it. On one occasion, when John Nelson was brought before an official and asked to state the offence for which he had been imprisoned, he replied: 'For warning people to flee from the wrath to come, and if this be a crime I shall commit it again, unless you cut my tongue out; for it is better to die than disobey God.'[2] Thomas Walsh was another such man. In 1755, when Wesley was in touch with him about his next circuit appointment, Walsh replied:

'You desire that I would go into the north; but you may judge how unfit I am for either at present. Dear Sir, I find, as it were, an infinite desire to preach the gospel, and, if I could, to set the nation on fire. But the providence of God keeps me weak, and often visits me with afflictions of body. I do not murmur, neither do I count my life dear unto myself; but I find need of patience,

[1] Ibid., p. 206.
[2] *Journal of Nelson*, pp. 145–6.

because I have not more health and strength to preach the gospel, which I love more than my necessary food.'[1]

Wesley once described his first helpers as 'poor, ignorant men, without experience, learning, or art; but simple of heart, devoted to God, full of faith and zeal, seeking no honour, no profit, no pleasure, no ease, but merely to save souls; fearing neither want, pain, persecution, nor whatever man could do unto them'.[2]

They were not always 'ignorant' – Walsh could use both Hebrew and Greek – but judging by university standards many of them undoubtedly were poorly educated and had often to face derision. That was no great affliction for men who might have to live on £12 a year, to face hostile mobs, and preach outdoors in all weather. Certainly in calibre and quality they were varied. Some proved disappointments. The best of them, however, would have been outstanding in any company, and they exemplified what Wesley regarded as a true calling: 'Give me one hundred preachers who fear nothing but sin and desire nothing but God, and I care not a straw whether they be clergymen or laymen, such alone will shake the gates of hell, and set up the kingdom of heaven upon earth.'[3] Irregular Wesley's Assistants may have been, but they exemplified the Puritan saying, 'They are the best ministers, that carry people unto heaven.'[4]

John Wesley was the undisputed director of his preachers, and it was to their welfare, usefulness and encouragement that he gave much of his time. His correspondence abounds with letters to these men in different

[1] Wesley, *Works* (Abingdon), vol. 26, p. 593.
[2] Tyerman, *Wesley*, vol. 3, p. 455.
[3] *Letters*, vol. 6, p. 272.
[4] William Fenner, *Christ's Alarm to Drowsie Saints* (London: Stafford, 1656), p. 8.

parts of Britain and sometimes overseas. These were no stereotyped letters, made to fit all; he knew his men individually and the counsel was often personal and particular. Some got very definite advice on their health. His medical knowledge was considerable and his pursuit of the subject life-long.[1] Most often his words to them had to do with preaching and personal devotion. The majority of the following extracts are from letters to his Assistants:

'Abstain from all controversy in public. Indeed, you have not the talent for it . . . Keep to this: repentance toward God, faith in Christ, holiness of heart and life, a growing in grace and in the knowledge of Christ, a continual need of His atoning blood, a constant confidence in him, and all these every moment to our life's end.'[2]

'People imagine the longer the sermon is the more good it will do. This is a grand mistake.'[3]

'Fight against *slowness*, not only in reading Prayers, but in all things small and great . . . Be lively! Be quick! Bestir yourself!'[4]

'Eat very little, if any, supper; lie down before ten, rise before six; every day use as much exercise as you can bear; or, murder yourself by inches.'[5]

---

[1] While some of his medical advice is inevitably quaint, at times he is right-up-to-date with current opinion, as for instance in recommending a tight bandage for a leg ulcer or a cold bath if suffering from a fever. Sea-bathing was high on his list for good health.

[2] *Letters*, vol. 4, pp. 158–9.

[3] Ibid., vol. 6, p. 255.

[4] Ibid., vol. 8, p. 210. The *Book of Common Prayer* was used in services, as well as extempore prayer.

[5] Tyerman, *Wesley*, vol. 3, p. 274.

'Read and pray daily. It is for your life.'[1]

'Read a little, pray and meditate much.'[2]

'The main point is, with all and above all, study the Greek and Hebrew Bible, and the love of Christ.'[3]

'I never spend less than three hours (frequently ten or twelve) in the day, alone.'[4]

'The right method of preaching is this. At our first beginning to preach at any place, after a general declaration of the love of God to sinners and His willingness that they should be saved, to preach the law in the strongest, the closest, the most searching manner possible . . . After more and more persons are convinced of sin, we may mix more and more of the gospel to *beget faith* . . . this is not to be done too hastily . . . it is only in private conversation with a thoroughly convinced sinner that we should preach nothing but the gospel . . . by this preaching it pleased God to work those mighty effects in London, Bristol, Kingswood, Yorkshire and Newcastle.'[5]

'Spend all the morning, or at least five hours in twenty-four, in reading the *most useful* books, and that regularly and constantly. "But I read only the Bible." Then you ought to teach others to read only the Bible, and, by parity of reasoning, to *hear only* the Bible. But if so, you need preach no more . . . "But I have *no taste* for reading." Contract a taste for it by use, or return to trade. "But

---

[1] *Letters*, vol. 4, p. 103.   [2] Ibid., vol. 6, p. 7.
[3] Ibid., vol. 3, p. 163.   [4] Ibid., vol. 6, p. 292.
[5] Ibid., vol. 3, pp. 79–82. There is much valuable advice on preaching to be found in his *Works*, i.e., vol. 8, p. 317, where his remarks include: 'What is the best general method of preaching? (1) To invite. (2) To convince. (3) To offer Christ. (4) To build up; and to do this in some measure in every sermon.'

different men have different tastes." Therefore some may read less than others; but none should read less than this. "But I have no books." I will give each of you, as fast as you will read them, books to the value of £5.'[1]

Wesley's Assistants were not only to be readers themselves but they were to do their utmost to lead their hearers into the same habit. To that end a Methodist publishing business operated from Wesley's 'Book Room' in London and Conference required every assistant preacher to act as an agent, ordering supplies and seeing to their sale. Failure in this regard Wesley noted with displeasure. Income was, of course, not the motive: 'Have a quantity of little books, partly to sell and partly to give among the poor – chiefly indeed to give.'[2] 'The spreading of books is always a means of increasing the awakening in any place.'[3] 'It cannot be that the people should grow in grace, unless they give themselves to reading. A reading people will always be a knowing people.'[4]

* * * * *

It would be a mistake to deduce from Wesley's letters to his Assistants that he saw preaching as the *one* essential for the spread of the gospel. Such was not his belief: communities of men and women acting as salt and light in society were equally needed, and for that reason converts had to be gathered together for their mutual help, instruction, and fellowship.

Confronted with Wesley's practice in this regard, the Church of England authorities objected that it was their

---

[1] Tyerman, *Wesley*, vol. 2, p. 582. Large societies were also to provide a library for the use of the preachers.

[2] Letters, vol. 7, p. 219.

[3] Ibid., p. 86.   [4] Ibid., vol. 8, p. 247.

role to supply pastoral needs. In that case, Wesley responded, they would not be supplied at all. Speaking of true Christians in the Established Church he wrote:

'Who watched over them in love? Who marked their growth in grace? Who advised and exhorted them from time to time? Who prayed with them and for them as they had need? This, and this alone, is Christian fellowship; but, alas! where is it to be found? Look east or west, north or south; name what parish you please: is this Christian fellowship there? Rather, are not the bulk of parishioners a mere rope of sand? What Christian connexion is there between them?'[1]

For Wesley, fellowship is a primary feature of New Testament Christianity and therefore the need for it had to be met. Hence the formation of his societies as already mentioned.

The care of the societies was a primary role for his itinerant men, the 'travelling preachers', as the Assistants were also called, one of whom became (in later years) the Superintendent in each circuit. But within the societies there was further internal organisation; members were divided into 'bands' or classes, usually from a dozen to twenty strong, divided by sex, and each with its own leader. Some class leaders were women, and occasionally some women were also local 'preachers'.[2]

---

[1] *Letters*, vol. 2, p. 295.

[2] In a letter of 1761 he discouraged the use of the title 'preacher' for women; their speaking at meetings was never sanctioned by Wesley's Conference but was practised and defended by Wesley as one of the 'extraordinary' things that 'do not fall under the ordinary rules of discipline'. See Tyerman, *Wesley*, vol. 2, pp. 398–9; vol. 3, p. 112. It needs also to be remembered that the Methodist societies at this date made no claim to be churches. He believed that women leaders were best for women's classes. When Methodism did become a Church the Conference disallowed the practice of women preaching.

Initial membership was not a profession of conversion but an expressed desire to 'flee from the wrath to come' and to live a blameless life. Membership required the duty of attending class weekly. There were also meetings for prayer, preaching, and 'love feasts' for those with assurance. Standards of behaviour were exact. There had to be a willingness to seek to please God in all things. Among things forbidden were uncharitable conversation; the misuse of money on clothes or jewellery, and worldly business on the Lord's Day. All members received a quarterly 'ticket' and this was withdrawn for conduct unworthy of the gospel. At times Wesley himself expelled members. At Newcastle, in February 1743, he expelled no less than sixty-four persons for such offences as wilful lying, swearing, and laziness, and a further twenty-nine for 'lightness and carelessness'. There was to be no respect of persons. When Wesley decided that a certain John Sellars was no longer fit to lead a class he told the assistant to stand him down, and if he refused, to 'put him out of our Society. If twenty of his class will leave the Society too, they must . . . Better forty members should be lost than our discipline lost'.[1]

The local preachers, band and class leaders, and stewards (who looked after local temporal matters), were all were subject to the travelling preachers who met with them in a Quarterly meeting; they, in turn, answered to the Superintendent, and he to Wesley himself. This unique Methodist organization was subject to much criticism, including, at times, objections from within to Wesley's authority. To such objections Wesley replied that he had asked none to join him, or to be his Assistants. If they

---

[1] *Letters*, vol. 7, p. 101. That Methodist societies grew under such standards as these says much for the spiritual commitment of the people.

were his helpers, and members of his societies, it was by
their voluntary decision. No doubt, at this and at other
points there was warrant for criticism, but the big thing
at which Wesley aimed should be kept in view. He wanted
a close, mutually-supporting fellowship. He wanted
strong, bright Christians – men and women for whom
God 'is their one desire, their one delight, and they are
continually happy in him'.[1] He wanted Christians to enter
more fully into the love of God and holiness of life.

These blessings, however, Wesley did not regard as ends
in themselves. True love to God involves love for all
people,[2] and so the societies, far from being inward-
looking groups, withdrawn from the world, were to be a
vibrant missionary force, with each member active in
Christian witness and service. The effectiveness of this
organization is a major part of the true explanation why
Methodism made such an impact upon society in the
eighteenth-century. The belief that the kingdom of Christ
grows as ordinary men and women, who know Christ,
live and speak for him had been almost lost, and it was
this that the Evangelical Revival recovered. 'In those days',
wrote Stevens, 'every Methodist, who could command
language for ordinary conversation, was expected to pray
and bear his "testimony" in his class.'[3] It was from this
fellowship within that there came the one-to-one evangelism without. In a true sense, in Methodism the outreach pattern of the Jerusalem church was seen again (*Acts*

[1] *Works*, vol. 11, p. 418.
[2] The case of John Oliver may be cited as typical of many others: 'He got
upon his knees in secret, and while praying received "the witness" of his
acceptance with God. "I loved God," he afterward wrote, "I loved all
mankind.' Abel Stevens, *Methodism* (London: Wesleyan Conference Centre,
1878), vol. 2, pp. 103–4.
[3] Stevens, *Methodism*, vol. 3, p. 104.

8:4). It was a startling phenomenon in an age when 'Church' virtually meant 'clergy'.[1]

For confirmation that the Methodist societies were often light-giving agencies we are not dependent on Wesleyan sources. The Rev. John Milner told his bishop 'what an assembly of worshippers there is at Newcastle – how plainly the badge of Christianity, love, is there to be seen'.[2] Henry Venn, another not uncritical observer of Wesley, could write, 'There are, doubtless, many very excellent Christians amongst his people'.[3] And Venn saw the connection between this fact and the high standard of Christian assurance that Methodists were encouraged to maintain. Writing to a younger minister on assurance of salvation, Venn said:

'A close walk with God is the best preparation for it . . . seeing the Holy Ghost, whose testimony alone can satisfy the conscience, will never dwell with the slothful or lukewarm . . . I judge, one great reason of the worldliness prevailing amongst the orthodox Dissenters, is, their teachers not pressing this point; and, amidst very much error, one great cause of Mr Wesley's success some years ago, was his urging Christians not to rest without joy in God from receiving the atonement. Indeed he erred in making this knowledge to be justifying faith itself, instead of a fruit thereof; and also as to the mode in which the

---

[1] A hundred years later J. C. Ryle complained of the same condition prevailing in the Church of England, see *The Upper Room* (1887; reprint ed., London: Banner of Truth, 1970), pp. 320–49.

[2] Wesley, *Works* (Abingdon), vol. 26, p. 467. 'When his lordship talked about order, I begged leave to observe that I had nowhere seen such a want of it as in his own cathedral.'

[3] Nonetheless he added, 'but the best are sadly harassed by this false doctrine [i.e., Christian Perfection],' and believed, 'How much more good Mr Wesley would have done, had he not drunk in this error!' *Life of Henry Venn*, p. 474.

knowledge is acquired: – yet, better even so, than that uncertainty which leaves believers and infidels on nearly the same footing respecting any anticipation of glory ready to be revealed, and which holds forth no peculiar blessedness to excite men to give diligence to make their calling and election sure.'[1]

That individual society members were much used in the spread of the gospel is borne out by many known instances. Martha Thompson, for instance, was involved in the beginning of the work in Preston, Lancashire, as we shall later note more fully. George Pearson, a tailor in Macclesfield, Cheshire, was converted at the age of twenty-eight and began a witness there. When he brought Wesley to preach, and used the bake-house of a farm as the place of meeting, a woman was converted. She was the mother of John Ryle, Sr., and her son and other members of the family circle became bright witnesses in the town.[2]

Possibly no one class of individuals was so influential in spreading the gospel as soldiers. At Limerick, in Ireland, Wesley noted in May 1749, 'I met the class of soldiers myself, eight of whom are Scotch Highlanders.' And a few days later, 'I spent some time (as I did once before) among the sick soldiers at the infirmary. Surely there is not so teachable [a] people under heaven.'[3] Hundreds within the British army were converted under Wesleyan Methodist preaching, and, wherever they were posted the

[1] Ibid., pp. 226–7.
[2] John Ryle, Sr. died in 1808. Another family member, 'Miss Ryle', died at the age of twenty-three in 1799 in full assurance of faith. An account of her death is given in *The Methodist Magazine for the Year 1800*, vol. 23 (London: G. Whitefield), pp. 115–20. J. C. Ryle, grandson of John Ryle, Sr., was born in Macclesfield in 1816.
[3] Works (Abingdon), vol. 26, pp. 360, 362.

gospel went with them. Repeatedly it was Methodist soldiers that were the means of starting a new witness, sometimes in places as far off as Canada (Quebec in 1780), Cape Town, Hong Kong, and Australia.

In the thirteen American colonies (where there were 3,418 Methodists in 1775) Methodism took hold in the first instance, not as the result of a formal decision to send preachers, but simply by the zeal of emigrants.

Wesley was to die just as the age of modern world mission was at its dawn. He was expectant himself and inspired the same expectancy in others: 'We have reason to hope that the time is at hand when the kingdom of God shall come with power, and all the people of this poor heathen land shall know Him, from the least unto the greatest.'[1] It was the recovery of evangelical Christianity in the eighteenth century revival that would provide the momentum and resources for a new age of mission and 'benevolence'. The Wesleyans contributed largely to the new agencies and Wesley saw several of them before his death. Methodists formed the 'Naval and Military Bible Society' in 1779, and a Tract Society in 1782. Two years later came the Methodist Missionary Society,[2] and in 1787 the Anti-slavery Society. Another new institution was the Sunday School. In 1784 Methodism had twenty-six such schools and within three years there were another 200.

Towards the end of Wesley's life his personal influence had never been greater and respect for him had become almost nationwide. The pulpits of the Church of England, long closed to him, were open again. His correspondence

---

[1] *Letters*, vol. 7, pp. 126–7.
[2] More formally instituted early in the next century; Tyerman, *Wesley*, vol. 3, pp. 480–84, gives reasons for accepting this date. The leading spirit was Thomas Coke, born in Wales in 1747, died at sea near India in 1714.

ranged from the Prime Minister to domestic servants. Every letter continued to be answered. His last, of 24 February 1791, carried words of encouragement to William Wilberforce, then at the beginning of his long campaign against the slave trade.

Wesley once summarized his life in these words:

'I have been wandering up and down between fifty and sixty years, endeavouring in my poor way, to do a little good to my fellow creatures . . . I can see nothing which I have done or suffered, that will bear looking at. I have no other plea than this:

> I the chief of sinners am,
> But Jesus died for me.'[1]

When the end of this remarkable life finally came at the age of eighty-seven, the testimony was the same. In 'low and distinct voice' he said, 'There is no way into the holiest, but by the blood of Jesus.' The Evangelical Revival began with song and, for Wesley, it ended with song. The day before he died he sang his brother's hymn, 'All glory to God in the sky', and Watts's, 'I'll praise my Maker while I've breath'. A final direction, moments before his death about ten a.m. on Wednesday, March 2, 1791, was that his sermon 'The Love of God to Fallen Man' should be 'scattered abroad and given to everybody'.

* * * * *

John Wesley's character was indeed complex. He was a man of action, never happier than crossing a windswept moor to preach in a cottage, or barn, or on a hillside. If,

---

[1] Tyerman, *Wesley*, vol. 3, p. 403.

as is commonly said, he took after his mother, what he used to say of her is relevant: 'She did not *feel* for others near so much as my father did; but she *did* ten times more than he did.'[1] But for all his public labours, he was a life-long student and one of the most prolific Christian writers of his or any other century.[2] While 'a man of one book', in the breadth of his learning he can have been exceeded by few of his contemporaries.

The contrasts in his make-up were many. He could antagonize others when it came to written controversy (not least by his magisterial tone and, sometimes, by unfairness), yet when strangers met him face to face they were often quickly won. James Hervey spoke of the kindness he received from him in his student days.[3] John Newton read Wesley in 1755, and was wary of him until a first meeting when, 'his prejudices were almost immediately removed and they struck up a warm acquaintance'.[4] So it was with many others. 'He is not the stiff, queer man that I expected, but of an easy, genteel carriage', said a Roman Catholic priest.[5]

Wesley remained the Oxford don, to which was added a natural imperiousness. His autocratic procedure was too much for some of his Assistants to bear, even his brother

---

[1] Concerning a woman prone to low spirits he gave the wise advice, 'The more active she is the more her soul will live.'

[2] Some 500 publications are credited to him and his brother. *The Works of John and Charles Wesley: A Bibliography*, Richard Green (London: Kelly, 1896) remains valuable.

[3] 'I can never forget that tender-hearted and generous fellow of Lincoln who condescended to take such a compassionate notice of a poor under-graduate.' Letter of Dec. 30, 1747, in Wesley, *Works* (Abingdon), vol. 26, p. 272.

[4] D. Bruce Hindmarsh, *John Newton and the English Evangelical Tradition* (Grand Rapids: Eerdmans,1996), p. 127.

[5] *Letters*, vol. 6, p. 370.

at times complained of it,[1] but the majority, as Frank Baker wrote, 'found it easier to bow to his will because they knew that he usually exercised his immense power graciously, and always for the advancement of the work rather than of his own prestige'.[2] While the existence of some pride has to be recognized, no one was less interested in 'social climbing' than Wesley, and his closest friends were generally 'plain, simple folk'.[3]

He excelled as a conversationalist; Dr Samuel Johnson said, 'I could converse with him all night'; yet Wesley thought one hour's talk with anyone was enough. From the time of his upbringing, with a devoted mother and five older sisters, he was an admirer of 'woman' but in his understanding of them as individuals he seems to have been remarkably inept.[4] His writings give the impression of a man opposed to levity and even to laughter, yet his speech 'was sprightly and pleasant to the last degree', said one who knew him, and especially marked by cheerfulness.[5] Those who met him when they were children said the same.

---

[1] *Works* (Abingdon), vol. 26, p. 479. John Berridge referred to the controversy of 1771 as being between 'Pope John and Pope Joan' [i.e. the Countess of Huntingdon]. Edwin Sidney, *Life of Rowland Hill* (London: Baldwin & Cradock, 1834), p. 428.

[2] 'The Real John Wesley,' *Methodist History*, July 1974, p. 191.

[3] He did not cultivate connexions with the evangelical aristocracy and commented to the Earl of Dartmouth in 1764: 'I do not desire any intercourse with any persons of quality in England. I mean for my own sake. They do me no good; and I fear I can do none to them.' *Letters*, vol. 4, p. 260.

[4] To encourage one single woman he told her that she had no husband or children to care about! To another, who had married, he said, 'Surely you was not designed to be shut up in a little cottage and fully taken up with domestic cares!' On his lack of wisdom with the opposite sex he had some plain speaking from one of his Assistants, *Letters*, vol. 6, p. 361.

[5] John Hampson, quoted by Rack, *Reasonable Enthusiast*, p. 527.

Perhaps the greatest contrast in Wesley has to do with the place of feelings in his make up. He was not an emotional man. His coolness and calmness were proverbial. His sister, Emilia, even thought that he was lacking in 'natural affection'.[1] Unlike many of his correspondents, he was certainly very reticent to say or write anything about his feelings. This absence of comment on himself is very marked. While he wrote, 'Everyone ought to declare what God hath done for his soul', he very seldom did so himself. Yet the quest for *felt* Christian experience dominated his personal life. While he knew that love is not all feeling, he believed there is no true love without it, and in this sense feeling had the highest place in his aspirations: 'I see abundantly more than I feel. I want to feel more zeal and love for God.'[2] 'I feel more want of heat than light. I value light; but it is nothing compared to love.'[3] The prayer of Jeremy Taylor was also his own: 'Lord, do Thou turn me all into love, and all my love into obedience, and let my obedience be without interruption.'

It may be that Wesley did not always rightly judge the relationship between faith and feelings, and that he gave too large a place to the latter.[4] But for Wesley, a person

---

[1] *Works* (Abingdon), vol. 26, p. 99.
[2] *Letters*, vol. 7, p. 549.   [3] Ibid., vol. 6, p. 153.
[4] Samuel Walker certainly thought so in the earlier years of the revival. Commenting on Wesley's Minutes for the Conference of 1744, he said, 'Religion in the heart, according to their notion of it, seemed nothing else but a continuation of rapturous impressions.' Quoted in G. C. B. Davies, *Early Cornish Evangelicals* (London: SPCK, 1951), p. 72. Wesley recognized the danger (if he did not always avoid it); 'I have much constitutional enthusiasm,' he wrote to his brother in 1753. *Works* (Abingdon), vol. 26, p. 527. In 1762 he told one of his Assistants, 'I dislike something that has the appearance of enthusiasm, overvaluing feelings and inward impressions: mistaking the mere work of imagination for the voice of the Spirit.' *Letters*, vol. 4, p. 193.

who has known Christ and the Holy Spirit will never be content with a cold heart. He once told one of his younger preachers, Samuel Bradburn, that his experience might almost at any time be expressed in the lines:

> O Thou, who camest from above,
> The pure celestial fire to impart,
> Kindle a flame of sacred love
> On the mean altar of my heart!
>
> There let it to Thy glory burn,
> With inextinguishable blaze,
> And trembling to its source return,
> In humble love and fervent praise.

Again the language is of aspiration rather than that of achievement. Perhaps one of the best conclusions that he came to on the nature of the Christian life, and corresponding with his own, is expressed in a letter of 12 April 1782:

'It is undoubtedly our privilege to "rejoice evermore", with a calm, still, heartfelt joy. Nevertheless this is seldom long at one stay. Many circumstances may cause it to ebb and flow. This, therefore, is not the essence of true religion, which is none other than humble, gentle, patient love. I do not know that all these are not included in that one word *resignation*. For the highest lesson our Lord (as man) learned upon earth was to say, "Not as I will, but as Thou wilt."'

* * * * *

The legacy of Wesley and of the Evangelical Revival has been frequently and variously evaluated. Initially there were historians who chose to ignore it as though it were insignificant. Referring to such authors, Thomas

Babington Macaulay (1800–1859) wrote: 'We have read books called Histories of England under the reign of George II, in which Methodism is not even mentioned . . . A hundred years hence this breed of authors will, we hope, be extinct'.[1]

In contrast with the authors Macaulay criticized, it was a general nineteenth-century belief that Methodism contributed a great deal to the saving of England from the Revolution which had occurred in France at the end of the eighteenth century. The French historian, Elie Halévy, brought that belief into prominence in academic circles in the early twentieth century with his book *The Birth of Methodism in England;* this was countered by others but has been defended again by Gertrude Himmelfarb.[2]

Of course, it is very possible to exaggerate what happened in the Evangelical Revival and evangelical authors have sometimes been responsible for treating revival periods as eras of unmixed blessing. I have not chosen to draw much attention in these pages to the failures, the relapses and the disappointments that attended Wesley's work (as they do all Christian work in this fallen world). Wesley's 'propensity for looking at life through rose-coloured spectacles' does not help to make him the most accurate recorder of events. His lifetime was certainly no golden age, nor did he think it was. But there are facts that cannot be denied in any assessment of Methodist influence upon society at large.

On one occasion, the Unitarian, Joseph Priestley, wrote to Wesley: 'By you chiefly is the gospel preached to the *poor* in this country, and to you is the civilization, the

---

[1] *Wesley Memorial Volume*, p. 671.

[2] See G. Himmelfarb, *Victorian Minds* (1968; reprint ed., Chicago: Ivan Dee, 1995), Chapter X.

industry and sobriety of great numbers of the laborious part of the community owing; though you are a body unknown to the government.'[1]

Priestley's last sentence is hardly correct. When, on account of his musical gifts, the son of Charles Wesley was once present with King George III, he was told by the monarch: 'It is my judgment, Mr Wesley, that your uncle and your father, and George Whitefield and Lady Huntingdon, have done more to promote true religion in the country than all the dignified clergy put together, who are so apt to despise their labours.'[2]

It is true that the number of Wesleyan society members at the time of Wesley's death 1791 (72,476), was not yet one percent of the whole population. But that figure does not include the thousands who heard Methodist preaching, and came under its influence without committing themselves to the membership. Henry Rack has estimated that the latter figure would have been near 300,000.

Then, again, the Wesleyan numbers are only part of the picture, for many who were outside Wesley's circle shared in the Evangelical Revival. As George III obviously understood, the influence went far beyond the boundaries of the Wesleyans. The historian, John Richard Green, gave the foremost place to Wesley, noting 'he was older than any of his colleagues at the start of the movement, and he outlived them all', and yet could write:

'The Methodists [i.e., Wesleyans] themselves were the least result of the Methodist revival. Its action upon the Church broke the lethargy of the clergy; and the "Evangelical" movement, which found representatives like

---

[1] Quoted by Rack, *Reasonable Enthusiast*, p. 44
[2] Quoted in Frederick C. Gill, *Charles Wesley, The First Methodist* (London: Lutterworth, 1964), pp. 188–9.

Newton and Cecil within the pale of the Establishment, made the fox-hunting parson and the absentee rector impossible.'

Of the moral change that slowly took place in England the same writer concluded:

'In the nation at large appeared a new moral enthusiasm . . . whose power was seen in the disappearance of the profligacy which had disgraced the upper classes, and the foulness which had infected literature, ever since the Restoration . . . A new philanthropy reformed our prisons, infused clemency and wisdom into our penal laws, abolished the slave trade, and gave the first impulse to popular education.'[1]

Nor would this impulse stop in Britain. All the ends of the Empire would know its power. Thus, in a crucial debate in Parliament in 1813 on opening India to missionaries,

'The Evangelical lobby swept all before it . . . Conversion of the heathen Indian was both a Christian and an imperial duty. For those of Wilberforce's mind, the Protestant faith was part and parcel of the civilisation that Britain was then spreading across the world. Enlightened Protestantism was the essential ingredient in Britain's greatness; it provided the cement which held the nation together and released the genius and industry of its people.'[2]

Such an outlook could never have existed without the Evangelical Revival.

---

[1] J. R. Green, *A Short History of the English People* (London: Macmillan, 1888), pp. 738–9.
[2] Lawrence James, *Raj: The Making and Unmaking of British India* (New York: St Martin's Press, 1997), p. 224.

Part Two

Men Who Followed

Far, far above thy thought
His counsel shall appear,
When fully He the work hath wrought
That caused thy needless fear.

John Wesley,
translating Paul Gerhardt

They knew no success but conversions,
and no applause but tears.

Anon.

Methodism is Christianity in earnest.

Thomas Chalmers

William Bramwell

Chapter 6

William Bramwell:
Friendship with God

O n the death of Wesley the country watched for the
demise of Methodism. There were a number of
reasons for that expectation. Despite hopes, Wesley had
never found another masterful leader to appoint in his
place. Men who were once in view to succeed him were
already dead, including his brother Charles in 1788, and
John Fletcher in 1785. Thomas Coke, who remained a
possibility, was too unpopular to command the acceptance
of the Assistants. The future of the curious organization
that survived Wesley's death, and which had for so long
depended on him, had therefore to be in doubt: 'To the
eye of an external observer, Methodism, as an ecclesiastical
system, appeared an unfinished, inharmonious mass,
without symmetry or cohesion, – something between a
fragment and a ruin.'[1]

Nor was this all. Wesley had left the problematical
relationship of his connection with the Church of England
unresolved. When he had ordained men for work in
Scotland and America, in the 1780s, he had rejected any
such step for England, certain that separation from the

---

[1] George Smith, *History of Wesleyan Methodism*, 3rd ed., vol. 2 (London:
Longman, 1863), p. 212. Cited later as Smith, *Methodism*.

national Church would mean self-destruction. But the half-way position of societies that were not churches, and of preachers who were not recognized as ministers, was one that could not be sustained indefinitely.

There was, however, one preparation for the future that Wesley had made and one which was to prove his wisdom. By 1791 there were about 400 meeting-houses belonging to his connexion and the deeds of these buildings were held by local trustees. From time to time these trustees were so attracted to certain preachers that they would have been glad to have them permanently. No such option was allowed in Wesley's lifetime but it suggested one possibility for the future: let the Assistants all become ministers settled in local churches. Wesley had foreseen such a scenario and put arrangements in place to prevent it. His reasons were twofold: first, such a change would put the appointment of preachers into the hands of trustees, men who were not called to be spiritual leaders. This would necessarily have been the case because the people in his societies knew nothing of the 'democracy' of independency, and were (not without reason) prejudiced against any form of Presbyterianism. Second, and more important, settling men in local churches would bring an end to the itinerant plan upon which, he was convinced, so much good depended.

Standing at the distance that we do from these events, and with our own predilections on forms of church government, it may be easy to suppose that Wesley was wrong in this judgment. But weight has to be given to the fact that it was not a Wesleyan but an independent, J. K. Foster, who, writing in the 1840s, argued that it was its distinctive structure which did much to make the Wesleyan branch of Methodism more flourishing than the Calvinistic. He wrote:

'The decrease of a spirit of zealous itinerancy in the Calvinistic body has doubtless contributed to the state of numerical inferiority; while the other section of the Methodists has, amidst all the changes of circumstances, preserved its youthful activity, and, almost heedless of what the other sections of the Church are doing, has maintained its earliest disposition to run to and fro, that knowledge might be increased; the followers of Whitefield and the Countess, associating more with regular pastors, have altered their habits, and rather devoted their energies each to a single congregation, than to a district or nation.'[1]

Instead of leaving any authority to settle men with local trustees, Wesley had set in place an arrangement that would prevent it. With no successor in sight, he had, in 1784, chosen one hundred of his Assistants and constituted them as the legal body to assume, on his death, all the authority that he had exercised. Thus in 1791 everything came to depend on these men. Other Assistants, and there were approaching 300, could come to the annual Conference, but authority would lie with the hundred. This arrangement provided no guarantee of success. The problems were many. Some of the preachers would leave the connexion in the years ahead, and take congregations with them.

Yet despite all this, and to the surprise of many, Wesleyan Methodism not only survived, but its greatest work was still ahead and it would spread its branches to the ends of the earth. The reason is best expressed in the

---

[1] A. C. H. Seymour, *Life and Times of the Countess of Huntingdon* (London: Painter, 1844) vol. 2, p. xii. Also reprinted by Tentmaker Publications, Stoke-on-Trent, 2001). The fact that the same Wesleyan structure could be well adapted to the mission fields of the world was also proving significant to an extent Foster could scarcely know.

words of George Smith who knew nineteenth-century Methodism at first hand. Referring to the testing difficulties that faced the connexion on Wesley's death, he continued:

'Beneath all the jars and collisions of sentiment and action by which Methodism was then distracted and distressed, the work of God in the conversion and edification of souls was carried on with diligence and godly zeal. The men who entertained and acted on conflicting views respecting the administration of the sacraments or disciplinary authority, retired from the arena where they had urged their individual opinions, to their closets for a fresh baptism of the Holy Spirit, and then went to the pulpit, the Class, or the Prayer-meeting, intent on saving themselves and those who heard them. This was the grand conservative principle of Methodism. Here was the secret of its vitality, power, and growth, under circumstances which would have destroyed any mere ecclesiastical or political organisation.'[1]

There is an abundance of biographical evidence to show that this assertion is true. The annals of early nineteenth century Methodism have some of the richest documentation in all church history and in this and the next two chapters I want to sketch three representative figures whose lives go far to illustrate what happened.

* * * * *

We have already noted how, as the work in England prospered, the circuits multiplied. In 1773 a circuit was formed in the West Riding of Yorkshire, with Haworth

---

[1] Smith, *Methodism*, vol. 2, pp. 212–3.

at its head, and covering the whole of North of Lancashire, Westmoreland, and Cumberland. This constituted an area some 120 miles long by 60 broad. In the midst of the spiritually destitute area of Lancashire was the town of Preston. It was in 1776, when Colne replaced Haworth as the circuit town, that Preston first appeared on the circuit 'Plan'. How a society came into being in that town is typical of what happened elsewhere. The first known evangelical in Preston at this time was a Martha Thompson who had become a Christian in London on hearing John Wesley preach. Her testimony (for which, at first, she was put into a lunatic asylum) led to the conversion of a Mrs Walmsley, owner of a local inn. It was probably at this inn that Roger Crane joined the small group of believers in 1777. Brought up among the Presbyterians, whose pastor had turned Unitarian, Crane had come to peace with God after a Methodist in Yorkshire had told him, 'Brother, you are inverting the order of God. Remember it is believe, love, obey; and you are trying to obey, love and believe.' Crane's home now became the centre of Preston Methodism.[1]

Crane was at once a bright witness. William Bramwell, a year his junior, heard his testimony but had no inclinations to Methodism. Already religious, moral, and in regular attendance at the Church of England, his family had warned him against the new religion. When he was loaned one of the works of John Wesley he returned the book unread. It took an unusual event to make him reconsider his attitude. An incident occurred when he was shocked by the blasphemous language of an evil woman; when he protested she at once attacked him as 'a

[1] For the above facts, see, John Taylor, *The Apostles of Fylde Methodism* (London: Woolmer, 1885).

Methodist devil'. The description surprised him and reflection on the text, 'They that will live godly in Christ Jesus must suffer persecution', led him to question whether his assessment of a people so disliked by the ungodly could be right. His doubts led him to decide to listen to Methodist preaching and slowly he was to enter a new spiritual world. At this time, it appears, he met Wesley in Preston and to the latter's question, 'Can you praise God?' he had to reply, 'No, Sir.' It is said that his position changed that same night on hearing the old preacher. Referring to his conversion in later years, Bramwell was to write to one of his sons:

'When I saw my need of Christ, I believed, as you do, that I must be saved, and that none but God could save me. But I found I possessed a degree of power to ask and to pray; and I exercised that power, praying for salvation frequently during the day. Though I sometimes felt but little, yet I continued to beg according to the Scriptures: "Ask, and ye shall receive; seek, and ye shall find." The Lord drew my mind to converse with his people, and to ask them to pray for me, to reprove, to correct, and to search me. This I found to be of great service; and I still see that this is the way of God with man.'[1]

By 1779, at the age of twenty, Bramwell was ready to join with Roger Crane and Michael Emmett (a third young man who had been disowned by family and friends on confessing Christ) in a 'band'. This was a private

---

[1] Thomas Harris, *The Christian Minister in Earnest: A Memoir of the Rev. William Bramwell* (London: Wesleyan Methodist Book-Room, n.d.), p. 257. The Harris biography leans heavily but not entirely on James Sigston, *Memoir of the Life and Ministry of Mr William Bramwell* (1820; reprint ed., New York: Waugh and Mason, 1833). Harris is more modern in style, Sigston fuller in documentation. Unless otherwise stated, it is upon these two sources that I am depending in this chapter.

commitment to help one another in service and devotion to Christ. Together the three spoke and prayed about the twenty or thirty villages around them with no gospel light and began to visit among them. 'Small and feeble was the work at first, for they were untrained and imperfect workmen. But they gathered experience and confidence after a few years of preparation.'[1]

There is no record of what happened in the next few years but by 1785 the Superintendent of the circuit could report blessing far and wide, 'the arm of the Lord was made bare; so that the whole Circuit, with the exception of the north of Pendle Hill, seemed to flame with the glory of God'.[2] It is certain that the three young men from Preston were closely involved in what the same author calls 'a gracious revival of religion'. Two early converts under Bramwell's witnessing were Ann Cutler and Ellen Byrom, and both were to play an important part in future developments. To Ellen he was soon to be engaged. Ann Cutler became a 'preacher' after the order of Acts 8:4. John Taylor wrote of her: 'Ann Cutler pleaded and prayed with overwhelming power. Her influence for good was incalculable. She lighted candles that flickered and flamed in remote cottages and farm houses for a generation.'[3]

By 1787 Preston had its own Methodist chapel; and twelve years later it was made the head of a new circuit and could report a membership of 373 in 1800. Summarizing this development, John Taylor wrote:

'These men and women who were the pioneers of the movement were made of sterling stuff. They were

---

[1] Taylor, *Apostles of Fylde*, p. 43.
[2] Ibid., p. 129.
[3] Ibid., pp. 61,131. Cutler, popularly known as 'Praying Nanny,' died in Macclesfield in 1794 at the age of 35.

whole-hearted, self-denying, holy men and women. They had a high standard of excellence. Their characters were pure and good. Their lives were holy, and active, and useful. They were spiritual giants – full of faith and of the Holy Ghost.'[1]

* * * * *

The various events in Bramwell's life do not form the staple of his biographies. Of such things as his appearance, his various homes, his family life and such like, we are told little.[2] This is not simply because his biographies were written before the age when the biographer's art was developed. It is rather that his biographers were pre-occupied with a greater purpose and with that in view they lent largely on Bramwell's letters and upon testimonies to his character by men who served with him in the gospel ministry. This purpose they certainly achieved. David Stoner, a circuit minister, who obtained James Sigston's *Memoir of Bramwell* soon after its first publication, wrote of it to a friend: 'My soul was ashamed, humbled and quickened in reading it. I do not know that the reading of any book ever produced such an effect upon my mind.'[3] Very many were to say the same.

The external course of Bramwell's life will not take us long to summarize. We pick it up again in Preston, where courtship with Ellen Byrom was not without its problems. These were not of their own making. By the mid-1780s Bramwell was both committed to the Preston society and settled on a business career; he had taken a house and

---

[1] Ibid., p. 133.
[2] That Bramwell had unusual physical strength is unmistakeable and Smith gives evidence of it, *Methodism*, vol. 2, p. 226.
[3] William Dawson and John Hannah, *Memoirs of the Rev. David Stoner* (New York: Lane and Sandford, 1844), p. 125.

shop in the town, with 'every hope of ease, honour and prosperity'. Family connections, and no doubt his future wife, supported his plans. One person, however, did not. This was Dr Coke, who was giving personal assistance to Wesley as the latter drew near to the end of his long life. Coke was confident that Bramwell's calling lay elsewhere and now repeatedly urged him to become a full-time circuit preacher in the denomination. This came to a head when Coke pressed on him the immediate need of the Kent circuit. After no small struggle, the Lancashire man gave up his business, bought a horse, and in the winter of 1785 rode to Kent. He took this step, however, on the condition that within two years he should be free to return to marry, a longer period being normally required of probationer ministers. Either Wesley did not know of this condition or did not agree with it, for at the 1787 Conference he directed Bramwell to the Lynn circuit. This was far removed from Preston where there were business commitments still to be finalized before the couple, now married, could leave for elsewhere. It says something for Bramwell's strength of character that he would not comply with Wesley's direction and it was only after a year's 'stand off' that he was given the Blackburn circuit (which had now taken over the Preston area from Colne).[1]

Bramwell was to spend four years in Lancashire, first at Blackburn then at Colne, before being appointed to

---

[1] The place which Scripture gives to marital and family obligations was never prominent in Wesley's thinking. Wives, and still less children, were not supposed to have opinions of their own. He held the conviction that no child should be allowed to cry aloud in his presence once ten months old! Sigston comments on this: 'The propriety of Mr Wesley's assertion on this particular has often been questioned, and some have said, that had he been a parent himself, he would have been better informed.' *Memoir of Bramwell*, p. 61.

Yorkshire where the greater part of his ministry was to be spent. He was there from 1791 to 1798, successively at Dewsbury, Birstal, and Sheffield. From 1801 to 1806 he was in the same county, at Leeds, Wetherby, and Hull. In 1810 he was re-appointed to Sheffield and in 1812 to Birstal. Apart from these Yorkshire stations he was at Nottingham, 1798–1801; in the North-East, at Sunderland, 1806–8; Newcastle upon Tyne, 1815–7; and in London, 1814–5. He was once back in his native Lancashire, at Liverpool, 1808–10, and back there finally for his last appointment at Salford in 1817.

Through all these years his manner of life as a travelling preacher is summed up in his own words as follows:

'I rise early, wash all over in cold water, meet the societies in every place after preaching, stay all night among the friends, and find this is the best way to receive and do good. I sacrifice my bed and home for the good of souls; and in this I am truly happy.'

The doctrines that he 'constantly pressed on his hearers' are summarized in this way by James Sigston:

'In a very masterly manner he displayed distinctly the attributes of God, the fall of man, the doctrine of free grace, the great atonement of Christ, repentance toward God and faith in the blessed sacrifice of Christ in order to be justified from the guilt of sin, and from the condemning power of the law of God. He was accustomed to maintain, that a sinner who feels himself thus redeemed and justified, is "a babe in Christ," and only a babe. It was necessary therefore, he insisted, that this incipient believer should hold fast the beginning of his confidence without wavering, and go on to be perfected in love, till he obtain the Divine nature, and recover the blessed image of God.'

Bramwell was present at the annual Conference held at Leeds in 1818, when he was re-appointed to Salford and made chairman of the Manchester district. But his attention was no longer on work here: 'It is my intention', he told his brethren, 'to be in heaven before next conference. I am hastening to that better country as rapidly as I am able.' A few days later, while still at his friend James Sigston's home in Leeds, a happy evening was spent in conversation with friends. The next morning, 13 August, he rose at 2.30 a.m., had coffee, bread and butter with a servant, and, with the words, 'The Lord bless you, Alice!', left to catch the coach to Manchester. A few minutes later he collapsed in the street and at the age of fifty-nine he was gone. It was all so sudden, a friend commented, 'We can scarcely call it death. It almost appears a translation.'

* * * * *

Bramwell was called into the gospel ministry at a period when God had determined seasons of remarkable success for the gospel. To look at what was achieved is to be convinced that a power was attending the ministry of the Word that cannot be explained in terms of the gifts of the human instruments. The facts all bear out that contention. For one thing, this power was not always present. His first year at Dewsbury he described as 'a year of hard labour and grief'. The next year saw 'a great revival'. The same sermons, preached by him at the same period, could have markedly different effects. At Leeds in 1802 he could report, 'Many are saved in the town, not so many in the country.' Or again, in 1804, when he was stationed at Wetherby: 'I saw a blessed work at Whitby, etc. I see souls saved nearly every night in this circuit. At Wetherby not many.'

It seems to have been at Sheffield and at Nottingham that awakening saw the greatest intensity. Writing from Sheffield in 1795, Bramwell reported to a friend, 'On the day appointed for thanksgiving the work broke out here in our chapel, at the evening meeting . . . I have clear evidence, and, to speak within bounds, I am persuaded of more than one hundred persons having found liberty in three weeks.' The following year he could speak of 'souls saved nearly every day', and by the time his first year at Sheffield was over 1,250 had been added to the society. A colleague who joined Bramwell in the work in May 1798, later wrote of what he saw:

'I was myself an eye and ear witness of those glorious seasons which will remain deeply imprinted on my re-collection to the latest period of my life . . . Certainly if ever I knew or experienced pentecostal seasons (those gracious and abundant manifestations of the Spirit which no language can describe), it was at that time, when, if not thousands, at least hundreds were added to the Church; many of them, I doubt not, such as shall be eternally saved. The arrows of conviction fastened on many; conscience did its office; the sword of the Spirit pierced "between the joints and the harness;" Gallios became serious; and before the presence of Jehovah the stout hearted bowed the stubborn knee, and rocks of impenitence flowed into streams of penitential sorrow . . . If ever I was conscious (as far as a human spirit can be) of the presence of supernatural powers, that was the time. Many felt and possessed unutterable things. It seemed that there was but a thin veil between us and the invisible world, and that Satan, for a season, was bound in chains, and the Church militant admitted into the presence chamber of the Majesty on high'.

The revivals at this time were clearly by no means identified with the ministry of one or two men. The work was much more widespread. Sigston could write in 1820: 'Many believers now living in the Leeds, Halifax, Bradford, and Huddersfield circuits, refer to that period as the time of their espousals to Christ. The Holy Spirit wrought powerfully.' Thus it appears that there was revival in Nottingham before Bramwell went there in 1798, but there had also been a controversy which took over 300 of the people into the secession which became the Methodist New Connexion. Even the Nottingham building had been lost to the other side. On his arrival there, Bramwell ignored the dispute that had affected so many, and 'left things flat', and continued to preach as he had done in Sheffield.

Within six months a new building was built in Nottingham, although soon to need enlargement. At a service for the church's renewal of their covenant and while Bramwell was praying, one observer wrote:

'The glory of God descended on all the society present in such a powerful manner as I never before experienced. Many were so affected, that, at the conclusion of the service, they could not come down the gallery stairs without assistance. That was the beginning of good days at Nottingham.'

Within a year the numbers previously lost had been made up and 800 more were soon added. At the 1798 Conference 1,100 members were reported for the circuit and 2,200 by 1801. One of his colleagues at this time was to write:

'Perhaps Mr Bramwell, in all his travels, never saw more glorious displays of the divine power, than in this circuit.

A great concern for religion discovered itself among all ranks; and many were "brought out of darkness into marvellous light". The societies were united and edified; "and walking in the fear of the Lord and the comfort of the Holy Ghost, were multiplied". The name of the Lord Jesus was magnified; and several Deists renounced their infidelity, and found redemption in the precious blood of Christ'.

Another member of his congregation noted: 'I heard nearly all the sermons which he preached in the town of Nottingham, and do not recollect having once had a barren season, except at one time when he was lame, and could not stand to preach. I have often seen a congregation of two thousand people so affected under his preaching as to be unable to restrain their feelings, till tears have afforded some relief.'

From the manner in which Bramwell conducted services it is apparent that to promote noise or emotional excitement was the opposite of his intention. His counsel was, 'Keep from everything wild, everything that goes before the Spirit.'[1] He required silence and would not so much as allow a crying child to remain in a service. Full attention, says Sigston, he demanded for the sake of the gospel and if ever this could not be obtained he would desist: 'It was his expressed determination not to preach to a people who trifled with the word of God. This com-

---

[1] The whole of Methodism was alive to the danger at this date. George Smith, commenting on the Conference of 1800, noted: 'In the two or three previous years, many extensive and blessed revivals have been productive of great good . . . But with these "times of refreshing" there had been occasional extravagances which justified the apprehension, that excitement and emotion had been sometimes mistaken for the work of the Spirit. It was ordered that Wesley's extract from Edwards' *Religious Affections* be reprinted and circulated without delay.' *Methodism*, vol. 2, pp. 332–3.

mendable practice produced a degree of solemnity in the people, that assisted him much in the impressions which he wished to make.'

It was his concern to see that the whole service be seen as an act of worship in the presence of God. Every hymn was carefully chosen and given out. Happiness, he believed, was no less important in worshippers than solemnity, and 'a little religion can never keep us happy' was one of his sayings. 'Slow singing, long prayers, long meetings', far from being a blessing he regarded as a sure sign of 'a low state of grace'.[1] Nor was an immutable formality a healthy sign, and he might well call on two or three men to pray before a service was concluded.

Those attending services were much larger than the number of society members. The usual Methodist practice of holding a prayer meeting of society members at the conclusion of services was followed. Others were free to attend and it was not uncommon for the unconverted to be awakened on hearing others pray. Sigston mentions a prayer meeting at Morley at which a stranger to the Methodists passing the door, stopped to listen. 'He was immediately seized with conviction, fell down on his knees, and, after remaining out of doors in that situation some time, entered.' It was for his lasting good – an incident surely akin to 1 Corinthians 14:24–5. Preachers, both circuit and local, would also meet quarterly to speak

---

[1] What he regarded as 'long meetings' is not stated. Referring not to Sunday services but to society meetings, Sigston notes that it was his usual practice 'to close the meetings at the expiration of one hour.' Bramwell's contemporary, David Stoner, advised this rule for prayer meetings: 'Let no individual pray long. In general, the utmost limit ought to be about two minutes. It will be found much better for one person to pray twice or thrice in the course of the meeting, than to pray once a long time. *Long* praying is, in general, both a *symptom* and a *cause* of spiritual deadness.' *Memoirs of Stoner*, p. 199.

and pray and a note of one such meeting, gives us an idea of what these Quarterly meetings meant:

'July 3, 1798. This Quarterly-Meeting of the Preachers far exceeded any other that any preacher present ever witnessed, in a fullness of love and glorious power. Mr Wood wished to speak his experience, but could not, he was so much affected. Mr Bramwell was so dissolved and overpowered that he could not pray: and Mr Pipe shouted, "Glory, glory, glory to God in the highest."'

Bramwell's convictions on the work of a gospel minister are very clear as can be seen in the following extracts from letters to three ministerial correspondents:

'Our work is of such importance that I frequently tremble exceedingly before entering the pulpit; yea, I wonder how I ever dared to engage in such a work. Yet when I am labouring to speak a little, I am frequently so much overpowered with the sense of the Divine presence, that I would not leave my work for all the world. O how merciful is God our Saviour; He strengthens our weak hands.'

'Let your end always be the salvation of men. Write all your sermons before you preach them: but do not write too much, neither determine to be too correct in keeping to your plan. Never be stiff, tiresome, or tedious. The English cannot bear this. Yet do not be too short. Let the people have all from you, but much in little.'[1]

'I understand you are quite satisfied you are in your place; I mean as a travelling preacher – a work which makes me, even to the present time, tremble in the presence of God.

---

[1] Elsewhere he says, 'I would labour night and day sometimes to have good sermons.'

I am still persuaded, that nothing can support us but that almighty power which raised the Lord Jesus from the dead. Yet it is quite possible for you and me to make this a worldly business, that it may become so formal as to create in us no more concern than any common business in life. Shall the Lord ordain us to this heavenly calling? Shall he empower us with the spirit of zeal and of power? Shall he send us forth into this labour, to save sinners from everlasting damnation? And shall we, after all, lose the true spirit of our calling? How can we then give in our account? How shall we stand before the judgment seat of Christ? Nothing less than the improvement of time, talents, etc, etc, can give us the least plea in that day.'

I turn now to some of the evidence that these revivals were a genuine work of the Spirit of God. In the first place, there was an overruling concern among the instruments to give all the glory to God. In Bramwell's life there is not a shadow of the spirit which came in with a later revivalism which was too ready to glory in numbers and results. Certainly he laboured for success but when it came he attributed no part of it to himself. Sigston wrote:

'Amidst all the fervour of the revival it was Mr Bramwell's constant cry, "Not unto us, O Lord, not unto us; but unto thy name be the glory!" The greatest fear he knew, was lest any of the instruments whom the Lord had honoured, by employing them in that cause, should forget their own littleness, and, beginning to think too highly of themselves, should neglect to ascribe all the praise to God, to whom it was entirely due. That sinful man should thus in the slightest degree encroach on the province of God, was an idea most revolting to his grateful spirit. He could not endure the bare contemplation of it; but in all the fervency of holy zeal, he bore his decided testimony against such presumptuous infringement of the Divine rights, and denounced the man who could audaciously attempt to rob God of his glory. In this way he was the happy instrument of preserving many unwary and aspiring souls from being dashed against the rocks of spiritual pride'.

Bramwell knew that there will always be false professions of conversion, but, for the glory of God and the purity of the church, he took care to avoid any practices which could encourage a premature profession and the easy introduction of new society members. At the end of his life he noted a slackening in this regard and wrote with regret of what he found in Manchester: 'As a vast number of children were taken in before I came, numbers have now gone back to the world. Young persons should never be in society without a real work of grace: I hope ever to abide by this discipline.'[1]

In regard to dealing with seekers and the distressed there is a significant difference between Bramwell's practice and that of a later generation. Whereas he would sometimes invite the awakened and the concerned to meet with him separately for spiritual advice, there is no record of his calling people to meet at the communion rail or 'the penitents' bench' at the end of a service. When the latter practice was first adopted by the Methodists it was only as a means to make counselling more easily and immediately available; but this was to prove a half-way to the practice of making coming to the front necessary for securing immediate professions of conversion. When that

---

[1] He also has strong words on the wrongness of bringing converts too early to public notice and witness, when their first need is to learn. Where this caution is not followed, 'ignorance is engendered, and pride fostered'.

final stage came, the prevailing understanding of evangelism was very different from that of Bramwell's generation.[1] And the final development encouraged the very danger of a premature profession that the earlier generation had been concerned to avoid. Bramwell's generation wanted to see repentance resulting in a changed life before they accepted any Christian profession.

Another evidence of the genuineness of these revivals was the spirit of love unmistakably engendered among the people. The description of apostolic Christians – 'of one heart and one soul' – was again seen to be true of people who previously had known nothing of brotherly love. Bramwell constantly held up this test: 'He considered the religion of Christ as an empty name when it was destitute of love; that perfect, powerful, operative principle.' 'Hearts irradiated with Divine love become one.' This love of God had marked effects in several of the congregations which he served. It made them irrefutable examples of the uniting and transforming power of the gospel; the communities of believers were eager to do good to all and to help every endeavour for the furtherance of the gospel.

Sigston mentions an opinion held by some in Leeds, before Bramwell went there, that if a minister had to 'exhort plain, simple people to unite in carrying on the work of God, – this is manifest proof of his being a person of only ordinary abilities'. At Leeds, as elsewhere, Bramwell put down such an unscriptural error, and in the words of the same author, 'employed the talents of the local preachers, leaders, and other individuals, in prayer;

[1] I have written of this more fully in *Revival and Revivalism: the Making and Marring of American Evangelicalism 1750–1858* (Edinburgh: Banner of Truth, 1994).

and they became important helpers to him in every place. The embers of love were kindled all around, and when he revisited the societies, he found them "striving together for the furtherance of the gospel".' 'Nothing produces such union of souls, such pity for sinners, such warmth of affection towards the Church', Bramwell concludes, as 'the great love of God our Saviour'.[1]

Love was no less demonstrated in the generosity of the people in their giving, the more striking because of the poverty of so many who made up congregations. Sigston tells us what happened when Bramwell went back from Nottingham to Sheffield to appeal for help in building a chapel. On his unexpected re-appearance among his former flock,

'Their joy was ecstatic. When the object of his visit was known, the people vied with each other, and seemed as if they would pour in their whole store. Their bounty was so lavish, that he had to restrain the feelings and limit the donations of many, till, oppressed with a torrent of love and gratitude, he suddenly left the town, to prevent the poor from exceeding the proper bounds of their ben-evolence'.

* * * * *

[1] The error of supposing that churches simply made up of individuals can ever make a true impact upon the world has been exposed in every period of revival. Ebenezer Porter, Congregational leader in the United States, refers to the same lesson when he wrote: 'The state of the church at – is such as that of every church must be, when merely associated at the communion table, without explicit union in any articles of faith, and without any explicit covenant obligations, hanging loosely together by a general, undefined influence from the pulpit. Oh, it grieves my heart to see such an assemblage of men and women miscalled a church. I do not wonder that Gideon, when going to fight Midian and Amalek, because "the people were too many," dismissed the promiscuous multitude, choosing to rely on *three hundred* true hearted men.' Lyman Matthews, *Memoir of the Life and Character of Ebenezer Porter* (Boston: Perkins and Marvin, 1837), p. 197.

It is not easy, from the limited information we have, to assess the natural gifts of William Bramwell. From the simplicity of his life and the fundamentals around which his ministry constantly centred, the impression might be that his attainments and education were comparatively small. This would certainly be a mistake. We know that for a time he wrote part of a journal (which has not survived) in Hebrew, and it is said that he also understood French and Greek. All testify to the strength of his mind, and to his ability in presenting truths in compelling and logical order. This part of his make-up has probably been underestimated on account of what was so evidently more spiritual than natural. That he possessed spiritual gifts to an unusual degree would appear to be evident. Sigston, who knew him well, says that the ability to discern the spirits of men 'Mr Bramwell at times appeared to possess'. He gives several instances of this which can scarcely bear any other interpretation. More than one hypocrite, whose falsity no one else had suspected, was exposed by him. Similarily there were instances of a gift of faith in regard to the healing of the sick. Clearly this was very occasional rather than usual; it was in special instances of need, when other means had failed, that he would, 'in submission to the will of God', plead for healing. That these prayers were sometimes answered with healing was evident.

To these unusual features in Bramwell's life Sigston gives no special attention and wisely advises us that 'they form no subject of instruction to other persons'. Bramwell himself, he adds, never spoke about it, 'neither in public, nor in the company of friends'.

More pervasive in his ministry was the gift of wisdom. In a few words he could often advise friends of points where their weakness lay. To one fellow-preacher he writes, 'We have great need to guard against our natural turn.' 'Instinct or natural affection has nothing to do with Divine love', he cautions another. To one he gives this counsel: 'Know your chain, and determine to go to its length. But also determine not to *break* it. "He knoweth wherof we are made", and indeed "we are but dust". Be filled with the Spirit; and yet the spirit will be subject to reason.' After confessing his own deficiency, he urges a preacher to give more attention to 'the great love of God our Saviour', and goes on: 'Do not condemn, but pity. Do not destroy, but heal. Do not drive, but draw.'

Sigston gives the following example of questions directed to Bramwell. Three society members once wrote to him with the following enquiries:

'1. In private prayer we sometimes feel power to wrestle with the Lord; at other times we feel no such power, but rather are distracted and our minds wander. What should we do in the latter case?

2. If we do not feel much liberty in prayer should we continue in the posture of kneeling?

3. Is what is called by some "burning love", to be attained *gradually* or *instantaneously*?'

It would only be to the ignorant that these questions looked simple. There is much spiritual wisdom, as well as experience, in his reply:

'1. When we find distraction in private prayer, we are often called upon to fight and wrestle, in order to obtain "a mind stayed upon God" . . . When we conquer through Christ, those seasons are often the most profitable.

2. Should we, however, still feel dissipated, we might then rise, and walk up and down in the room, and sing, or read some portion of the word of God, and then kneel

down and pray again. Or if the body be weak, we may occasionally pray standing, or even sitting.

3. "Burning love", that is, a warm glowing feeling in the heart, is no necessary consequence upon full salvation. It may exist with or without it. It is seldom given for more than a day or two: and then often previous to some peculiar trial, or some extraordinary outpouring of the Spirit.'

When we turn from Bramwell's gifts to his character there can be little doubt which two features are most prominent; they are love and humility.

The love which appeared among his people was first of all in himself. He loved all and even non-Christians could recognize it. Sigston wrote: 'What is very remarkable, notwithstanding his uncommonly faithful admonitions, and his great plainness of speech, the ungodly part of mankind flocked to hear him in preference to a great number of his brethren in the ministry.' A major part of the explanation for this is surely indicated in the following words of Bramwell to a younger minister:

'Get all your nature moulded into love: lose self in God, and dwell there. In your preaching, discover by every word and look the strongest affection for the congregation, and let everything declare your earnest desire for their salvation. Show the greatest respect, and keep from everything harsh. Say strong things, but let your edge be smooth. This will make all men love you, even if they do not leave their sins.'

Other preachers often received similar counsel from him. To a James Drake he wrote: 'One thing has been on my mind concerning you: – I think you should fully try every place in your circuit, in the consolatory way. Preach in an encouraging way . . . Dwell much on the love of Jesus.'

His personal life was conformed to this same spirit. To keep oneself in the love of God was for him the mainspring of the Christian's life. It was a privilege requiring constant watchfulness for 'Satan will use a thousand means to damp our love'. 'To be clear in pardon of all our sins, to be pure in heart, to live in love – this is heaven on earth. What is all the world compared with this! To live in profession is so far well; but to enjoy the kingdom, to live in God, to have union with him, to bear his image, to glorify our God, and finish the work, – this is our grand business on earth.'[1]

Involved in Bramwell's thinking at this point is the whole subject of 'perfect love' or 'entire sanctification'. It would be a serious misrepresentation of his life and ministry to minimize the importance he placed on this aspect of Wesleyan teaching. Elsewhere I comment on this. All that I would point out here is that he fully believed that the higher the Christian's attainments the lower will be his view of himself. For him this was a clear principle: 'Of this I am fully assured. I grow, and am less; I am become more ashamed of *myself*, and more dependant on God.' 'The love of Christ is my study', he writes to a friend, 'but I am frequently at a loss to understand how it is that my love to him is so small.' His language about himself is consistently the same: 'I nothing have, I nothing am.' 'I have stood to look back on all my works, but I cannot fix my mind on one that yields me joy.' To a fellow minister he writes: 'It is no proof of your not being

---

[1] This spirit assumed the most practical form in his giving to the poor. 'In nothing did he approach more nearly to an imitation of our Lord, than in his benevolence. It cannot be thought singular that he was courteous, and pitiful, and kind; for all the ministers of the gospel ought to exemplify these virtues. But he relieved the necessities of others, by making frequent sacrifices of his own personal comfort. We have known him give his only top coat in severe weather to one who had not a coat.'

called to the work, when you see yourself so unfit, and feel so ashamed before God. At sixteen, we think we know; at twenty, we think we know much; but if we increase in true knowledge, we shall know ourselves to be nothing.'

To another he writes from Durham in 1807:

'The Bible becomes more than ever my delight, and I am ready to say – "I know nothing: I am nothing." O how I sink, yea, I lie before the Lord! Everything that I say or do, preaching, praying etc, etc, seems to me to be nothing compared to what it should be. Here I am, here I live, wondering that even the Lord himself should notice me for one moment.'

* * * * *

The above quotations give us some idea of what Bramwell was as a Christian but to understood the man aright we have to go to what he saw as the whole purpose of the Christian revelation: *The gospel is to bring men into the presence of God.* Its objective is not forgiveness, nor even holiness (in itself); it is union with God and all other blessings are related to that end. In Paul's words, the end is 'that you might be filled with all the fullness of God' (*Eph.* 3:19). This is the belief that leads to the wonder expressed by Charles Wesley,

> And will this sovereign King
> Of glory condescend?
> And will He write His name
> My Father and my Friend?

For Bramwell, the first need of the Christian is 'to live in the closest fellowship with God'. 'To retain a constant sense of the presence of God is our glory in this world.' And he was sure that 'to live in God' is the only source of the believer's usefulness. This is the repeated note in his letters. Christians are to 'do all in God': 'We may do all things in him. You may see, talk, walk, and suffer in the Lord.' Giving his own testimony, he writes: 'I view him [Christ] in all my acts, take hold of him as the instrument by which I do all my work, and feel that nothing is done without him.' This is how he understood the command, 'Be strong in the Lord, and in the power of his might' (*Eph.* 6:10).

In practice this meant living by prayer and faith in all the promises of God. There were occasions when he knew 'a baptism of the Holy Spirit',[1] but these times were not the norm: the norm was habitual walking with God by faith. In the words of Thomas Harris:

'He experienced daily, and many times daily, what he called "the Divine touch" . . . The glories of the Divine presence which irradiated his soul, filled him with profound humility, and shone forth with uncommon lustre in his conversation, prayers and daily walk. His preaching, his pastoral visits, conversations and letters, were full of this holy unction.'

To prove that this was no eccentricity but genuine Christian experience, Harris gives a number of quotations from authors of other centuries, including Bishop Hall, who wrote:

'The more familiar acquaintance we have with God the more do we partake of him. He that passes by the fire

---

[1] He wrote, for instance, to his daughter from Newcastle in 1815: 'I hope you will unite in praise to God, when I tell you that I have received what I call *an extraordinary baptism of the Spirit.* I do not know that I shall preach any better, or look in any thing more like an angel; but my soul has experienced such a fellowship with God, and heavenly things, as I never felt before.'

may have some gleams of heat, but he that stands by it has his colour changed. It is not possible that a man should have any long conference with God and be no whit affected. If we are strangers to God it is no wonder that our faces become earthy.'

Where this element is too largely missing in Christians and gospel ministers, Bramwell believed, the cause was commonly twofold. First, the day is not so planned that private prayer takes first place. 'Go to bed earlier'; 'Spend less time talking to others – never be too long even in the best company', were his common counsels to fellow preachers. Sometimes he spent unusual lengths of time in prayer ('What is so beneficial as a whole night spent in prayer?'), but it is the regular daily times of devotion, he insisted, that are essential. Second, he believed that failure in a prayerful living near to God was due to failure in faith, to an absence of dependence on God and trust in his promises. Persistence in prayer is bound up with belief in God's Word. Because he *believed* that men are dead in sin, and that all means for their salvation can accomplish nothing without the Holy Spirit, he knew that the gospel could have no success without prayer being heard. Scripture teaches that believing prayer *will be* heard and so, when prayer is given up without a reception of the promised blessing, he saw the cause as unbelief:

'God works by his ministers, and gives the Holy Spirit to them that ask him. He says, "Ask and it shall be given you." But how much is implied in asking rightly? – what strong desires, what agonising faith! What importunate prayer, what holy wrestling, persevering supplication, and imitation of the poor widow, when she cried, "Avenge me of my adversary!" or, like Jacob, when he said, "I will not let thee go, unless thou bless me." O, if all Christians prayed as they ought, – if every Christian minister entered fully into this duty, and more seriously considered the necessities of the church of Christ and the world, – what a different state of things would soon be witnessed!'[1]

Faith was at the centre of all Bramwell's thinking and desires. His cry is, 'O for this mighty faith that brings the blessing!' But, as the previous paragraph shows, he did not see 'faith' as an exercise which frees the suppliant from effort ; it was not the 'easy believism' of a later day. On the contrary, Harris says that at times when Bramwell left his room in the morning to come to breakfast, his hair was wet with perspiration 'as if he had been engaged in the extremity of manual labour. Like Jacob he would not cease to plead till a blessing was imparted'.

Of all the blessings that he sought in prayer success for the gospel was ever foremost. Sigston says, 'It appeared as though he could scarcely bear to live unless he was made useful. He often entreated the Lord, that he might be delivered from that bitter cup – a useless life.'

Sometimes, after such praying, we find Bramwell saying that he received an assurance of coming blessing and went to his work with the firm expectation of success.[2]

[1] It is significant to note prayer for 'revival' is not apparent in Bramwell's biography; instead there is frequent reference to pleas for the immediate, present giving of the Spirit, according to Christ's promise in Luke 11:13. Harris summarized Bramwell's thought when he writes: 'The power of the Spirit is to be diligently sought.' Bramwell tells us something of his prayer life when he says in a letter, 'I am receiving more love; it comes by drops, after agony of prayer.'

[2] This happened at Birstal where, after initial discouragement, 'I received an answer from God in a particular way . . . I could say, "The Lord will come; I know he will come, and that suddenly.' A parallel experience to this occurred in the ministry of John L. Girardeau at Charleston, South Carolina, before the revival which occurred there in 1858. See my *Revival and Revivalism.* p. 420. At the same time it is important to notice what Thomas Harris honestly included in his biography of Bramwell: 'He was occasionally led astray by too great reliance upon sudden impulses and impressions.'

For Bramwell the essence of Methodism was living before God in private. The inner life must go before the outward; the secret prayer, seen by the Father, must go before his 'reward[ing] you openly' (*Matt.* 6:6). Consequently he warned of the danger that too many were ignoring:

'Too much conversation with the world, too much preaching and hearing, and too little self-examination and prayer. A number of Methodists now will be in public the whole of the Sabbath; and if they heard angels all the time they would be backsliders. It is astonishing how the devil is cheating us, and at the same time filling our heads, and emptying our hearts.'

It is on this note that Harris concludes his *Memoir of Bramwell*:

'He saw that the mere letter of the truth might be preached without the power and demonstration of the Spirit; that a preacher might appear as a man who can play well on an instrument, but see no fruit. A showy lifeless ministry; the substitution of beautiful chapels, large congregations, formal worship, for the power of godliness; a departure from the inward power to the outward splendour; were what he most dreaded.'

To the very end Bramwell was repeating the lesson which he had first learned in his youth at Preston. 'To retain a constant sense of the presence of God is our glory in this world.' At the last annual conference in 1818, when told by a friend that he had been made chairman of the Manchester District he, without seeming to hear what had been said, responded, 'O brother, live to God.' What he meant by that was repeated again in one of his last sermons, preached in the month of his death, on words he so much prized in 1 John 4:16–17: 'God is love; and he that dwelleth in love, dwelleth in God and God in him. Herein is our love made perfect, that we may have boldness in the day of judgment.'

Bramwell's life was greatly used of God to keep a great many in Methodism from drifting from real Christianity. His warnings were heard, and even more important, his life shone with the lesson, 'Be much with God and your face will shine.' He believed in 'the necessity of a conscious and habitual sense of the presence of God in order to successful Christian work'. Surely to read him is to understand why one who knew him could say, 'I never left him without a determination to live nearer to God.'

Chapter 7

Gideon Ouseley:
Methodism in Ireland

In a country church in the west of Ireland in the early 1790s a priest was reading Mass, while the kneeling congregation trusted that the souls of the departed were being remembered before God. Trust it had to be, for of the language the priest spoke the people understood not a word. So long had this been the case that none ever expected anything different. But on this day, amid the intoning of Latin, another voice was suddenly heard. The speaker was a thick-set stranger, of medium height and about thirty years of age, who turned every sentence in the Roman liturgy that expressed scriptural truth into Irish. These sentences he repeated aloud after the priest, adding with evident feeling, 'Listen to that!' The service ended, the same man 'with a face beaming with affection, urged upon the people the necessity of having their peace made with God, and telling them that they must become reconciled to Him, and that it was possible so to do by real repentance and true faith in the Lord Jesus Christ'.[1]

---

[1] William Arthur, *Life of Gideon Ouseley* (London: Wesleyan Conference Office, 1879), p. 61. I am using Arthur's work repeatedly in the following pages and quotations are from him unless otherwise stated. An earlier, and at certain points larger biography of Ouseley was written by his friend, William Reilly, *A Memorial of the Ministerial Life of the Rev. Gideon Ouseley* (London: Mason, 1847), hereafter Reilly, *Ouseley*.

The man departed as unannounced as he had arrived, leaving the priest to face the people's question, 'Father, who was that?' More awed than annoyed at the strange occurrence, the cleric confessed that he had no idea. Today in Ireland, although the shelves of bookshops are loaded with biographies of the nation's benefactors, the *Life of Gideon Ouseley* is not among them. For most he is again a stranger. Yet he was one of the truest lovers of the Irish people who ever lived. Of him it has been said, 'Among all the eminent men raised up by God in Irish Methodism, I doubt if any other was ever so successful in winning souls to Christ as Mr Ouseley.' Another has written that our subject was 'one of the most successful and illustrious evangelists who ever proclaimed Christ to perishing sinners'.[1]

The evangelization of Ireland in the eighteenth century went through two phases. Ouseley belonged to the second phase. The first began in 1746 when the evangelist John Cennick came to Dublin. What followed was very similar to what had begun with the Evangelical Revival in England some eight years earlier. First there was the inevitable opposition, and a contemptuous name was coined to deter anyone from taking the new message seriously. When preaching in Dublin, Cennick had referred to 'the Babe that lay in Mary's lap wrapped in swaddling clothes'. The word 'swaddling' was so unknown to his hearers that a wit coined a derisory nickname: these evangelicals should be called 'Swaddlers'. Although the label persisted in parts of Ireland for over a hundred years it was soon superseded by the term of

---

[1] C. H. Crookshank, *History of Methodism in Ireland*, vol. 2 (London: Woolmer, 1886), p. 39. Crookshank's *History* has been reprinted as *Days of Revival: History of Methodism in Ireland 1747–1859* (Clonmel, Tipperary: Tentmaker, 1994).

reproach already being popularized in England. The new preachers were 'Methodists'. John Wesley first visited Dublin in 1747 and thereafter the work in Ireland became one of his enduring concerns. Altogether he made twenty-one visits, constituting something like six years of his lifetime. To any who doubted such an expenditure of time, he would reply, 'Have patience and Ireland will repay you.'[1]

Wesley grasped the nature of the spiritual problem in Ireland. He described his first contacts in Dublin as people who exceeded all he knew for their 'sweetness of temper, courtesy and hospitality', but they were 'English transplanted into another soil'. They belonged to the Protestant establishment and it was from their number that the members of his first Society in Dublin came. Noticeably absent from that first Society were the native Irish-speaking people, of whom Wesley said, 'At least ninety-nine in a hundred remain in the religion of their forefathers.' For this sullen majority he had genuine sympathy and he regarded it as no surprise that they should live and die Roman Catholics 'when the protestants can find no better ways to convert them than penal laws and acts of parliament'.[2]

Wesley's conviction on how the Irish need should be faced were outlined in a twelve-page booklet which he

[1] Tyerman, *Wesley*, vol. 2, p. 3.
[2] Tyerman, *Wesley*, vol. 1, pp. 559. From Mediaeval times Ireland was divided between the Anglo-Norman ruling class and the native Celts whose language was a form of Gaelic. At the Reformation, while the formal Church structure became nominally Protestant (the Church of Ireland), Roman Catholicism survived and soon redeveloped its independent life. Roman belief and Irish nationalism coalesced and the South at last gained independence from Britain as the Irish Free State in 1921. From that solution, Ulster (the six counties of the North, largely settled by Scots Presbyterians in the seventeeth century) stood apart and Ulster's religious history has been largely distinct from that of the rest of Ireland.

published in Dublin in 1752. The title was: *A Short Method of Converting All the Roman Catholics in the Kingdom of Ireland*. The advice it contained was directed chiefly to the clergy of the 'Church of Ireland', the Protestant and episcopal church that had come into being after the Reformation and which was viewed by the majority of the people as an English institution imposed upon them. The Irish still gave first place to their Catholic priests, and Wesley's argument was that this situation could not change until the people learned of a ministry more holy and wise than their own. The first apostles were just such a ministry and, therefore, let all the clergy of the Church of Ireland, instead of being merely nominally Protestant, 'only *live* like the Apostles, and *preach* like the Apostles, and the thing is done'.[1] He went on to state how the apostles lived, and what they taught, with the conclusion that if the Protestant clergy would only follow the same pattern then 'Popery will vanish out of the kingdom'.

The problem with this proposal was that the clergy of the Church of Ireland were themselves a principal cause of the prevailing conditions. In no sense were they apostolic. When Whitefield was on a second visit to Ireland in 1757, he could say, 'Not one minister, either in the Church or among the Dissenters in this kingdom, as far as I can hear, appears boldly for God, even a God in Christ.'[2] If revival had to depend upon the episcopal

---

[1] *Works*, vol. 10, p. 130.
[2] *Works of George Whitefield*, vol. 3, p. 206. Whitefield's previous visit was in 1751. He had also passed through part of Ireland in 1738 when he noted: 'As far as I can find by all I converse with, they place religion in being either of Protestant or Roman Catholic communion, and are quite ignorant of the nature of inward purity and holiness of heart. Lord, the Christian world is cast into a deep sleep; send forth, I beseech thee, some faithful and true pastors to awaken them out of it.' *Whitefield's Journals*, p. 183.

clergy – or upon the moribund dissenting ministry – the outlook was bleak. The remedy was to come initially by a different route. Preachers there had to be, but their coming was not in fulfilment of Wesley's proposal. Rather it was through the ranks of his own followers, unordained men whose authority lay in an anointing of the Holy Spirit and in the truth of their message. A number of such preachers were raised up in Wesley's societies in Ireland in the forty years after 1747. By the time of his death in 1791 there were seventy five of them. They had laboured patiently amid great difficulties and, by that year, membership of the societies stood at around 15,000.

Within ten years of Wesley's death, a second phase in the evangelization of Ireland had begun, and it was to be still more remarkable. The *Methodist Magazine* for 1800 contained a lengthy letter on 'Revival in the West of Ireland' in which its author said: 'The Lord is now fulfilling the desire of his servants, by pouring out his Holy Spirit, in a greater or lesser degree, upon almost every circuit in this kingdom . . . I never saw a more genuine work of God.'[1] This was confirmed when the Irish Methodist Conference for 1801 reported an annual gain in membership of almost five thousand (4,941). In 1802 the total increase over the previous three years stood at 10,473. Clearly something extraordinary was happening and there is no better way to understand it than to look at Gideon Ouseley as a central and representative figure. To know him is to get at the heart of the change in Ireland.

* * * * *

[1] *The Methodist Magazine for the Year 1800*, vol. 23 (London: George Story), pp. 317–319.

Gideon Ouseley was born at Dunmore,[1] County Galway, on 24 February 1762. His background had prepared him to be a bridge between the two divided communities in the land. In name and genes he was English, for a hundred years earlier his royalist ancestors had removed from Northamptonshire to be landowners in the west of Ireland. But by the circumstances of his upbringing, among Irish-speaking country people, and far removed from Dublin, he was as Irish as his Connacht brogue. Attuned in sympathy to the population's oppressed and poor majority, he could get into their hearts 'before one trained differently could have seized the tips of their fingers'.

Ouseley's life had a comfortable beginning and his father's ambitions for him rose no higher than a continuance of that comfort. These were the days when a clergyman's position offered 'a good profession', so, although a deist and no church-goer, John Ouseley planned a Church of Ireland career for his son. A second son, Ralph, was destined for the British army where he rose to the rank of Major-General and to a knighthood. In view of Gideon's anticipated career he was early put under the private tuition of a priest possessed with special ability in Latin and mathematics. But before the days of his youth were over a change in the family fortunes put the Church out of his father's mind. John Ouseley was left a valuable farm in Roscommon and so his eldest son's prospects for a good life-style seemed well enough secured without the aid of the Church. These prospects were still further improved when, at the age of twenty, Gideon married Harriet Wills. Harriet's father marked the event

---

[1] *Dun-mor* (big fort) took its name from the fort of a twelfth-century King of Connacht. It is approximately in mid Galway as the county extends east and west, forty one miles north of the town of Galway, and in the province of Connacht.

by the gift of a house and lands, adjoining his own at Wills Grove.

Gideon had entered upon manhood well placed to be a leader among the fashionable younger set of Connacht gentry. Work was peripheral to their life-style. Most days could best be filled with field sports, horse racing, and hunting, while the evenings were too short for all the drinking, dancing, card playing, and gambling which were expected of them. Describing the attitude of those among whom Ouseley now spent his time, William Arthur wrote: 'On the whole, the calling of a real gentleman was to do nothing and spend much. The honour of ladies was tenderly prized, but the purity of gentlemen was another matter.'

Yet Ouseley's existence was not as carefree as it appeared to be. There were mounting gambling debts and then 'out of the blue' came a more severe blow. His wife's father died and the chief beneficiary contested the validity of the deed which had conveyed the gift of land and property to Harriet and himself on their marriage. Perhaps pride prevented Ouseley fighting this apparent injustice and insisting on their right. Possibly Harriet even thought that her wayward husband would be better back at Dunmore where he proposed they should go. The circumstances are obscure, but if such was her hope it was soon to be disappointed. Once back at his birthplace Gideon soon found companions as worthless as those he left around Roscommon, indeed, it was their friendship that now nearly ended his life.

One day in Dunmore he met some of these friends returning from a day's shooting and joined them in the village inn. Fortified by the ensuing 'refreshment', an argument broke out and, in a scuffle that followed, one man's gun, still loaded, went off and shot Ouseley in his face and neck. He was instantly blinded in one eye and so wounded that he looked like a dying man. A long convalescence was to follow, during which Harriet tenderly nursed him back to health, although he never recovered the sight of his right eye. But his forgiving wife recognized that it was more than a recovery of physical strength that he needed, and she began to read the same religious book to him as his mother had done years before. This was Edward Young's poetical work, *Night Thoughts*, which had much to say on death and eternity.[1] Young wrote of men who knew neither God nor their own hearts, and Gideon Ouseley now discovered that the description fitted himself. Believing that God had spared his life, he now resolved to be a changed man and to live righteously. The resolution was sincere but time was to prove that he had no power to execute it. In truth, he had no real heart for such a change. Awakened to his guilt, he remained a prisoner to the life he loved.

Such was Ouseley's condition in the year 1791 when something strange happened in Dunmore. The Fourth Royal Irish Dragoon Guards were at that time occupying the local barracks. That was common enough. What had never been known before was that some of the soldiers had hired a room at the main inn, and this not for drinking and carousing but for hymn-singing, prayer, and preaching. Equally strange, was the fact that they appeared to need no book for their praying and preaching apart from the Bible. The local clergy dismissed the phenomenon with laughter but it gained the attention of Ouseley whose reaction was a mixture of curiosity and suspicion. He was used to playing tricks on others and did not mean

---

[1] Young, 1681–1765, rector of Welwyn in Hertfordshire, published his once-famous *Night Thoughts* in 1742–44.

to be fooled by soldiers. So cautiously, in April 1791, he went to view the proceedings in the inn room for himself and to hear the speaker, a Quartermaster from the cavalry by the name of Robins. The result was that, for the first time, he received some glimmerings of an evangelical understanding. The next month, when a Methodist visiting preacher arrived to speak, Ouseley was present again and now he determined to change his ways:

'I more fully resolved upon reformation, and changed from evil practices, and withdrew from the society of my ungodly associates.'

By this time he had started a serious reading of the Bible and while thus engaged, alone in his home, a further turning point came. He had learned from Isaiah 1:18 that God invited him to receive mercy. But he also knew there would be a cost. This he reviewed as follows:

'I am a young man, and may live, say forty years, and to be under restraint all that time, as if buried alive, would be dreadful. I am not willing to undertake to be tied down to obey that book [the Bible] for the remainder of my life. Then I considered the possibility that I might die before the morning; and even should I survive forty years, and then be cast into hell for all eternity! This decided the matter. I had such a clear view of eternity, of being cast into everlasting misery, never, never, never to be released! I fell upon my knees, and cried, O God, I will submit!'

Yet Ouseley was still in the dark over how pardon could come to him and supposed it must somehow be connected with works he had to do. On this subject he did not know who could guide him. Even now his suspicions of the soldiers and of the Methodists remained; he could not trust himself to them; and he was convinced that neither the Roman priests nor the Church clergy could be of any help. The one thing of which he was sure was that he must stick to Scripture. Before the end of May 1791 he attended the inn meeting again on a weekday evening. On this occasion it was indicated that a meeting of the Society would follow the ordinary meeting and that 'any seriously-disposed person' was welcome to remain. With hesitation, lest there be any 'tricks', he decided to stay. No record exists of how many were present at that Society but what Ouseley then discovered is well described by William Arthur. He found himself among a people

'of one mind, giving themselves up with feelings of cordiality to communion on the things of God. It was Brother this, and Sister that. The hymns sung were such as speak of mercy in possession; of peace as felt and flowing; of God as a Father near at hand and strangely loving; of Christ as perfect Priest, Sacrifice, Mediator, Righteousness, and Redemption; and of heaven as a happy, happy home, only on the other side of a thin cloud . . . The words of each particular person would vary, and yet, somehow, all would support the testimony of others. The great theme was the pardoning love of God, and simply believing in Christ crucified was constantly alluded to as the means by which it came to be felt and known.

'What he found was very far from being the discovery of a new religion; yet it was the discovery of a Church in a new aspect . . . Here was a Church in a house, not a Church with her tongue always tied, except when vicariously opened on Sunday in the pulpit; but a Church seated at home like a joyful mother of children, with her sons and daughters holding free fellowship in family communion.'

Although now thoroughly awakened and convinced, Ouseley was not yet delivered. That came one Sunday morning not long after. On going into his room at home he determined not to come out until he found peace. Once again he cried, 'Lord, I submit, I submit', but this time there was a new light:

'I saw Jesus – Jesus the Saviour of sinners – Jesus the Saviour for me. I saw Him as the gift of the love of God for me. Jesus loved me, and gave Himself for me, and I knew – yes, I knew – that God had forgiven me all my sins; and my soul was filled with gladness and I wept for joy.'

In the weeks that followed he still had doubts and difficulties but the one thing that was beyond dispute was that God had done something for him and in him. 'God poured His Spirit upon me so that I felt wonderful happiness. God did give it me.' In August of the same year, 1791, he told the Society prayer meeting of his joy. His change of interests was immediate:

'From this time forth, wherever I went I spoke of the "things of God", telling of a kingdom, not in the golden clouds of a distant world, but within you – a kingdom of righteousness, peace, and joy in the Holy Ghost.'

Ouseley, at twenty-nine years of age was a new man, and his testimony to the fact soon brought disturbance to Dunmore. Trouble seems to have started with the local curate of the Church of Ireland. He was a charitable man who, we are told, 'allowed every man to go to heaven in his own way'. Every man, that is, except a Methodist whose beliefs he held up as 'rank nonsense'. 'They teach', he complained, 'that man is fallen, utterly done from righteousness; and that he cannot recover himself from sin.' Hearing this kind of talk one Sunday morning in the Church, Ouseley rose to his feet when the sermon was done and declared that the teaching they had all heard denounced was indeed that of the Bible and the Liturgy. 'Do you know what you are doing, sir?' demanded the curate. 'I do, sir', replied his hearer; 'I am striving to persuade you that you should not preach false doctrine, and to guard those who heard you from its effects.'

Instead of being deterred by the anger of many – including that of his own father – Gideon Ouseley was filled with compassion for the people who were as ignorant as he had long been. So it was not only in church that he seized opportunities to speak. His powerful voice was to be heard in places not usually connected with any evangelism. The holding of 'wakes' – a watch over the body of a deceased person prior to burial – was at this time integral to the culture. Apart from the collection of fees for mass to be said for the soul of the departed, wakes were not religious occasions; rather they were generally characterized by heavy drinking and entertainment. Arthur says: 'Folly and vice were formally presented in the chamber of death, and installed there as if fit for any presence.' Ouseley now joined such gatherings not as a participant but as a witness. Among the mourners he would speak and pray in such a manner that all present began to know something of the realities of death and eternity. His endeavours of this kind soon led him, as already noted, to go into parts of the surrounding countryside where he was unknown.

Within a year of his own conversion, his wife, Harriet, also came to real faith. Religious before, she had learned 'that the Holy Spirit was not merely a solemn name in the Creed, but a living agent, operating on the hearts of ordinary people'. The Methodist Society was now transferred from the inn to the Ouseleys' home and when, Gideon was away on gospel excursions, as he often was, Harriet was the spiritual helper. The Society, it appears, had about a dozen members, of which half were their relations.

Ouseley received no income from his self-appointed labours and how he had enough to sustain his wife and family we do not know. He cannot have been relying on his father for it was the latter's opinion, as he told Harriet, that Gideon 'will ruin himself and bring you to beggary'.[1] It may have been financial pressure which led them to remove from Dunmore and settle at Ballymote, Sligo, in 1797, for there is record of his opening a girls' school at that place. Even so all his endeavours for the gospel were unabated. His biographer writes:

'Mr Ouseley seems to have had no idea of anything short of constant itinerancy. Not only in every one of the five counties of Connacht, but in several towns of Leinster, and a few in Ulster, he made his appearance on horseback, the people wondering who he was, where he came from, what had sent him, and altogether feeling as if a voice from the unknown had reached them, and brought strange things to their ears. In fair or market, at burial or patron, he took his stand, and cried aloud. He also succeeded in gaining access to the jails, visiting both the debtors and criminals.'

'It is more than sixty years since I first heard Mr Ouseley', Edward Rigley once said. 'I see him now as distinctly –

---

[1] Harriet replied nobly: 'Sir, why are you so violent against your son? When he has spent nights in sin, and when you have seen him scarce able to walk home, you administered no reproof.'

his gestures, his fire, his pathos, his smile, his benignity, his powerful persuasiveness and tact, and his peculiar shake of the hand – as ever I did. If ever heart went with hand to a brother or sister, it did so in Gideon Ouseley's shake.'

The removal to Sligo brought Ouseley into closer contact with Methodist preachers, and this led in 1799 to a decisive change in the organization of his life. The Irish Methodist Conference met in July of that year under the shadow of the 30,000 or more lives that had been recently lost during nationwide bloodshed. The year 1798 had been the year of the Great Irish Rebellion. Multitudes, armed often with little more than pikes and a few muskets, but hopeful of French aid, had risen against British rule in various parts of the land. Some of the revolutionaries were nominal Protestants, most were republicans and Roman Catholic (although one of the oaths they took was 'to form a brotherhood of affection among *Irishmen* of every religious persuasion'[1]). Irish Methodists, believing in a different brotherhood, took no part in the rising and sometimes suffered on that account. Given the weakness of French aid, the outcome was inevitable as peasants fought disciplined troops. Widespread misery ensued and the 1799 Conference of Methodists in Ireland met with a deepened pity over the state of the Irish-speaking people. At the instigation of Thomas Coke a new plan was introduced and named a 'General Mission to the Irish'. Coke was convinced that in addition to circuits and the local preachers, general missioners were needed to preach across the land and *to preach in the Irish*

---

[1] Thomas Pakenham, *The Year of Liberty: the Great Irish Rebellion of 1798* (London: Abacus, 1997), p. 253.

tongue.[1] Two names were proposed for this endeavour, both regular preachers among the Methodists, then a third name was brought forward, that of Gideon Ouseley. The nomination of Ouseley was irregular, for he had not been recommended by any Methodist district meeting, he had not been examined as to his doctrinal beliefs, and he was married. Previously all his labours had been independent and spontaneous, and there was no proof of his being able to work with a colleague as the Methodist preachers normally did. Nonetheless he was appointed and when he heard the news he was happier than if he had been given a fortune.

The man appointed to work with Ouseley by the decision of the 1799 Conference was Charles Graham, and this launched the two men into six years of the closest partnership. Graham, a man of like spirit, was forty-nine, and Ouseley was now thirty-six. Their years together were the years which coincided with a general revival in various parts of Ireland and while numbers of faithful men were engaged in the work, it was these two who ever seemed to be at the front of the advance. From August 1799 they always worked together, riding everywhere and generally used their horses as their pulpits. With regard to Ouseley's dress, it is said, 'He always wore thick cord breeches, with top-boots – *mahoganies*; and his dress was that of a man who spent a great portion of his time on horseback, and was constantly exposed to all sorts of weather.' Both men

---

[1] The difference the native language could make is well illustrated in the life of another Methodist evangelist. Thomas Walsh writes that when a man raged at him, 'I reproved him in Irish. He was instantly amazed; and replied, "Why did you not speak so to me in the beginning?" The lion was a lamb; and so I then let him know, still speaking in Irish, what Christ had done for sinners.' 'Thomas Walsh', in *Wesley's Veterans*, ed. John Telford, vol. 5 (London: Kelly, 1913), p. 54.

were distinguished by their black velvet caps which seems to have been a Methodist dress (hence another nickname, 'the Black Caps'). Their usual method was to draw up their horses outside a chapel, as a congregation was leaving after Mass, or in a village street, and then begin with a hymn before they spoke in turn. The practice was as unusual as the language the people heard; the words were not the customary Latin, nor the English they disliked, but the very tongue they spoke at their own firesides.

Frequently, it seems, it was not so much the preaching as the praying that arrested attention. The two men might join a burial party, and in the midst of those kneeling and wailing in the traditional manner at a graveside, pour out fervent and sympathetic prayers. It was thus that many for the first time heard of eternal life and of a loving heavenly Father. The missioners were ready to pray in every place. On one occasion a priest looked out of his church door for an overdue wedding party he was expecting. To his surprise he saw them kneeling on the road outside, with Ouseley also on his knees praying and tears flowing. Long before, Augustine had once said, 'The Christian teacher will succeed more by piety in prayer than by gifts of oratory.'

In the providence of God, the two men had been sent out as a new day was dawning in the land. One man who had belonged to the Methodists for thirty-one years said that he had never seen a year like 1800 'for a deep-spreading work'. We find Ouseley and Graham reporting: 'The spirit of deep conviction seized on the people; it was like the Day of Pentecost'. Another preacher said of the two men:

'The mighty power of God accompanied their word with such demonstrative evidence as I have never known, or indeed very rarely heard of. I have been present in fairs and markets while these two blessed men of God, with burning zeal and apostolic ardour, pointed hundreds and thousands to the Lamb of God that taketh away the sin of the world. And I have seen the immediate fruit of their labour, the aged and young falling prostrate in the most public places of concourse, cut to the heart, and refusing to be comforted until they knew Jesus and the power of his resurrection . . . blessed be God, hundreds of men now stand and adorn the gospel of Christ Jesus. These two men have been the most indefatigable in their labours of love to perishing sinners of any that I have yet known . . . I am wanting both in memory and language to set forth the wonders I have seen wrought by the mighty power of the Holy Spirit.'

The occasional letters which Ouseley and Graham were able to write tell the same story. Writing from near Enniskillen on 23 December 1800, Ouseley said:

'Every day souls are converted; we cannot ascertain how many, the number is great, and the multitudes who throng around us are so immense. We found it so impossible to find out all the mourners, or those who are made happy – we did not attempt to count. We conversed with a priest on Tuesday, and the result was pleasing. Many appear *literally to devour* the word . . . These Roman Catholics love us, and are anxious to get pamphlets from us. Near Enniskillen we had a blessed meeting; scarcely a dry face. Glory, glory, to our God.'[1]

---

[1] W. G. Campbell, *Charles Graham: the Apostle of Kerry* (1868; reprint ed., Clonmel, Tentmaker Publications, 1995), pp. 126–7.

A few weeks later Graham wrote:

'At Oldcastle the Catholics flocked to hear us as they did before, and the Lord blessed His Word to them; at the market, next day, they seemed as much athirst for the Word as the gaping land for the falling rain.'[1]

This is not to say that they saw uninterrupted success. By no means. The devil stirred up many to hate them. Threats were commonplace, and as with all the early preachers they had sometimes to suffer physically; anything from dirt thrown in their faces to stoning. When in villages they would often back their horses against the glass window of a Catholic shop to deter stone throwing. But despite all precautions they might take, a readiness to die was a precondition for open-air preaching in many parts of Ireland at this date. Persecution was commonly stirred up by the Catholic priests and in some localities, had it not been for the presence of British troops, open-air preaching would have been impossible. At Kilkenny the preachers needed the protection of the army barracks.[2] On such occasions Ouseley, ever mindful of what he owed himself to the witness of Christians in the army, took every opportunity of addressing the soldiers. This is not to say that officers invariably allowed him to do so; at one point we read of him being put into 'the Black Hole of the barracks in Sligo for disturbing the peace'.

---

[1] Ibid., p. 127.

[2] This did not deter them from making a second visit when there was no such uproar. John MacDonald of Ferintosh, Scotland, visiting Kilkenny in 1827 found Roman Catholics to Protestants in the proportion of twenty-four to one. By this date there were a number of evangelicals in the Church of Ireland and it was by their invitation that MacDonald was there. J. Kennedy, *The Apostle of the North: the Life and Labours of Dr M'Donald* (London: Nelson, 1866), p. 163.

As general missionaries, Ouseley and Graham were annually appointed to wide areas of the country although they were not tied down to any strict boundaries. They preached across the whole island from east to west. In 1801, the Conference designated their area as the south and the west, together with Ulster. We hear of them riding 230 miles in five-and-a-half days, and preaching each day, morning, noon and night. Snow, rain and the want of food were no deterrents to them. Frequently their bed was no more than straw and a blanket, in a loft or on a damp floor; it was a case of wherever they could find lodging.

A correspondent in the north wrote about the same period:

'Graham and Ouseley travelled this country, but two such men for an apostolic, fearless spirit, I never saw. Great success attends their ministry. At Fivemiletown a hundred and fifty have joined the society since they left. Prisons and death seem no more to them than liberty and life. There is a revival in all the neighbouring circuits, namely, Brookborough, Clones, Ballyconnell, Sligo, Enniskillen, Ballinamallard, Newtownstewart, Belfast.'[1]

Reviewing the six years that Ouseley and Graham shared together, one writer has conjectured, 'Never perhaps, in the same space of time, or by any two men, was a larger portion of this *native seed* of Divine truth scattered in any country or in any language than by those two men'.[2]

---

[1] Campbell, *Graham*, p. 151.

[2] Ibid., p. 94. The love and understanding between the two was unbroken. William Reilly, who knew them both, noted: 'Mr Graham was *naturally* gifted with persuasive powers; Mr Ouseley with reasoning powers. Mr Graham's voice was soft and musical; Mr Ouseley's rough and sepulchral. Mr Graham brought the Scriptures, with a mind filled with holy truth, to bear upon errors and prejudices convincing to all: Mr Ouseley, by logical arguments and varied research, would stop the mouths of gainsaysers. Both were perfect masters of the Irish language . . . They were sons of thunder.' Ibid., p. 262.

In 1805 the General Mission instituted a major change by appointing Graham and Ouseley to different areas and each with a new worker. There were now ten general missioners and no doubt it was believed that the gifts possessed by the two veterans would be best shared among others. At this date the membership of the societies stood at 23,321. From 1805 Ouseley's colleague was William Hamilton; he was changed in 1809 for a younger man whose health soon broke down. In 1810 William Reilly and John Nelson were appointed by Conference to work with him. Reilly remained with him for five years and was later to write of his older friend, 'No language could adequately describe the veneration which I entertained for that singular man – veneration increased by every day's acquaintance and blended with tender affection which time cannot efface.'[1]

Reilly's initial shock at the difficulties of the work was soon countered by the encouragements he found alongside Ouseley. A notable instance was what he saw at Burrisokane. In 1809 Ouseley had visited this 'very destitute neighbourhood' where there were many nominal Protestants and found very few with religious interests. But in following visits there was a remarkable awakening and in April 1811 he could report, 'We have more than 150, perhaps 200, in society, in Burrisokane, there and about it, and six blessed class-leaders; and about 500 at times in our congregation.' Of his own first visit to this place, Reilly says: 'I had now the happiness of witnessing the character and spirit of this infant society, resembling, as it did, the church in primitive days, when –

> They all were of one heart and soul,
> And only love inspired the whole.'[2]

---

[1] Reilly, *Ouseley*, p. 210. [2] Ibid., pp. 171, 189.

Growth was to continue and while the extraordinary general conversion work of blessing seen at the beginning of the century was not repeated there were powerful movements of the Spirit at various times, especially in 1819 when 400 joined the societies in the counties of Wicklow and Carlow; and also in 1826 when 'thousands turned from lying vanities to search for Christianity in the Volume of divine truth'.[1] Reilly is, however, careful to point out that growth and success were by no means invariable in Ouseley's ministry. The same sermons that had brought so much light in other areas found no response in others.

* * * * *

I turn now to the subject of Ouseley's methods. He had no 'methods' in the modern sense of the term. When a candidate for gospel preaching once asked him what plan he followed, he replied:

'I have no plan to give you, my son: the country is before you: go into every open door; and, if admitted, preach and exhort and pray, proclaiming the grand truths of our holy Christianity, and while you thus preach with divine power, and the love of God burning in your heart, you will never want hearers.'

There were, however, some things in his practice which might be called methods. William Arthur says that all the Methodist preachers used the 'interrogatory style', which is to say that they employed questions to awaken interest and attention. Certainly Ouseley did this to a marked degree. He did not preach on the assumption that people

[1] Ibid., p. 265.

were *already* interested. Awakening attention he saw as part of his responsibility. So to a suspicious and maybe hostile Catholic crowd he might begin by saying, 'The Virgin had the best religion in the world.' 'What do *you* know about the blessed Virgin? We don't want to hear a word', a member of a mob once shouted at him. 'More than you think', he replied; 'and I am sure you will be pleased with what I have to tell you, if you'll only listen to me.' He then launched into an account of the wedding at Cana of Galilee, and from Mary's words, 'Whatsoever he says to you, do it', he went on to preach Christ without further interruption. Ouseley's aim was always to 'individualize' the message and to press home it home with such questions as, 'Is *your* soul happy in Jesus? Are *you* sure you love Him?'

Reilly indicates something of the demands that Ouseley's readiness to engage with his hearers placed on him. For instance, while preaching at Ballina on a market day, he was interrupted by a questioner. Ouseley asked him to be patient till he had finished then he would answer. With the sermon concluded, discussion followed and the able questioner pressed him on texts which a preacher less familiar with the Bible would have been hard put to answer. 'He was on his feet for three hours', reported Reilly, 'during which time the people heard him with the utmost attention; and this indefatigable servant of God exerted himself until he was bathed in perspiration'.[1]

Reilly gives the following example of Ouseley dealing with questions from a crowd. A critical schoolmaster asked

[1] Ibid., p. 249. After an hour's rest, Ouseley then rode five miles to another opportunity. 'What should these people do? How could they ever get enlightened?' he commented to Reilly, 'had not God put it into the hearts of some persons to stand in the open streets and instruct them.'

him for the loan of his Bible. When the preacher handed it to him, the man checked it was the Rhemish version (approved by his Church) and then turned to the words of Matthew 6:5 which he asked Ouseley to read aloud to the people. Ouseley did so: 'And when thou prayest be not as the hypocrites; for they love to pray standing in the synagogues and in the corners of the streets.' This provoked a general smile at the seeming criticism the preacher had read of himself. But he immediately went on to read from chapter 5:9, 'Let your light so shine before men . . . ', and handing the Bible back to the schoolmaster he asked him to read Acts 17:7. The man then read aloud, 'Therefore disputed he [Paul] in the market daily with them that met with him', and, having done so, exclaimed, 'I declare, sir, here is a contradiction.' 'What!' said Ouseley, 'a contradiction in your own book? No, my dear fellow, the contradiction is in your head, not in the book. The doing good works in secret has regard to motive, that of pleasing God with a single eye; the command, to let them appear before men, as did Paul, is for an example to men to lead them to do good.' The subdued questioner said, 'I am thankful to you, I never understood this before.'[1]

In everyday conversation with strangers, Ouseley commonly used varied and well-chosen questions to break through an initial indifference. His first question, and the answer received, would lead to another, and a discussion would thus begin in which the other person would often find it hard to remain uninterested. 'Do you think that Jesus Christ was at least a good man?' was his opening enquiry to one sceptic. A hesitant but positive response led straight to the next question, 'Do you not think He

---

[1] Ibid., p. 275.

was a good teacher?' A real conversation was soon taking place.

Meeting a man who had been on an eighty-mile pilgrimage to a holy mountain, Ouseley asked him, 'What were you doing there?' 'Looking for God', the man replied. 'On what part of the hill did you expect to find him?' To this enquiry the puzzled pilgrim admitted, 'I did not think of that.' The next question was now at hand: 'Where is God?' 'Everywhere', was the immediate reply. 'When the sun is up, 'Ouseley went on, 'where in Ireland is the daylight?' 'Sure, sir, it is everywhere.' 'So, then, it is about your cabin as much as in any place. Would it not, then, be a strange thing for you to go eighty miles, and bruise your poor feet so, looking for the daylight?' This meeting ended with the man vowing he would never go on another pilgrimage.

An old soldier was asked by Ouseley one day, 'How is your soul?' 'Oh', he objected, 'I am not of your way of thinking.' 'Well, what way of thinking are you? Don't you wish to go to heaven?' 'Oh, I do', replied the man. Thus the questioner had his opening: 'Then, sure, I wish to go there too. You see we are of one way of thinking.' And Ouseley proceeded to take the old soldier by the hand and to talk to him of the love of Christ till the tears streamed down his face.

At another time he met a Roman Catholic, who said he was returning from confession. 'And what good did you get from that?', was the question. 'Och, and I got plenty, your riverence. I got absolution, and everything is put right for my soul.' 'And how long does it last?' 'Och, and shure enough, not long; for I'm soon back to my old ways, and I'm in need of absolution again.' 'And so, my child, you're no better. Your old sin has still the power over you. You're not cured.' Ouseley then went on to ask him what he would think of a salesman, hawking a medicine in his village that promised to cure fits. Supposing he suffered from this complaint, bought the remedy and rejoiced in his 'cure', but only to find another fit coming on before he reached home. Would he not feel cheated? The way was open to speak of the lasting healing found in the gospel.[1]

The above already give some indication of his approach to the Roman Catholics – easily the majority of his hearers. But his wisdom in this regard warrants further comment. In a letter on the subject, he set down his whole method of approach. The Roman Catholic religion, he believed, contained two parts:

'Some of the professed tenets are exquisite, pure, and apostolic, and essentially Protestant; but its practical doctrines, framed by men of great parts, and by Councils, in order to uphold the glory of the Papacy, and support of its numerous clergy, are the very reverse, and are with all diligence passed on to the credulous for *divine mysteries of faith, without which none can be saved*, and which to even doubt in any one point is heresy. While these latter are diligently inculcated from infancy to hoary hairs, the former, though constantly extolled and professed, are with equal diligence neutralized and set aside, as the unceasing opposition to the Scriptures of truth clearly shows. Thus are the poor unsuspecting people taught darkness for light, and are deceived and ruined.'

---

[1] Another anecdote illustrates the same thing. One fine summer's day Ouseley approached some men cutting peat with the question, 'What are you doing, boys?' 'We are cutting turf, sir.' 'Sure, you don't require it this fine summer weather?' 'No, sir, we don't want it now, but we will want it in the cold days of winter.' 'And won't it be time enough to cut it when you want it?' I need not add how the conversation proceeded.

'Now the Christian missionary, knowing these things, must see it his wisdom to bring forth these *pure tenets*, as found in their catechisms, standard writings, in the three ancient creeds, and in the gospel, and to insist that all doctrines contrary to them must be false and damnable. To all this the people will freely agree. Then should he mildly adduce the contrary tenets, and, *without ridicule or sarcasm*, contrast them with the pure . . . This blessed plan have I adopted, and for many years past have been endeavouring to follow, both in my preaching and writings, and not wholly in vain.'

William Arthur emphasizes how Ouseley's aim was always to win over opponents. Roman Catholics he would ever treat with sympathy and respect. When his exposure of the errors of Roman beliefs met with the curses of priests, he 'at once impugned their system, exhibiting its antagonism to revealed truth'. But there were a number of instances where priests responded very differently to his friendship and even subscribed to the cost of Methodist chapel buildings. One such priest, we read, 'clung to Mr Ouseley with the greatest affection, and such was the impression that his conversation had upon his mind, that, when he was dying he cried out, "O, Mr Ouseley! Mr Ouseley!"'[1]

In addition to the spoken word, there is another method to which Ouseley gave much attention. He constantly carried tracts and books with him, some of the most influential of which he had written himself. His best-known work, *Old Christianity Against Papal Novelties* ran to more than 140 pages. When a fifth edition of this work appeared in 1828 a reviewer said, 'The author is a veteran

---

[1] Reilly, *Ouseley*, p. 294.

polemic: he was fighting the battle orally and with his pen, when others were yet supine.' Not all that he wrote was of that character. Ouseley was also a witness for greater unity among all evangelicals and one of his publications was entitled, *An Earnest Appeal on Calvinism and Arminianism, etc, to Promote Christian Union.*[1]

* * * * *

We have only touched upon the early period of Ouseley's life. Yet this is enough to convey the spirit of the man and the truth is that the story varied very little right down to his last days. This made it very difficult for Reilly and Arthur to convey a sense of development in their biographies of Ouseley. There could have been a major change in his life in 1813, for at the annual Irish Conference Thomas Coke pleaded for missionaries to go with him to the East Indies. Reilly writes:

'Mr Ouseley was one of the first to volunteer for this new and arduous undertaking – He stood forth in the Conference with tears streaming from his eyes, lamenting that he had been comparatively unsuccessful among his own countrymen, and that he believed he would be more useful in a strange land.'[2]

Those who heard Ouseley on that occasion understood his standards for success: 'Mr Ouseley could not be satisfied, in holding any meeting, unless souls were brought to God.' However, they refused to accede to his judgment and were inflexible in their disagreement with his proposal. 'His place on the Irish mission could not be supplied.'[3]

---

[1] I have not been able to see this piece.
[2] Ibid., p. 212.   [3] Campbell, *Graham*, p. 187.

Thus in the mid-1820s Ouseley was still in the same work and writing, 'My mind is in it day and night; my vigour, my tongue, my pen in it, almost wholly so.' It was impossible for him, he said, to preach, as he easily could, 'to the few Protestants to be found here and there, and pass by the multitudes of dark Papists, as if they had no existence in creation'.[1] In 1830 he wrote to a friend that for several years he had not lost any blood preaching in the open-air, apart from a recent exception, when, assailed by a shower of stones, turf, dirt, and eggs, he had been hit in the mouth and this 'made me bleed a little'. The truth, Arthur says, is that two of his teeth were knocked out and that, as he went on preaching, he had to pause at times 'to relieve himself of blood'. The same writer says, 'Had some men been as often mobbed and stoned as Mr Ouseley, they would have made something of it.'

At the age of seventy-five we find him preaching thirty-six times in sixteen days, eight of these being in markets and streets. His horse, 'that had carried him the previous seven years many thousands of miles', failed before he did and, with reluctance, he had finally to exchange horse-riding for a gig. In 1836 he was in England preaching. Two years later he was still evangelizing in the open air but friends noticed his health failing, and that he could not sing as once he did.

In April 1839 he was taking services at Mountmelick from whence he wrote to his wife of 'fresh revival'. His sermon there, on the morning of April 11, was to be his last. On April 19 he closed his last letter to his wife with the words:

---

[1] Reilly, *Ouseley*, pp. 258–9.

'My work was the Lord's, who never left nor forsook me, but blessedly sustained me in my labours and dangers. Glory, glory, glory be to Him, Amen.'

They had been married for over fifty years and Harriet had been a wonderful helpmeet. A few days later she was nursing him at his bedside, as she had done so tenderly nearly fifty years before. But, says his biographer, what a difference separated their present experience from that dark time! It was not Young's poetry now which occupied them but the Bible, and 'the future opened to the eye of both, filled with light and gold'. If he had any wish to recover, Gideon told a friend, 'it was to hasten the downfall of the dire apostacy that overspread the land'. To another, in a voice barely audible, he said, 'Hear what the great Master said, Learn of me, – not of councils of popes and cardinals, but of ME.'

Gideon Ouseley died on 14 May 1839, in his seventy-eighth year. The inscription on his grave includes the words:

'During nearly half a century he was ceaselessly engaged in his Master's work in Ireland especially, in its towns and villages, fairs and markets; regardless of personal ease, fearless of danger, uninfluenced by the policy of those "who are prudent in their own sight", he persuasively called on men to "repent and believe the Gospel".'

His wife, to whom he owed so much, survived him by fourteen years. A friend said of her: 'Not to be great, but how to be holy and happy, was the example presented by Mrs Ouseley'.

* * * * *

How Ouseley was called to the gospel ministry is instructive. No one recommended or advised him to do what he did. In a lonely part of Ireland he acted simply because he was constrained to do so. In some respects he lacked the knowledge that was needed, and he was aware of it, but when the lack prompted him to stay silent other thoughts compelled him. He would say to himself, 'Do you not know the disease? And do you not know the cure?' And his conclusion had a divine authority about it, 'Go then and tell them these two things, the disease and the cure; never mind the rest.' On how Ouseley was called of God, William Arthur makes this comment:

'When God seeks labourers, He goes not to the places we should have thought of, nor does he cast in the moulds we should call most becoming . . . The theory of the Methodists is that no training for the work of God is like training in it; and that, however valuable study in preparation for the ministry may be, actual service is absolutely indispensable: and when that is voluntarily rendered, in such a way as to give full proof of call and qualification, it offers a certificate with which no other can be admitted into comparison.'

Certainly Ouseley's call had the element of the extraordinary in it, and he was not called to the regular oversight of a congregation, yet the contrast it presents to the formal channels into Christian service that are so often regarded as essential gives food for thought. We have gone too far from the Methodist pattern.

* * * * *

There are many references to individuals converted under Ouseley's ministry. One of the earliest of these, brought in while Ouseley lived in Dunmore, was a man named William Cornwall. Cornwall was later to become a preacher himself and was the instrument used in the conversion of Ouseley's own father in his later years. Arthur Noble was another in whose conversion Ouseley was instrumental and who later became a missioner alongside him. Reilly speaks of many other converts 'who became able ministers of the New Testament, not only in the Methodist connexion, but also in other churches'. Still larger numbers, without becoming ministers, were to be bright witnesses in many parts of the world. Soldiers, as mentioned earlier, were often particularly significant in this regard. George Smith says that at Cape Town, thirty four men in the 93rd Regiment owed their salvation to the Methodist preaching they had heard in Ireland, and in the 21st Light Dragoons 'five Methodists were found, the spiritual fruit of Ouseley and Graham, three or four others were discovered in the 21st Foot, and in the 72nd'.[1]

For Ouseley himself, figures had no prominence. The later practice of inducing men to 'decide for Christ', with a prompt announcement of results, was foreign to him. The addition of individuals to the Methodist societies he took as a very serious matter and not one to be hurried. Recording the names of new class members he was known to say, 'I write your name before God, and the Lord Jesus Christ, who shall judge the dead at His appearing, and His kingdom.'

The numerical increase around 1800 and later we have already noted and additions continued for many years thereafter. It would appear that the figures given were not produced by lowering the standard of what is required for a Christian profession. This was not a time when there was superficial dealing with souls and the entrance at the

---

[1] Smith, *Methodism*, vol. 2, p. 457.

'strait gate' was made easy. Ouseley followed the same approach as the other Irish Methodist evangelists before him. Thomas Walsh, for instance, when asked by enquirers for further instruction, would speak as follows:

'I told them that as to religion, that it was not a bare profession which would avail anyone: that the true way was to forsake sin, and follow Christ; and that in order thereto, it was needful that a person should (1) Be poor in spirit; feel that he is a sinner (2) Mourn on that account, with a broken and contrite heart; (3) Forsake sin, by applying to the Lord for strength; (4) Believe in Christ, and Him only, for salvation; as it is His blood alone that cleanseth from all unrighteousness; and (5) Obey the gospel, by conforming to the rules there laid down; living "soberly, righteously and godly in the present world".'[1]

Ouseley could have written these words. He had no slight views of human sinfulness. A fellow-missioner wrote of him: 'It is beyond my power to describe him as a preacher. He clearly expounded the moral law in its spirituality, extent and requirements; and then the depravity of the heart as a fountain, sending streams of corruption continually. Then the meritorious cause of human salvation, by the redeeming work of the Lord Jesus; and then he pressed the present acceptance of pardon through faith in His blood.'

This point is noteworthy lest anyone should think that the numbers quoted as evangelized in Ireland at this period have to be regarded with the same suspicion that becomes necessary when one reviews figures later in the nineteenth century. In 1876 the total number adhering to the Methodists in Ireland, including Primitive

---

[1] *Wesley's Veterans*, vol. 5, p. 54.

Methodists, was only some 29,000, and, therefore, a question remains: If the blessing accompanying this evangelism was so extensive, how was it that the numbers in the second half of the nineteenth century were no greater than they were? Two things need to be said in answer to this:

First: the lasting good done by the earlier Methodist witness in Ireland is not to be judged solely in terms of how their own denomination benefited. The good done was much wider. Thus a non-Methodist could write in a Presbyterian journal of the fruitfulness of their witness:

'It awoke the Protestant Episcopal Church of Ireland when it was asleep, or worse; it stimulated by its zeal and labours the other great Protestant Church [Presbyterian] of Ireland; it showed all the Churches how to labour, how to live, how to give, how to suffer for Jesus and His cause. It created a taste for reading among the poorest of its members. It carried the gospel into regions where, from the days of St Patrick and Columcille [Columba], it would seem to have been almost if not altogether unknown. It brought multitudes to Christ.'[1]

---

[1] W. Irwin, 'Methodism in Ireland: Life of Gideon Ouseley' in *British and Foreign Evangelical Review*, vol. 29 (London: Nisbet, 1880), p. 288–9. This result was in part due to the way in which Ouseley and his colleagues, while possessed with some of the foibles of Wesleyan Methodism, rejoiced in the work of Christ wherever they met it. Ouseley could write: 'The grace of God saved me from a sectarian spirit. I loved other Churches, not heeding peculiarities with which I could not agree, and availed myself of every opportunity of conversing with persons belonging to them, on topics tending to our mutual benefit.' Thus he was thankful for the labours of the eminent Dr Henry Cooke in Ulster 'for he regarded the purgation of the Presbyterian Church as certain to be productive of much good.' On this spirit Arthur comments: 'Unity placed in the construction of the fold, is a poor substitute for that unity which lies in the person of the Shepherd and the nature of the sheep.'

Second: the figure given above for membership in 1876 has to be understood in the light of the vast numbers of Methodists who were lost to Ireland by means of the extensive emigration of the nineteenth century. At its height, between the years 1845 and 1850, the population fell from about eight and a half million to four and a half million, and, while slower at other times, the drain continued. Yet in this way Ireland made the world its debtor. In 1849 an Address of the British Methodist Conference to the Irish Conference spoke of their 'emigrant witnesses for Christ' as providing 'a blessing beyond calculation'.

Twenty years later the British Conference believed, 'You cannot place your foot on any colony of the British Empire that does not include a convert of that little Irish Methodist Church . . . She has yielded more ministers than any Church of similar size in the world'.[1] In 1866, when there were only 167 Methodist ministers in Ireland, there were reported to be 'not less than 170' ministers in Canadian Methodism who were 'directly or indirectly the fruit' of Irish Methodism.[2] The *Cyclopaedia of Methodism*, published in 1881, said that 'all the ministers ordained' at a recent session of the Methodist Conference in Australia, 'were of Irish birth', and believed that the fruit of Irish Methodism, 'is beyond reckoning in the United States'.[3]

Wesley's conviction, 'Ireland will repay you', was not disappointed.

* * * * *

[1] Norman W. Taggart, *The Irish in World Methodism 1760–1900* (London: Epworth, 1986), p. 45.

[2] Ibid., p. 73.

[3] Matthew Simpson, *Cyclopaedia of Methodism* (Philadelphia: Everts, 1881), p. 485.

Problems in the history of the church have often arisen on account of wrong views of the relationship between dependence on the sovereign power of God and earnest human endeavour. Both divine action and human responsibility are clearly taught in Scripture, and if either is emphasized out of the proportion to be found in Scripture, the life of the church is bound to suffer.

In theory, Methodists denied divine sovereignty as commonly taught by the Reformed churches, yet the prayerfulness which characterized their lives gives the clearest practical proof of their dependence on God.[1] They saw prayer itself as the gift of God. Ouseley and his colleagues had no doubts on the necessity of divine action to make all human endeavours effective. 'God did it', is his witness. 'A gracious visitation of saving power', is the kind of language used. It was not men who were praised for the formation of the crucial Irish General Mission in 1799, rather, in the timing and raising up of preachers, it was the hand of God which was recognized.

So these were not men who in any way thought that they could produce revivals, yet their dependence on God increased rather than lessened their zeal. The necessity for God to work in no way diminished the urgency with which they acted or weakened their sense of duty. Instead of

---

[1] The following anecdote is typical of Methodist prayerfulness. In 1798, the year of the Rebellion, a soldier was found to be leaving his barracks regularly every night and was sentenced to be shot on the assumption that he was communicating with the enemy. The plea of the man (a Methodist) that he was engaged in prayer at these times was dismissed. The unusual nature of the case attracted the attention of the Commander-in-Chief in Ireland, Lord Cornwallis, who asked to interview the prisoner. Hearing the man's defence, Cornwallis said to him, 'Well, if that be so, you must be pretty expert at that business now. You had better kneel down, and give us a specimen.' The Christian soldier obeyed and in such a manner that he was soon interrupted: 'Quite enough. A man of such intercourse with God could never be a rebel.' Campbell, *Graham*, p. 198.

waiting in the hope of better days they were marked by the way they redeemed the time and seized opportunities. Given the strength of their convictions they could not do otherwise. The outlook of these Irish missioners in this regard is well seen in notes of a discussion that took place at their annual Conference in 1804. The question was proposed, 'What can be done for the revival of the work of God in Ireland?' and the following points were set down by way of answer:

'1. Let us humble ourselves before God. The revival must begin with ourselves. Let us use self-denial.

2. Let us be more careful in giving to God, through Jesus Christ, the entire glory of all the good wrought in and by us. He must be our "all in all".

3. Let us, as preachers, be more simple, evangelical, practical, and zealous in our preaching.

4. Let us not aim at what sermon-hunters call *fine* preaching, in order to be popular.

5. Let us frequently insist on the doctrine of original sin. It is not stale or worn out; it is fundamental.

6. Let us, above all things, be zealous to bring our hearers to the fountain opened for sin and uncleanness.

7. Let us press upon believers the necessity of increasing in holiness, and of dying daily and walking with God.

8. Let us faithfully preach practical holiness, and tear the mask from the face of the hypocrite.

9. Let us never omit a pointed, faithful, yet loving application at the close of our sermons'.[1]

[1] Campbell, *Graham*, p. 158. Lest it be thought this quotation contradicts my statement on the previous page that these men did not think they could

Ouseley and his friends were possessed with a spiritual common sense. To preach in a quiet building, where few would hear them was, for them, a virtual denial of Scripture. 'Behold, I make you fishers of men', was one of Ouseley's favourite texts, on which he would comment, 'Fishermen seek after fish; but we find those who are called fishers of men waiting for the fish to seek after them.' This was a note he often struck in speaking to fellow Christians:

'Preachers are fishers; they catch men. Some fishers like to have full nets, but do not like the toiling to fill them. If their nets never contained fish but of their own catching, they would be empty indeed. Be not ye like unto them . . . Preachers are hunters. Hunters do not wait for the game to come to them; they go in quest of it.'

Charles Graham believed: 'We do more in spreading truth in one fair or market day than we do in weeks or months in private places'.

* * * * *

An account of the life of Gideon Ouseley leaves deep impressions on the reader. Ouseley spoke with unction and persuasiveness; he 'had power over the consciences of his hearers'; he was unwearied in labours and in denying

---

'produce revivals,' it needs to be remembered that the word 'revival' had no standard meaning in 1800. That failing churches could be 'revived' by earnest endeavour the Methodists certainly believed. But a 'revival' in the sense of an outpouring of the Spirit, bringing large numbers suddenly into the kingdom of God, they did not regard as belonging to the sphere of Christian duty. They understood the meaning of 1 Corinthians 3:6, 'I have planted, Apollos watered; but God gave the increase.' I have written further on this subject in *Pentecost Today? The Biblical Basis for Understanding Revival* (Edinburgh: Banner of Truth, 1998).

himself legitimate things. These, and other characteristics, are all features rather than explanations of the man. It is in what happened in secret, in his fellowship with God, that we find the key to understanding him. 'Richly replenished in spirit by close communion with God', takes us to the source of his usefulness. Prayer to him was a proven reality and everything about him proved it to others. A colleague reported, 'While Mr Ouseley prayed, the heavens opened, and "there was a shaking among the dry bones".' 'I shall scarcely ever forget his power with God in prayer', writes another.[1] When people in grave-yards, or amidst the bustle of a market place, were awed by his praying it was through the conviction that the man, in truth, was speaking to God. William Reilly writes:

'He was pre-eminently a man of prayer. His ardent zeal and vehemence in his public ministrations, were but the result of his private meditations, and his earnest wrestling with God, for poor sinners, and for the accompanying of the Holy Ghost. This too under the most solemn impressions of the mysteries of Calvary. Some of the most hallowed reminiscences associated with the character of that saintly man, are those in which I witnessed his pure and fervent devotions. He made it a rule when we travelled in company, and sometimes we were several weeks together, that when we retired, we should alternately pray with, and for each other, and for the work in which we were engaged. But his devout breathings when alone, which I often overheard, were most affecting. It was difficult, on such occasions, to determine whether the love of lost men, or the love of Christ, predominated: – "My gracious Master! My gracious Master," had generally an accompaniment, "O,

---

[1] Campbell, *Graham*, pp. 86, 94.

poor lost sinners, O, my deluded contrymen! O Lord, save my country.'[1]

The love of God was in him and shone through him. His pity for others was part of the love of Christ which he enjoyed. Here indeed was his strength. He took seriously the maxim, 'Let me never fancy I have zeal until my heart overflows with love to every man living.'

It was this same love which delivered him from all the disheartening effects of opposition and persecution. He quotes with approval the words of a young girl, 'Oh, if you would but get the love of God, you would never be afraid of the priest again.' After a stoning at Kilkenny he could write, 'I felt real pity for their blindness.' A man can be known by the hymns he loves, and one of Ouseley's favourites which he often sung in the open air in English and Irish was this:

> Behold the Saviour of mankind
> Nailed to the shameful tree!
> How vast the love that Him inclined
> To bleed and die for thee!

Ouseley's hearers *saw* as well as heard of this spirit. It is said that in his preaching of both law and gospel, love 'was expressed in his every tone and movement, and could not fail of making its impression on their hearts'.[2] Not

---

[1] Reilly, *Ouseley*, pp. 181–2. With reference to his private praying, another wrote: 'How often have I known this blessed man, when all the family with whom he lodged had retired to rest – how often have I known him to spend hours together, wrestling with God in ardent, mighty prayer for the conversion of lost souls.'

[2] It is important to note that he did not treat the law *only* as a display of the severity of God; there was also emphasis on love as the fulfilment of law. Thus on the first commandment he would say: '"Thou shalt love with all thy heart," affectionately; " with all thy mind," intelligently; "with all thy soul," passionately; "and with all thy strength," the energy of all thy powers.'

surprisingly, this affection for his hearers often gave birth in them to a like affection, and we read that 'a favourite name for Mr Ouseley among the country-folk was *Sheedd-no-var*', which meant 'the silk of men'. Roman Catholics themselves acknowledged that he loved them.

So he was to the last. When he was dying, the last text he quoted in a message to a friend was 'God is love' – a testimony, says Arthur, 'that, in life and strength, he had made to resound in the ears of many a thousand'. The dying words of his one-time colleague William Hamilton were on the same theme, 'If I could shout so that the world might hear, I would tell of the goodness and love of God my Saviour.'[1]

It is not for every branch of Christian instruction that we would go to the evangelists of Ouseley's school, but if we want some of the highest of Christian lessons we may well find them here. It is not surprising that the only biography of Ouseley in the twentieth century came from the Salvation Army and contains the prayer: 'May God ever touch us with the compassion that, instead of denouncing any people or their errors, rushes to their rescue with sufficient power and wisdom to rescue them.'[2] And in a different branch of the Christian church, we can understand why Thomas Chalmers, the Scots Presbyterian leader, spoke as he did to Thomas Waugh, one of Ouseley's colleagues. Near the end of his life, after a meeting with Waugh, Chalmers, in a brogue as strong as his visitor's, declared to him in parting:

---

[1] Ibid., p. 161.

[2] Commissioner G. S. Railton, *Gideon Ouseley: An Old-Time Irish Salvationist* (London: S. A. Book Dept., 1904), p. 81. This biography of 133 pages appears to be based entirely on the work of Reilly and Arthur.

'You hae your doxy, and I hae my doxy. I think I could show you that I am theoretically richt, but I am sure you are no' practically wrang. Fare ye weel, and Guid Almichty bless you'.[1]

---

[1] *British and Foreign*, vol. 29, p. 290.

Gideon Ouseley

Chapter 8

Thomas Collins: the Spirit of English Methodism

Thomas Collins might appear to have little lasting significance in the annals of the ministry of English Methodism. He never served in London, he was not an author, did not serve as President of the Conference, and never became a household name. His life was possibly no more eventful than that of many of his colleagues whose names have long since past from remembrance. The most he would say of himself, before his death at the age of fifty-four, was, 'I have always stood up for plain, honest, Bible Methodism'.

In the course of a letter to Collins, dated 31 October 1843, the Free Church of Scotland author, James Douglas of Cavers, wrote concerning England:

'In what a state would that country have been, if the multitudes rescued by Wesleyan exertions from vice and ignorance had been left to augment the mass of crime and discontent! The narrative of the work of God you have recently witnessed in central England – of the nature of revival – has given me much pleasure. It is very desirable that accounts of such seasons of refreshing as from time to time gladden the labours of your ministry should be set forth. Though, perhaps, well known in the Wesleyan body, they escape general attention.'

No copy of Collins' letter which prompted this reply from Douglas has survived, and we would know little or nothing of him were it not for the fine biography, *The Life of the Rev. Thomas Collins*, written by his nephew, Samuel Coley.[1] If Collins was in any way typical of the rank and file of Methodist pastors in the early-nineteenth century then 'Bible Methodism' was no ordinary thing. In his diary for 8 August 1854, he noted: 'Many recent tractates have dealt with the polity of Methodism. When will some able man give us a good one on its spirit?' He little thought that his personal diary – never intended for publication – was to be so ably used to that end in the biography published four years after his death.

In the Preface to his biography of his uncle, Coley wrote: 'Why another Biography? Because it pleased God to enrich this man's life with special endowments of grace of which the church ought to be told. If it bless those who read, half as much as it has done him who has written, a great end will be answered.' Few could come to the end of Coley's 493 pages on his uncle without being similarly thankful.

Thomas Collins was born on 12 April 1810 and brought up by devout Methodist parents near Redditch, in a country district of Warwickshire. It was there, at the age of nine, and under the preaching of Gideon Ouseley, that he first came (as he believed) to a saving knowledge of Christ. A portrait of the Irish evangelist was to remain with him through all his life. The spiritual earnestness of his childhood was, however, to wane and to give way to 'mirth and trifling'. This permanently changed when he,

---

[1] Samuel Coley, *Life of the Rev. Thomas Collins* (London: Hamilton, Adams and Co., 1868). All my quotations are from this source unless otherwise stated.

along with many others, saw a revival at Redditch in 1826. The main instrument appears to have been the local Methodist minister, the Rev. W. Davies, who received Collins into the class meeting and soon encouraged him to take a lead among young men who were organized to evangelize surrounding villages. His first endeavour at public speaking was at Stratford-on-Avon, which meant a round trip on foot of thirty miles. Soon he was combining an apprenticeship in business with local preaching but after an experience in a prayer meeting in March 1830 – a 'fire baptism' – his calling was decided and the District Meeting recommended him as a candidate for the Wesleyan ministry.

An unusual trial was to mark the years that intervened before Collins was finally received as a minister in full connexion in 1837. It appears that from an early age he had been led to think of an overseas mission field as his final destination, and the Methodist Conference for 1830 granted his request to be placed on a list of those available for such service. In the meantime he remained at Redditch, again the scene of revival as the circuit membership rose in twelve months from 290 to 400. Then, as there was no immediate need for new candidates for overseas work, Collins was directed to Wark in Northumberland in October 1831. Here, covering a rugged country district, some fourteen miles by twenty, a Methodist Mission had begun in 1827. Little impression had been made on the prevailing spiritual darkness and few men could have been given a harder field, supported, as he was, by only by a small Methodist society. Of his early impressions of this new scene he wrote:

'Darkness covers the people. Dullness freezes the Society. Some, indeed, are well-meaning and very sincere, but completely ignorant of the short and straight Gospel way. There is not much religion; and the little there is, not of the type that gives promise of diffusion. Professors here seem to have no idea of God's mighty saving purposes: they have not learned to care for others, and, as in such case generally happens, are everlastingly full of complaints about themselves. Sinners are perishing all around. My heart yearns for them. I am racked, and torn, and rent in pieces, because men *will* go to hell. Lord, give me converts; raise up for me helpers, men who in the freshness of first love will joyously go to and fro and tell Thy simple plan. O for more men of God!'

A stirring of the members of the Wark Society marked the New Year 1832, and he saw the beginning of an answer to this prayer. After that date we hear of neighbouring societies requesting Collins to 'send over to us some of your lively souls'. It was with reluctance he had to leave his first field in August 1832 at the direction of the Conference. There was still no overseas appointment and for the present he was to join the Wesleyan Superintendent in the Kent circuit. He took up lodgings at Sandhurst, from where he was to preach in many parts of the county.

It was at this period that some ministers were leaving Wesleyan Methodism, alleging that it was insufficiently evangelistic. The controversy which this occasioned led Coley to include some valuable pages on Collins' convictions on evangelism. The nature of faith was a main point at issue. Those seceding from the denomination were apparently of the opinion that evangelism would be more successful if the simplicity of 'faith' was pressed more exclusively upon men. Collins agreed that the call to faith in 'a present salvation' was indeed essential to gospel preaching, but he was concerned that salvation should not be presented to the lost *solely* in terms of their need to exercise faith. Commenting on this, Coley noted:

'The great themes of Methodist preaching in early times were Repentance, Faith, and Holiness: may it in this be *semper eadem* [always the same]! We depreciate any salvation by wholesale, achieved by slurring over any of these individual experiences . . . Celerity obtained by omission is theologically fashionable just now. In many quarters convincing speech is denounced as legal. The fallow ground is unbroken. Men are in such haste to sow that they cannot wait to plough.

'May God give unto his ministers seals multitudinous as the converts of Pentecost! But let them – far rather let them – be few and true, than count up into crowds and be spurious . . . "Jesus died for me", minified [diminished] into the mere premises of an argument in an impenitent lip, is as worthless as any Shibboleth bigot ever framed. Thousands can get through the narrow steps of that poor mental exercise only to realize that in its bosom lies a sophism, and that its conclusion is a lie. Woe befalls any church multiplied by such accessions; as John Bunyan would say, "They have tumbled over the wall, not come in at the Wicket Gate." A Gospel minus repentance, a salvation without conviction of sin, a faith without trust, an assurance by logic, and a religion without holiness – what will it all issue in but an eternity without hope?'

In these words Coley was reflecting on new teaching in Methodist circles that said that 'saving faith is not wrought in the human mind by divine influence as the gift of God; but is simply an exercise of the powers inherent in our nature, and employed at our will'. When this teaching was opposed by Methodist preachers in the Derby circuit, a secession of nearly half the membership of that circuit occurred in 1832, the seceding group calling themselves, 'Arminian Methodists'.[1] This shows how Methodism, at this date, was not 'Arminian' in the later sense of that word.[2] The leaders believed that faith has not only to be exercised, it has also to be received: 'The Holy Ghost gives not the act of faith, but the light, power, and disposition to believe.' Accordingly, Collins said:

'In preaching I deal with man . . .In prayer, on the contrary, I deal with God, and ask the gift, the plenitude, and the continuance of the Spirit. Addressing the penitent, I bid him believe: addressing the Lord, I say, "Lord, help this poor creature!"'

Although Collins was to some extent drawn into this discussion, he was never in his element in controversy and was quick to acknowledge the merits of men with whom he disagreed. To a friend perturbed at the disagreement he wrote:

'Talk as little as possible of the secession . . . A general revival would – best of all things – heal the wounds, hush

---

[1] Smith, *Methodism*, vol. 3, pp. 171–2. He adds: 'In connection with this dogma they encouraged young women to preach' and 'introduced great disorder under the plea of revivalism'.

[2] There was further evidence of this in the way in which the Methodist Conference later excluded the American 'revivalist', James Caughey, even although he was a Methodist. Prior to that action (in 1846–7) a preacher pointed out to Jabez Bunting how 'the credit of religion and the welfare of Methodism' were involved. Under Caughey's type of preaching in the States, he was informed, 'that the same people are converted again and again; and that if all the announced conversions could be found, the entire population of the States, would be converted in four years; that they proceeded in this "converting" work, as deliberately and mechanically, as a builder to raise a house: and nowhere is true and fervent and established piety more scarce, than when these proceedings are most frequent.' W. R. Ward, *Early Victorian Methodism: The Correspondence of Jabez Bunting 1830–1858* (Oxford: OUP, 1976), pp. 340–1.

the murmurs, supply the wants of Methodism. Work, full work for God, would leave us little time for quarrelling; and devotion, full devotion, would leave us no inclination.'

* * * * *

Meanwhile, Collins remained a candidate for the mission field, and it was this which brought on the unusual trial to which I have already referred. It began when, at Sandhurst, he received a direction to join a group being sent out to strengthen the West Indian Mission. His Superintendent, who himself had worked in the West Indies, strongly opposed this appointment on the grounds that Collins' health could not stand the climate. Medical opinion supported this view. Collins was thus forced to re-examine his original intention, and to listen to friends who believed that his gifts fitted him better to revive churches at home than to be a pioneer abroad. The issue was referred to the Conference of 1834 and he was given another year in Kent. But when the Mission's call on him was renewed at the 1835 Conference, without the response that was wanted, his character was called in question by some present. A representative of the Mission declared: 'Well, if the work for which he offered himself be now distasteful to him, we give him up; we will not have him.'[1] Even the President of the Conference, Dr Bunting, referred to him in slighting terms.

By the same Conference Collins was sent with another man to what almost amounted to a foreign field. The

---

[1] Collins was not at this Conference. It was typical of him that when he heard of the severe language some had used, he commented: 'I expected censure. Nor is it wonderful that they, who can neither see my heart, nor know all my case, should misjudge, or, under the circumstances, think hardly of me.'

Orkneys, in the wild ocean to the north of Scotland, had never had a Methodist ministry, and, noted Coley, 'A post so cheerless was refused by many.' To Collins, he adds, 'it was not penalty; it was a providence'.

The contrast Collins found between Orkney and sunny Kent was far greater than the 600-mile journey would suggest. Windswept and treeless, with many poor people housed in huts and hovels, the islands presented a different world. The spiritual contrast was still greater. At Sandhurst he had come to a Methodist membership of 366, and when he left, after three years, the number stood at 912. At Stronsay, where Collins made his base, there were only forty who could be gathered into a Society. They seem to have been made up mainly of poor seafarers and fishermen, who had come into contact with the life of Methodism elsewhere. The majority of the population 'at first neither wished the presence of Wesleyans, nor came to hear them'. A non-evangelical Calvinism seems to have reigned for, as Coley wrote, 'Free Kirk zeal had not yet stirred the heart of Scotland. The world mastered the Church . . . Present faith in Christ was not urged. All talk of being saved here and now was thought to be sheer enthusiasm. Assurance of sin forgiven was neither preached, enjoyed, nor expected'.

Collins quickly recognized the need for making some changes in facing this new situation ('wise men are wedded to usefulness, not to methods'). He dropped his former practice of asking seekers to meet at the communion rail for counsel and prayer,[1] and, on being

---

[1] Calling the concerned to come to the communion rail, or 'the penitents' rail', had become common among Methodists at this period but no one thought that such action was a part of conversion. It was regarded only as a useful means for counselling, and so could be laid aside without the loss of anything essential to salvation.

impressed by its value, he adopted the Scots' practice of public catechizing.[1] His Sunday programme he describes as follows:

'I hold a prayer meeting at ten; preach at eleven; meet the Society at half-past twelve; preach again at three; commence the School at five; close at seven. The children recite texts; the young men and women undergo examination upon a theme allotted for the week's meditation and research on the previous Lord's day'.

Before this date, personal prayer was already at the centre of Collins' ministry; now its necessity impressed him in a new way: 'I must have more of the Divine image, more of the Divine power, and more of the Divine fellowship, if I am successfully to labour here.' Accustomed to pray aloud, and unable to do so with freedom in his simple lodgings, he made it his custom to go to a cave on the shore for that purpose. When his colleague arrived at Stronsay in February 1836 it was in this same cave that they spent their first morning together. Collins adopted the same practice elsewhere as a diary entry at Skarfskerry on 9 June 1836, shows:

'I found, on the shore, a secret place, where, from ten o'clock until four, I had a very humbling yet comforting season, and came away in the strength of renewed dedication to God.'

Collins' eagerness to see conversions was rewarded; forty-two 'clear cases' are mentioned, yet, to his regret, the

---

[1] Coley writes: 'This Scotch catechizing, if we could import it into English churches, would be the best thing that ever crossed the Tweed . . . Catechizing keeps attention awake; trains the reasoning faculty; tests attainment; explains things before ill understood; methodizes, summarizes, and puts into the scholars hands what they know.'

August Conference of 1836 decided to scale down the Orkney work and to move Collins back across the Pentland Firth on to the mainland, to Wick in Caithness. Here he was to have the first home of his own, for he married Emily Graham in London, in August 1836, and together they settled in this busy fishing port. In Wick there was much more real religion than in the Orkneys. 'A goodly number were really pious', yet the conservative Scots remained suspicious of such a new thing as Methodism: 'This is a very humbling station. I am learning that the excellency of the power is of God. How helpless I feel in the presence of Scotch pride, hardness, formality, reserve, and prejudice!'

His acceptance among the people was eased by the manner in which he responded to the distress caused by famine and typhoid, prevalent in the far north at this time. Half-fed and half-clothed people possessed little resistance to infection. From his own purse, and more largely by help from friends in England, Collins was able to provide meals, clothes and blankets for numbers; taking care, wherever possible, to avoid the stubborn pride of the needy by charging half the cost. 'By his efforts', Coley writes, 'many lives were saved, and many souls were blessed.' His wife was no less busy in visiting victims of the plague.

Additional help came by means of his father. John Collins, in his own words, saw 'twenty years of life's prime expended in desperate, despairing sin'. Even when grace ended his unbelief, his progress as a Christian was small. The following twenty years were 'only half improved. I lingered in a low, doubting, unworthy state'. All this had changed by the time Thomas was ready for the Methodist ministry; his father was now a local preacher and letters to his son show the brightness of his testimony. In the spring of 1837 John Collins paid a prolonged visit to

Wick, in order to take care of his son's people while the latter went on an evangelistic itinerary. The nine pages that Coley includes from the father's Journal show him to have been no ordinary man. Coley calls him 'a man of strong individuality, utterly unconventional, of great faith'. The advice Thomas gave his father for carrying on the work in Wick constituted no problem for him: 'Be prepared to preach ten or twelve times a week; to hold many prayer meetings; to visit many sick; and to live on barley loaves and fishes.'

A converted theatre in Wick, seating 400, was now in use, with 191 members. In spite of this success, a few years later, in an act of Christian catholicity, the Methodist Conference handed over all their work in the North of Scotland to the Free Church of Scotland. Before that time, now in full connexion, and with the shadow of criticism behind him, Thomas Collins had been moved to Durham City in August 1838. The next three years in this location were among the busiest of his life, despite sharing the work of the circuit with two colleagues. In addition to the large chapel in the city itself, there were over thirty scattered preaching places on the Plan, and only one horse for the three men. Problems of that kind were no strain on the unity of the preachers: 'We labour together in love', he wrote, 'knit together and refreshed by a common devotion.' By the close of the March quarter in 1839 there was an addition of 100 members, with 150 'on trial'. These figures seemed small to Collins in the face of the rapidly increasing population. Durham had become one of the wealthiest areas in England for its resources in salt, lead, iron, marble, freestone and, above all, coal. Collins wrote:

'Need of evangelistic activity daily increases. New collieries are starting all about. Thousands of fresh inhabitants are

clustering round them. Alas! we have neither chapels built
to receive the people, nor time left to look after them.'

The excitement of such developments was not without
its effect on those within the church: 'Of all speculation,
mining speculation is most absorbing and everybody here
seems drawn into it. Hurry forbids thought. Business
continually growing keeps all heads in a whirl.' In his diary
for October 11, 1840, he wrote:

'I rose at five to seek the Lord. He drew near to me. He
helped me preach in Durham with liberty and power. We
had a great shaking. I felt so strongly for the work of God,
that I thought my heart would have broken. The church
here has been sadly world-pressed, sluggish, and dull. I
was led to declare simply how much I felt in their behalf.
Having done this, I solemnly charged upon them the
delay of the revival of God's work. The word smote. The
fire burned. In the prayer meeting salvation work was
done.'

Four days later his diary noted:

'A blessed revival is in progress at Shotley Bridge. The
Lord is affecting sinners at their own firesides. One of
our members, a travelling dealer, when on his round that
way last week, found that in the cottages, for some miles
on his route, he could scarcely get in a word about
worsted and small wares, the people were so taken up
with talk of Christ and things Divine.'

Until the summer of 1840 the village of Shotley Bridge
had been part of the Durham circuit. It says something
for the growth in Durham itself, which had 909 society
members when Collins came in 1838, that although it
was depleted on the separation of Shotley Bridge, the

number of members stood at 1016 in 1841. His diary contains the record of numbers of individual conversions, seven persons at Pittington, for instance, yet such figures remained overshadowed in his mind by the numbers who remained unsaved. As Coley commented, 'Where desire is large, it makes increase seem small.'

* * * * *

While Coley's record of Collins' time at Durham is full of interest, a large part of the narrative – as throughout the biography – is taken up with his subject's inner life. On this matter he repeatedly drives home the same lesson. A typical statement in Collins' diary reads: 'When we are fully devoted to the work of God, then are we happy; then the Spirit comes and fills us with intelligence, purity, tenderness, energy, and bliss.' On which Coley comments: 'Convinced that evangelistic power, not being of self, is only at the full when the man becomes the channel, instrument, and minister of the Spirit, Mr Collins most diligently marked the promises which pledge such Divine condescension, pleaded them, and in expectant faith yielded up himself for their fulfilment.' Again: 'One great cause of Mr Collins' spiritual growth lay in his habitual seasons of seclusion, fasting, self-examination and prayer.'

The use of the word 'habitual' underlines another prominent characteristic. Far from regulating his devotional life by impulse or mood, Collins was a typical Methodist in his determination to 'live by method' not the impulse of the moment. His diary of this date records this daily programme:

'I will arise at quarter to six. Till half-past six shall be spent in devotion. Chosen divines will afterwards occupy me till eight. Breakfast and family worship may be allowed an hour. From nine to ten, Greek and Hebrew on alternate days. From ten to twelve, compose [sermons]. From twelve to one, read the Scriptures and pray. From one to two, dine. During the afternoon, visit among the people either in town or country'.

The 'chosen divines' at this period included Thomas Goodwin and John Owen and their works on the Holy Spirit.[1]

From Durham, Collins moved on in 1841 to another mining area, Dudley in the 'Black Country'. He remained only a year. In part it was the very success of the work at Dudley that accounted for the shortness of his stay and his willingness to take another appointment. The numbers in the societies were simply too great to be cared for by only two men – a Superintendent and himself. Sufficient funds were available to support another man but the local trustees refused to allow it.[2] This was not all. For the first time in his experience he found his colleague and superintendent, the Rev. Samuel Dunn, very difficult to work with. In all his dealings Dunn was authoritarian and 'most injudicious'. A spirit of contention among the people thus became inevitable and it was more than Collins could bear.

From 1842 to 1845 Collins was the Superintendent of the Coventry circuit. The city had then some 32,000 people, of whom it was believed 24,000 were without any church connexion. The phrase to be 'sent to Coventry'

---

[1] Whether he was reading these authors in their original, or in the abbreviated versions of Wesley's Christian Library, I do not know.

[2] It was at Dudley that Coley first speaks of hearing his uncle preach. His text was Jeremiah 13:27: 'Unction richer than was wont, even to him, came down. Such power I had never felt under any ministry, nor, after the lapse of these years, have I ever yet again experienced anything approaching to it.'

already existed and not without reason as Collins noted in his diary for September 9, 1842:

'Ignorance, sensuality, and all kinds of immorality abound. There is much poverty, and more sin: much degradation and desperate wickedness . . . Our people are few; our Circuit bowed down with debt. Lord, I give up the Circuit to Thee . . . I bewail the unbelief of Coventry: many read infidel books, gather in infidel assemblies, and answer rebuke with infidel flippancy. I bewail the lack of family care: parents neglect, children run riot, and neither pray. I bewail the strifes of Coventry: in business, in politics, in religion. O Thou, who didst weep over Jerusalem, give me tears for the sins of this people: help me to live for the good of this people.'

Again prayer was answered. Amid a rising tide of interest, Collins noted and adopted Asahel Nettleton's practice of holding a special series of services. In the course of these meetings, which he held in February 1843, the fear of God took hold of many. 'Sir, you hit me too hard', said one distressed man to the preacher. On which conversation Collins noted: 'As he was both convinced and alarmed, I now set myself patiently to show him how *in Jesus justice has had its course*. The Gospel seemed new to him. He drank it at once, eagerly as would a thirsty deer the stream'.

Within two months of this date two hundred had been added to the Society. Hearing of this sudden success through Collins' instrumentality, a friend warned him wisely: 'Sudden and striking results lead to idolatry of instruments. The healthiest and safest condition of things is when progress comes of the lively, spiritual, aggressive action of Christians in general. Such common effort – with the least possible individual peril of pride – spread the Redeemer's kingdom apace.' This was a basic Methodist principle with which Collins would have heartily concurred.

Certainly there were bright witnesses among his people. One of his hearers spoke of 'the heavenly benignity that beamed in his happy face'. One of his aged members whom he was visiting when she was close to death, could say to him, 'You do not seem cheerful, what is the matter?' To which he replied: 'Nothing is the matter; I am all right: but then our cases differ. Happy woman! You are near your labour's end: I am in the midst of mine. What wonder that, looking at it out of the sunshine of Beulah country, my joy to you seems dim?'

Apart from constant regard for the poor, Collins did not regard action in the community at large as part of his responsibility. But Coventry was an exception. It seems that from the reign of the dissolute Charles II there had been an annual Lady Godiva pageant, involving a naked woman riding horseback through the streets. Collins, by tracts, letters and protests to authorities, raised such a protest to the practice that there was no more nakedness – much to the anger of the promoters of the event. His effigy was burned outside his front door. 'Paul, found "beasts at Ephesus",' he noted, 'I have found some here . . . Man can do nothing but what shall turn to my good. "Woe unto you when all men shall speak well of you." The friendship of the world is dangerous; the enmity of it, safe.'

Shadowed only by the death of an infant son, the years at Coventry were particularly happy years. Among his diary entries we read:

'I have a comfortable house, and every person in it is alive, fully alive, to God. I have a people, humble, teachable, and who have learned by what they have suffered; I have a thick field of unconverted; I can generally secure the forenoon in the study: I have God, All Sufficient; I am happy, well assured of being in my right place.'

The next appointment for three years (1845–48), at St Albans, in Hertfordshire, was to be something of a contrast. He found things in the church in a low condition, nor was the adjustment from Coventry easy to make: 'Coventry is scarcely off my mind. Christ, and Christ alone, can keep all Circuits and all men in His heart at once.' St Albans was to prove that 'revival principles', if faithfully employed, do not always secure abundant success. The contrary belief was gaining acceptance in some Methodist circles, but it was evidently not a conviction upon which Collins acted.[1] After three months in the new situation he noted: 'The harvest is not ripe, the time of sheaves is not come. I have had new lessons to learn in every Circuit hitherto, and new ones lie before me here.'

The year 1846 did bring a heartening increase, and his preaching was as earnest as ever, but thereafter difficulties in the congregation increased. Differences of opinion on political issues brought a disunity which, he feared, 'it will take years to amend'. In his diary for 4 January 1848, he wrote: 'This diminution of success has tried me . . . I trust, if the Lord will, that my next appointment may set me among a more sympathetic people. The people here will not – no, they will not – stir towards the land of perfect love . . . The poor are distressed for bread, and the

---

[1] For an example of the argument that faithfulness will always produce revival see, Richard Treffry, Jr, *Memoirs of the Life, Character, and Labours of the Rev John Smith* (1832; reprint ed., London: Wesleyan Methodist Book Room, 1902), pp. 159–61.

wealthier are not thoroughly on the Lord's side'. His biographer adds, 'The whims and worldliness, sins and misfortunes of men, alike concurred in these three years to throw difficulties in his path.'

There were also wider concerns that troubled him at this period. Coventry elected a Roman Catholic to a Parliament in London that was already willing to weaken the Protestant constitution of the nation. He believed that the government was being led by expediency, and his attitude to Roman Catholicism is well summarized in his sentence: 'Towards the adherents of Rome, as men and as fellow-citizens, we entertain a cordial good will; but to the corrupt and corrupting system of which they are at once the votaries and victims, we are irreconcilably hostile.'

His attendance at the Methodist Conference at this time was not as congenial as it had been for there was an element of disharmony which contrasted with former years. No increase of membership was reported in 1847. On a decision to allow the government to share responsibility for the education of their young he believed the leaders were making a wrong decision: '*Not that I should at all object to a truly Christian State helping*: but can our Government now claim to have that character?' Other matters also led him to fear, 'A blight is on us.'[1]

Collins' reaction to these setbacks is instructive. The St Albans years are among the richest in his diary with regard to his communion with God. 'In these evil times Christians need more closet work. The dovelike Spirit retires from strife to nestle in the hearts of sons of peace.'

---

[1] Coley records some discussion among ministers on the reasons for existing difficulties. These included the opinion that pride and a lack of reverence had grieved God. A new reluctance to enter into the responsibilities of church membership was also noted.

'God has wonderfully opened His heart unto me. Oceans of delight are there. Many things are amiss in the earth; but, hallelujah! All in God is right. While looking there, the mass of evil in the universe, huge as it is, seems but as the dot of a pen by the side of a planet, which compared with the measureless abysses of purity and good which exist in Him. The Lord is, – and the Lord reigneth: let the earth be glad.'

This spirit of devotion was by no means confined to his study as the following note about a journey he made in May 1848 illustrates:

'I asked myself, How may I best improve these three hours upon the coach top? It darted through my mind, with vivid light, as a beam from the Lord, that a man can do no better things than believe the love of God to himself and his species. I saw – as I never saw before – how all stimulus to holy work comes out of that. I therefore at once gave myself up to a believing meditation of the truth which, with unusual demonstration, the Spirit had borne home upon my heart. As I did so, the *meaning of the cross* marvellously shone out. My faith strengthened. I took hold of God's love to me and to man as I had never done before. The journey seemed done too soon. I got down from that coach-top with an indelible lesson and a soul on fire.'[1]

Throughout his ministry Collins sought to observe the providence of God in his life. Looking back later on the St Albans years, he observed: 'I intended well, but in many things performance lagged behind intention. The work

[1] He later wrote to a friend: 'Since I saw you, I have found a fountain of happiness in God. He has taught me that firmly and always to believe God's great love to me and to all men, is itself the highest form of obedience.'

of mortification, necessary for a Minister who has been in a degree successful, was carried on there. I learned, by experience, the great profit of abasement before God, and, remembering the lesson, can say that I rejoice more in the good St Albans Circuit did to me, than in any good I did to it.'

* * * * *

When Collins moved to Camborne, Cornwall, in September 1848, it was to be to the last area where he could continue, at least at the outset, to work physically at full stretch. If Methodism was stationary in the country at large it was not so in Cornwall. Soon whole pages of his diary were taken up with news of conversions. At the Quarterly Meeting at Camborne the following January, 218 members were added 'on trial'. 'We have not yet the overwhelming power of a great revival', he wrote to his mother, 'yet conversions are continually taking place' (28 February 1849). The spirit of some of his people may be judged from an event he records. Visiting one of his older members, confined to bed, one Sunday afternoon, he heard the woman's daughter urge her to take a drink. The conversation then ran: 'I cannot, child; I am too weak.' 'Do not say so, mother dear. You will be down among us again yet.' 'Who says so?' 'I do, mother.' 'You! *you are always a-foreboding.*'

As the year 1849 went on, notes such as the following appeared in his diary: 'Melting influence'; 'Divine presence powerfully manifested'; 'Blessing filled the place'. From the beginning of the year a revival had broken out in neighbouring Mousehole. Coley writes: 'The zeal of the new converts was remarkable. The idea of concealing what God had done for them, entered none of their heads. Whole days were spent in going from house to house, telling all, without fear or exception, of the love of Jesus.' By the summer of 1848 a general awakening was present 'which swayed the people through several Circuits', including Camborne. One minister noted: 'One great momentous concern seemed to pervade the mass of people. Domestic engagements and worldy business seemed superseded until the great question of salvation was settled.'

At the December 1848 Quarterly meeting at Camborne, 171 members were added, and 935 'on trial'. The demands of this situation took Collins to new levels of diligence. His daily reading of Hebrews had to be laid aside for 'revival work' but time for prayer was not lessened, on the contrary we find him up at 4.30am on Sundays for that purpose. This was not in vain, as an entry for 7 January 1849, records:

'About five o'clock on Lord's day morning, in anticipation of the solemn service of Covenant renewal, I was waiting upon God in believing acts. He mercifully drew near to me, as once, only once before – He did, years ago, on the Rock of Skarfskerry. His coming darkened and distanced all earthly things. My soul felt as if within the cloud of Tabor. While it hung around me, I cried, "I know Thee! Yes, I know Thee!" That ineffable glory did not long abide, such specialities of manifestation never do; but in its gentle ascent it left a sweet life, a calm, and a tenderness which cannot be expressed.'[1]

Collins was now only in his fortieth year but his strength was being taxed beyond endurance. For 5 July 1849 his

---

[1] The main effect of this experience, he wrote to a friend, was to humble him before God: 'Learning of Him more, I think less of myself.'

diary contains this unusual entry, 'I was too unwell to rise.' This illness was only temporary but by June of 1850 his health was so broken that he was compelled to ask Conference for rest from the Camborne circuit. Without doubt his condition was aggravated by a controversy that quenched the revival. Three ministers, including Samuel Dunn who had been his Superintendent at Dudley, had long been agitating for change in the Methodist church order. Now deposed, they arrived in Cornwall and made every effort to spread dissension. It was neither the first nor the last time that controversy has interrupted revival. Some who had been Collins' eager supporters now turned against him. Coley records: 'Times of extreme trial passed over him; yet no bitterness ever tainted his soul. He was firm without acrimony; true, yet charitable.'

The response of Conference to Collins' request was to send him only twenty-six miles to St Austell, still well within the area affected by controversy. It was 'one of the most unquiet and perturbed of the Cornish Circuits', and the hope was that the weight of Collins' character would settle the people. Given the state of his health, it was an unwise decision and against his own judgment. In October 1850 he took a break in his beloved Kent – the first love of all his circuits. On the night he returned to St Austell he was surprised to find lights in the chapel. On asking what was happening, he was told that 'a mighty revival' had begun. It was true and once more in the following days he was to be kept up to midnight, directing seekers and those under distress. The blessing came as oil on troubled waters and for the time all differences were forgotten. On 1 January 1851, he could write: 'The good work progresses. Every week increases the number of conversions. Labour increases; and, in fact, overpresses my weakness.' By the end of the year, however, the damage done to his health was unmistakable. Although complaining was far from his make-up there were repeated diary entries that noted the reality of his condition: 'My nervous system is unstrung.' 'I am not at all the man I was. I cannot rise as early as I did.' 'My elasticity is all gone. I flag. I get drowsy in the daytime. I cannot work half as hard, or walk half as far, as I used to do. My legs feel as if coated with lead.'

In the meantime church strife had resumed, interfering with his sleep and further undermining his health. At length medical opinion demanded his absolute rest. Thus he said farewell to Cornwall on 26 August 1851, and, with a year's leave granted to him, settled at Hemel Hempstead. The leisure here did good but he was never to regain the strength of body and voice so long associated with him. In 1852 he applied for another circuit appointment – unwisely in Coley's opinion: 'Mr Collins' power had so diminished that – a new thing in his experience – slumberers could repose under his pulpit.'

In January 1853, at the urging of the President of the Conference, he took up the work in Bradford, a place not yet as begrimed as later in the century. 'I learned how exceedingly beautiful Bradford looks at night from the hill sides, when the lights of all its mills are gleaming.' How far his ministry here was affected by his declining health, and how far to a measure of resistance in the congregation, it is impossible to tell. Certainly the old fire was still there. 'I have seen some of the most hardened wretches in Bradford weep under those prayers', recalled one of his hearers. His personal dealings with individuals were as direct as ever though not always appreciated. 'Have you peace with God?' he asked one of his congregation. 'No, Sir'. 'How long have you been among God's people?' 'Fifteen years'. 'Fifteen years! Ah, I see how it has been; *ding, dong, bell; ding, dong, bell.* Ordinances round and round, but no Divine conviction of sin; no tears at the Saviour's feet; no clasping of the Crucified; no agonizing resolve, "Lord, I will not let Thee go." How long is this inertness to last? Down on your knees man.' Words of this kind, uttered with Collins' spirit, were hard to resist, and, as on this occasion, they were not without result. 'I have seen him', wrote Coley, 'bring a drunken sinner to tears by a single sentence.'[1]

His diary entries show that he had not forgotten the lesson of St Albans. After a six-mile walk home from a service at which no conversions were known, he wrote: 'Once I should have been miserable without visible fruit. I strive as faithfully as ever for it; but, in troublous times, and in stony fields, the Lord has taught me that hardness of men must not abate my gladness in Him. In Him I will rejoice, even "though the fig-tree shall not blossom".' At the beginning of 1854 the Circuit Stewards surprised him with the information that they intended to seek a successor in his place. At the next Quarterly Meeting this was overturned by a large majority of the people: 'Upon this', he writes, 'I appealed to the minority to say whether they would work with me and with their brethren. No response was given. I then felt that, as one in humble fellowship with my great Master, as one who could do nothing but for the edification of the body, my work there was done. I could not stay to be a party man.'

---

[1] The same power often evident in his praying was similarly evident in the impromptu words he spoke to individuals. To a soul in distress and claiming he saw nothing for himself but condemnation, he exclaimed, 'Nothing? why man, all the hill of Calvary belongs to you!' To those distressed, but showing no sign of saving repentance, he could speak very differently. To a desponding Christian who said to him, 'What talents have I?' He replied: 'Well, at all events, two: leisure and God's word: time and truth. Let them be well used, and your crown will be bright.'

Collins' biographer notes that a happy providence had led Collins to Bradford for this short period. For the first time since 1831 his location brought him much closer to his parents who lived in Leeds. He was thus at hand when both died in December 1853. Ever since his visit to the Orkneys, John Collins had been fully employed in the work of Christ, interrupted only by a final eighteen months of illness. Of his mother's death, Collins wrote: 'Her departure was beautifully tranquil. Nearly the last thing she did was to repeat the Hundredth Psalm, – ever a favourite with her. Her cough compelled a pause at the words: "O go your way into His gates with thanksgiving." She never finished the recitation, and was only able to add: "His gates, – His gates. Go into them; yes, I may for they are wide open – wide open – to me; and have been for some time."'

Sowerby Bridge in Yorkshire was to be a charge where, relieved of the duties of superintendence, he spent the next three years (1854–57). Compared with the pressures of former times this was to be a peaceful and quiet situation – his 'house pleasant, the country beautiful, friends cordial'. He could no longer itinerate as widely as once he did – 'In strange beds now my rest gets broken' – yet we still read of him preaching in many places, even as far away as Caithness where he was pleased to revisit the 'Bethels' on the shores of the Pentland Firth where he had met with God. Of those former occasions he noted: 'Formerly, God came *strangely* nigh unto me in those places, giving me a mysterious, ineffable, awful, yet happy, consciousness of His presence. That *speciality of manifestation* He gives not now, but He enables me to exercise unwavering faith.'

Yet his times of 'retirement' remained as regular as ever. On January 2, 1857, he wrote in his diary: 'I have given myself to the Lord for this year. I cannot fast, as once I could; but by taking a biscuit at one o'clock I am still able on Fridays to have the seclusion of my room, without injury until tea time. Now, if I feel the need of it, without any scruple I take a chop with my tea. It is not penance, but retirement with God that I want.' Another time he wrote: 'My humble joy, in anticipation of the home in heaven prepared for me, was so great that, though I wished and tried to express it, I found all words to be a failure.'

His last circuit for three full years was to be at Leamington (1857–60) in his native Warwickshire. He loved this area of childhood memories and says, 'It somehow became a fixed idea in my mind that after serving the Lord awhile in rougher fields He would lead me hither.' The one material defect of the new situation is wisely noted by Coley: the study where the preacher spent so much of his time 'had the chapel wall for a prospect, and was sunless and cold. The nerves of steel that once accepted pleasantly wood, or damp sea-cave, as closet, now thrilled with agony in the currents of a draughty room.' Yet, on the whole, the time at Leamington was to be a happy one. A diary note read: 'The sense of Divine goodness bowed me down.' A hundred were added to the fellowship and, when the farewell eventually came, he could say, 'I have ever been solaced by your sympathy and prayer.'

Few active years remained. To his disappointment, an appointment to Pontypool in 1860, with its cold hills, proved impossible for his health. In 1861 he was sent to Bristol South and, for a time, all the old characteristics of his thirty years' ministry were again in evidence. In the pulpit he was 'full of fresh thoughts and baptized with heavenly power'. His hearers spoke of his 'winning tenderness' and evident happiness. Ever ready to rejoice in the work of others, he was especially moved to visit the 1,100 orphans in the Müller's House: 'At the sight of it I was both amazed and humbled. By the side of that God-honoured man I felt ashamed and humbled. I abhorred myself for my unfruitfulness, and adored the Lord for His mighty acts.'

His public work was suddenly ended by a partial stroke in December 1862. In the eighteen months ahead he was still able to travel, though an inability to control his emotions made public speaking impossible. There was a last visit to Kent in May 1864, the month after his fifty-fourth birthday. Many of his children in the gospel still stood and 'wept to see the strength of one who had been among us such a Samson, so utterly broken'. He paid a last pastoral visit on 3 September 1864. On 14 September he came down stairs for the last time, and died peacefully in the arms of his daughter on 27 December.

* * * * *

Coley neither tells us where Thomas Collins was buried nor what inscription his grave bore. For many no text would have come more readily to mind than Luke's description of Barnabas, 'He was a good man, and full of the Holy Spirit and faith.' In our all-too-brief summary of his life we have omitted one outstanding influence without which his ministry would never have been what it was. The wives of Methodist pastors, ever in the background, were commonly the heroes of the work as much as their husbands. Emily Collins was eminently so. Coming from Clapham, London, her background was more genteel than that of her husband, yet from the beginning of their lives together in Caithness, she was ever a blessing to him. In a home life of repeated changes, and rarely enjoying his company as much as she wished, her self-denial for the sake of Christ never faltered. Often separated from her, he could write to her with the confidence that she understood: 'Absence from you is painful; but, that I may win souls, I am obliged to prolong it. I, with you, make the sacrifice for Christ's sake.'

Emily Collins had added needs when three children were added to the family circle and Thomas' later letters show him ever mindful of this. 'I never need to say to you, Care for my children; but, pray, care for yourself. Do not overdo.' Perhaps she smiled to herself at such an exhortation coming from one who too closely followed the spirit of Baxter's question, 'What is a candle for but to be burnt?'[1]

Coley, a welcome visitor to his uncles and aunt, could say, 'I never saw home life more happy, godly, and beautiful.' This circle was broken before Collins' own death. One of their daughters, Emmy, was not long married before she died at Loughborough in July 1863, with her father at her bedside. 'Many', he said, 'wept her loss, but only few could know her worth.' She appeared to have known Christ from her childhood.

In May 1863, on leaving Bristol, Thomas and Emily had moved to their final home at Warwick Lammas, within sight of the Malvern Hills. Emily, now suffering from asthma and heart-failure, had set her eyes on a better country, and to this she went at the beginning of 1864. Coley wrote of her: 'Religion was her life. She was very prayerful, and more manifestly unworldly than almost any one I ever met.' Her husband, who had one more year to live, wrote of her:

'For more than a quarter of a century her truthful love

---

[1] The admission of his latter years is important: 'If I had taken things more quietly, and sometimes rested my back against a tree when I was weary, I might, perhaps, have kept longer in the field.'

has been to me a steady stream of consolation and refreshment . . . her prayers have, all through, upheld my hands and brought a blessing on my work. Since dear Emmy died, her thoughts have turned unceasingly towards eternity. The last six months have been months of retirement and rest. Repose was upon her spirit. Sabbath and assurance dwelt with her. In her last hours . . . for the sake of others, I brought myself to ask, "Is your eye wholly on Christ now?" She had little breath to spare. Her answer was necessarily brief. With a look as if of wonder that I could question it, she replied, "Of course." Then I remembered the word of the Lord, "Have I been so long time with you, and yet hast thou not known me, Philip?"'[1]

Of the lessons that may be drawn from the life of Collins, one of the foremost must be the evidence it gives of the supernatural power bound up with the gospel. Nothing else can explain the glorious changes he so often saw. None proved to be too guilty or too depraved for his message, and the fresh and artless language of such converts witnessed to the reality of the new life. 'I feel', said one, 'just as if I was somebody else.' To a poor almswoman Collins put the question, 'What part of God's Word do you love the most?' 'Those glorious Epistles', was the immediate answer. One of the last works of grace he saw at Bristol concerned a prostitute. 'Her soul to him seemed as precious as a queen's and her end was

---

[1] John Henry Newman, a contemporary of Collins', reflects a very different view of the place of women in the evangelization of the poor in industrial cities. The men needed for such work, he believed, ought to be celibate: 'The Church wants *expeditos milites* – not a whole camp of women at its heels, forbye brats.' Quoted in Ian Ker, *John Henry Newman, a Biography* (Oxford and New York: OUP, 1988), p. 46. Newman evidently knew nothing of the work of the Methodists.

brightened with hope.' Another Bristol case was that of a blind man whom Collins taught to read. The man at length could say: 'O, this Bible is a treasure. Thank you, Sir, thank you much, and thank God more; for I can now, for myself, in these holy words, feel the way to heaven with my finger tips.' It would have made a fine book if Collins could have brought together many similar testimonies uttered during his ministry.

To what source Collins attributed all such usefulness the preceding pages have repeatedly witnessed. Coley summarizes it in the words: 'Marvellous results come not of nothing. What then were the causes of this unusually triumphant good? There was the concurrence of grace, in the people, and in the man. We reverently acknowledge, first of all, the plentiful descent of that power by which "God giveth the increase".' 'The secret anointing of the Holy Spirit' was the explanation.

One prominent theme in Collins' biography provides another impressive lesson. Unity was for him an indispensable need in Christian work. To see a work united in a brotherly spirit was his first priority in every field where he laboured. Where this was missing he anticipated little success, for it was proof of an absence of the anointing of the Spirit. For this reason he was dismayed at first in Wark. 'There is', he reported, 'a coldness one towards another, which prevents co-operation, which sets men back to back when they should be embracing.' The whole Methodist system was organized to bring ministers and people close together, so close indeed that Collins knew it could not work unless the love of God consciously filled hearts. 'Sacred sociality is the spirit, life, and leaven of genuine Methodism. Colleagueship in the ministry, and class-meetings for the members, are its result. They are our strength: but the strength of them is love. Let love decline, and such a system must at once be felt to be a bondage and a fret.'

Where such a unity is genuine and Spirit-given, it will never result in a denominational narrowness. The love of God knows no such limitations. With reference to the branch of Methodism that took the name 'Bible Christian', Collins queried, 'Is it right for one sect to assume as its own a title which belongs to every branch of the Protestant Church alike?'. While he remained an upholder of the distinctives of Wesleyan Methodism he ever followed with interest and prayer God's blessing on other communions. We find him rejoicing in the revival at Kilsyth, Scotland, in 1839; in the early prosperity of the Free Church of Scotland; and in the ministry of the young Baptist, C. H. Spurgeon, in London.[1] Where a wider unity was practicable he always aimed at it, holding services with evangelicals of other denominations, and giving eager support to the Evangelical Alliance in its beginnings. For Collins the beauty of holiness and a catholicity of spirit were ever companions. In all this his wife was a kindred spirit: 'Life through, her heart never narrowed to the limits of a sect. Jesus, the joy of every believer, being her joy, to Him, in all things she gave the pre-eminence.'[2]

* * * * *

[1] A diary entry in 1857 reads: 'Heard Spurgeon at the Surrey Gardens. He did three capital things: he spoke vital truth, he spoke out, and he spoke home. The vast hall was crowded. I rejoiced at the sight. The Gospel has its old power yet.'

[2] Coley introduces a number of good remarks on unity throughout the biography. For example: 'When will love of Jesus draw forth more gifts than love of party? . . . Earnest work found for everybody keeps unity in a church better than any devices of polity, however wise, can do. Heart-hold is the strongest link, and fellowship in toil rivets it . . . Christian unity is felt by spiritual men to be a fact; but how to make the fact visible has been a problem puzzling many ages. Solution has been immensely delayed by the error of counting uniformity essential to unity. Uniformity is the bigot's dream.'

Finally, it must be said that the life of Collins sheds a great deal of valuable light on how Methodism viewed the work of the gospel ministry. From one standpoint it might appear that, at the time Collins entered the work, the appointment of men for the preaching office was all too informal. There was no denominational selection committee for candidates, or theological college to train them. But such a judgment fails to face the question how such a supply of *effective men* came to be present in the Wesleyan pulpits at this date.

The truth is that a very thorough system of checks was in place before a man even became a candidate for the ministry. The apostolic rule, 'let them first be proved' (*1 Tim.* 3:10), was taken very seriously. If a man gave 'evidence of decided piety, and talents for public usefulness by Christian teaching', he was put on trial as a local preacher and subject to the enquiry of every Quarterly Local Preachers' Meeting. Thereafter the Superintendent minister could recommend the individual to the Quarterly Meeting and, if his name was approved by that Meeting, to the District Meeting of the circuit where there was further examination with such questions as the following:

'Do they know God as a pardoning God? Do they desire and seek nothing but God? And are they holy in all manner of conversation? Have they a clear sound understanding? Have they a just conception of salvation by faith? And has God given them an acceptable way of speaking? Have they had any fruit of their labour? Have any been truly convinced of sin, and converted to God, by their preaching?'[1]

---

[1] For this procedure, see Smith, *Methodism*, vol. 2, pp. 151–3.

This was the system through which Collins had to pass, and having done so, he remained as a candidate only for four years, with his name on the 'Reserve List', before he was received into 'full connexion' by the Conference of 1836. This was before he went to Wick. By that date a 'Theological Institution' was coming into existence in London but its role was carefully stated. It was not to aid in the selection of men for the ministry, for none was to be allowed to enter before his gifts were proved, the selection completed, and his name placed on the Reserve List. There was no idea of *making* preachers by education and training. George Smith, commenting on the change, was apprehensive lest the introduction of formal theological training would gradually change the way men came into the ministry, and his fears would later be proved well founded.[1]

One ingredient in the training of the men in Collins' period is too important to pass over. A model of gospel ministers was before them in the example of the older generation. For successive generations Methodism would have a common ideal. The day when the message and methods of the fathers would be seen as antiquated was not yet come; rather, 'The young felt that they were connected with by-gone times, and associated with the fathers of Methodism, to catch their mantle, and a double portion of their spirit.'[2] Their vision was that the lessons that had been passed to them should be kept alive. 'The history of our fathers is encouraging', said

---

[1] 'The Institution was never meant to be the means of introducing men into the ministry who could not be respectable preachers without it . . . Let the persons recommended by Superintendents and Quarterly Meetings be only such as commend themselves, by their piety, energy, ability, and aptness to teach, and the advantages of the Institution to such men will make them all that Wesleyan ministers ought to be.' Ibid., vol. 3, p. 510.

[2] Ibid., vol. 3, p. 380.

Collins. 'When they were few, and their external aids few; when the opposition made to them was frightful on all sides, they yet made progress. They had power with God and through God, power with men.'[1]

The lesson of this high tradition shines through the whole of the Collins' biography. It came to him through the praying people he knew in youth; he saw it in days of revival; he received it by the frequent counsel of his elders in his early years of ministry; and he passed it on faithfully to others in his maturity. The biography abounds in sound and often inspiring counsel on what the life of the pastor ought to be, as a Christian, as a preacher, and as a pastor. The following counsels will give a good summary of some of its chief maxims:

'Be a preacher, not a reciter. Admit no anxiety about mere words. Sound doctrine, godly unction, manly reasoning, and free speech, answer all evangelical ends. Whatever else you be, be holy.'

'The old power can be obtained by three things: experimental consistency with our own teaching of truth;

---

[1] On the importance of knowing church history, Coley writes: 'History lengthens experience. Men unacquainted with it often waste time in experiments which old attempts have proved to be useless.'

In connection with the subject of candidates for the ministry it is worth adding the question Wesley put to Dr Lowth, Bishop of London, when the latter turned down three men whom Wesley recommended and needed to serve in America. He asked the Bishop by what standard he accepted men and believed he already knew the answer: "Why, whether they understand a little *Latin* and *Greek* and can answer a few trite questions in divinity! Alas, how little does this avail! Does your Lordship examine whether they serve *Christ* or *Belial*? whether they love God or the world? whether they ever had any serious thoughts about heaven or hell? whether they have any real desire to save their own souls or the souls of others? If not, what have they to do with Holy Orders? And what will become of the souls committed to their care?' *Letters, vol. 7*, p. *31*.

freedom from the manners, maxims, and spirit of the world; and passion for souls.'

'Be always tenderly yearning for sinners. This is a happy unhappiness. A man full of Christ-like tears is a noble creature. Such concern melts men, and tells with God.'

'In selecting the sermon to be preached consider the people, not yourself . . . Choose your hymns carefully. Give them out heartily, and with much inward devotion. In your first prayer plead until the people move; wait until the baptism of power falls. You must not preach without power.'

'Never doubt either God's presence, God's word, God's pity, or God's power.'

'Carry paper with you everywhere; and if God gives you a good thought, *nail* it immediately.'

'As to study, calculate your time, prize it, consecrate it, apportion it. Every man can best form his own plan. Let your system be simple and easy to be practised. Remember, the master rule of all is, "Stick to it." But whatever else you do, deal much with God. People say, "This man has talent," and "That man has talent;" depend upon it, the great secret of usefulness is close dealing with God.'

'Have a horror of sinking into a tattling, twaddling, trivial sort of man, talking much and achieving nothing. Steer clear of a young man's rock, self-importance. Walk humbly with God. Acts of self-condemnation are, next to acts of faith in Christ, the most profitable of devotional exercises. I have grown best and done best when most frequent in them.'

'Wesleyan Theological Tutors have all been pastors. May it never be otherwise! Theory, unsobered by necessity of practical application, is a great source of German scepticism. Who would trust the therapeutics of one who never healed? Medical professors reach their chairs through hospital wards. According to Wesleyan usage our "masters in Israel" have to do the same.'

'Make what you read thoroughly your own. Have a book always in use for analysis, reviews, and extracts. Stick close to Wesley's writings; he wrote, as I would have you live, for God and souls.'

Maxims such as these will surely appear again wherever the gospel ministry approximates to the New Testament.

Thomas Collins

Wesley preaching the first sermon in
City Road Chapel, London,
1 November 1778

Part Three

Against Unquestioning Following

I believe there are many things unscriptural among us all; that is, either defective, redundant, or erroneous: but human nature is very fallible; ten thousand circumstances produce prejudices, which warp the judgment; and the Lord seems to illuminate his people but in part. There must therefore be differences of opinion.

Thomas Scott, 1795
Letters and Papers (1824)

Wesley in later years
(from the portrait by Henry Edridge)

Chapter 9

Justification

Despite the clear statements on justification quoted in earlier pages it was on this doctrine that Wesley, at times, departed from the evangelicalism of the Reformation. In 1773 Richard Hill faced him with words of Luther in the question, 'Is Justification by Faith the article of the standing or the falling Church?' That is to say, is it *the* doctrine that determines whether churches live or die? Wesley replied, 'In the beginning of the year 1738, I believed it was so. Soon after I found reason to doubt. Since that time I have not varied.'[1] To this claim for consistency of belief, Hill responded by pointing out that many years after 1738 Wesley was still using the very words of Luther:

'Nay, but in the year 1765 you say, "This is the name whereby he shall be called, *the Lord our Righteousness*. A truth this, of which may be affirmed (what Luther affirms of a truth nearly connected with it, justification by faith) it is *articulus stantis vel cadentis Ecclesiae* [the article of the standing or the falling church].'"

To this Wesley answered:

'It is certain, here is a seeming contradiction; but it is not

[1] *Some Remarks on Mr Hill's Farrago Double-Distilled* (1773) in Wesley, *Works*, vol. 10, p. 432.

a real one; for these two opposite propositions do not speak of the same thing. The latter speaks of justification by faith; the former, of trusting in the righteousness or merits of Christ. (Justification is only mentioned incidentally in a parenthesis) . . . But Mr Hill thinks, "justification by faith, and by trusting in the merits of Christ, are all one."[1]

Without clarification – which Wesley did not give – this reply is mystifying. Is it not God's action in counting the merits (righteousness) of Christ as the believer's own that constitutes the doctrine of justification? Faith justifies, not because of what it is in itself, but because it receives Christ and his righteousness. Certainly this is what was taught in all the Reformation and Puritan standards, as in Article 11 of the 39 Articles which begins, 'We are accounted righteous before God, only for the merit of our Lord and Saviour Jesus Christ by Faith'. So Wesley himself believed in 1738 and 1739;[2] but replying to Hill in 1773 he now wanted to distinguish between the believer being accepted on the basis of Christ's righteousness and his being personally 'accounted righteous'. By means of this distinction he meant to reduce the content of 'justification' to forgiveness only.

Wesley's variation from the historic teaching had developed gradually and for many years was scarcely noticeable. In the Minutes of his private 1744 Conference, justification was defined as 'To be pardoned and received into God's favour', but a caution against the older belief was added in

---

[1] Ibid., pp. 432–3. The words from Hill are taken from Wesley's pages.

[2] In 1739 Wesley published *Two Treatises*, taken from the writings of the English reformer, Robert Barnes, one on Justification and the other the Sinfulness of Man's Natural Will. He did not reprint these in his Christian Library. Barnes wrote: 'We say with blessed St Paul, that faith only justifieth *imputativè*; that is, all the merits and goodness, grace and favour, and all that is in Christ to our salvation, is imputed and reckoned to us, because we hang and believe on him.' *Fathers of the English Church* (London: Hatchard, 1807), vol. 1, p. 588.

the words, 'We do not find it affirmed expressly in Scripture that God imputes the righteousness of Christ to any.' From caution on imputed righteousness, Wesley moved to criticism in a letter to James Hervey of 15 October 1756. The subject of Wesley's letter was the well-known book by Hervey, *Theron and Aspasio*. With much of the book Wesley was in full agreement but not with what it taught on Christ's righteousness imputed. To such sentences as the following in Hervey's book Wesley objected:

'Believers who are notorious transgressors in themselves, have a sinless obedience *in Christ.*

'The claims of law are all answered.

'Your sins are all expiated thro' the death of *Christ*, and *a Righteousness given you*, by which you have free access to God.

'Faith in *the imputed righteousness of Christ*, is a fundamental principle in the Gospel.'[1]

---

[1] The quotations are found in Wesley, *Works*, vol. 10, pp. 326–33. Hervey responded to Wesley's criticism in a series of letters which were not, however, sent or published before his death on Christmas Day, 1758, at the age of forty-four. The letters were subsequently published by William Cudworth. Hervey's brother regarded Cudworth's work as faulty and inaccurate, and so issued his own edition, in which he printed all Wesley's criticisms before the letters of response. I am here quoting from this source, *Eleven Letters From the Late Rev. Mr Hervey, to the Rev. Mr John Wesley; Containing an Answer to that Gentleman's remarks on Theron and Aspasio*, ed. W. Hervey, 3rd ed (London: Rivington, 1790), pp. xxii–xxxiii. Hervey himself had not favoured publishing his letters in reply to Wesley. He wrote to a friend on 3 January 1758: 'I am sometimes apprehensive that he [Wesley] would draw me into a dispute on particular redemption. I know he can say startling and horrid things on this subject; and this, perhaps, might be the most effectual method to prejudice people against my main point.' *Whole Works of James Hervey* (Edinburgh: Brown and Nelson,1834) p. 912. Hervey had no confidence in Wesley as a controversialist: 'He is so unfair in his quotations and so magisterial in his manner, that I find it no small difficulty to preserve the decency of a gentleman and the meekness of a Christian, in my intended answer.' Ibid., p. 917. His *Eleven Letters* run to nearly 300 pages and are a thorough examination of imputed righteousness and its scriptural basis.

Wesley published his critique of Hervey in 1758, and republished it in 1764 as a Preface to a reprint of part of John Goodwin on *Justification*. Prior to that, in 1762, he published a tract *Thoughts on Christ's Imputed Righteousness*. The latter contained no direct attack on the received evangelical belief except to question alleged scripture proofs and to argue that the teaching of imputed righteousness took away the need for sanctification: 'For if the very personal obedience of Christ . . . be mine the moment I believe, can anything be added thereto? Does my obeying add any value to the perfect obedience of Christ?'[1]

By the mid-1760s it was being openly questioned whether Wesley was orthodox on justification. At that date Hervey was dead but at the end of 1764 his brother published posthumously, *Eleven Letters From the Late Rev. Mr Hervey, to the Rev. Mr John Wesley; Containing an Answer to that Gentleman's remarks on Theron and Aspasio*. These letters centred on justification and imputation. Hervey was the ablest evangelical who ever wrote against Wesley. In evident response to him, and to other criticism, Wesley preached and published a sermon on *The Lord our Righteousness* in 1765. In this sermon (referred to by Richard Hill above) he rejected the charge that he had departed from the historic Protestant teaching. To allege that he denied imputed righteousness he calls an 'unkind and unjust accusation. I always did, and do still continually affirm, that the righteousness of Christ is imputed to every believer.'[2] He held, he assured his hearers, what Calvin taught.

In the light of this strong disavowal, and taking his sermon in the most charitable light, there was reason for

---

[1] *Works*, vol. 10, p. 315.   [2] *Works*, vol. 1, p. 242.

many to suppose that concern over Wesley's teaching on justification might be unfounded. It is only what he had written *before* the 1765 sermon, and what he would write *after*, that forces one to read that sermon with the conviction that he was not using words in their customary sense. The meaning of righteousness imputed, he said in the sermon, was that 'God justifies the believer, for the sake of Christ's righteousness'. That sounds correct, but for Wesley it did *not* mean that the sinner is declared righteous because God counts Christ's righteousness as the sinner's own.[1]

Further debate lapsed until 1770 when the Minutes of Wesley's annual Conference re-opened the issue. Among other things, they contained this proposition:

'Does not talking of a justified or a sanctified *state* tend to mislead men? Almost naturally leading them to trust in what was done in one moment? Whereas we are every hour and every moment pleasing or displeasing to God, "according to our works"; – according to the whole of our inward tempers, and our outward behaviour.'[2]

These words revealed Wesley's real problem. It was not simply with imputation but with justification itself, for if it is a once-for-all act, resulting in a believer's permanent acceptance, would that not be a sure charter for careless living, rendering needless such warnings as 'without holiness no man will see the Lord'? So he was against any idea of justification being understood as complete when

---

[1] In reply to Hill, Wesley confirmed in 1773 that this was how his words of 1765 were to be understood: 'When I have either in that sermon [i.e. of 1765] or elsewhere said, "the righteousness of Christ is imputed to every believer," I mean, every believer is justified for the sake of what Christ has done and suffered.' *Works*, vol. 10, p. 428.

[2] *Works*, vol. 8, p. 338.

the sinner first believes. This came out plainly in his dispute with Hervey. The latter had written, 'Justification is *complete* the first Moment we believe, and is incapable of *Augmentation*.' Upon which Wesley wrote, 'Not so: There may be many *Degrees* in the *Favour* as in the *Image* of God.' Here lies the crux of his objection to imputed righteousness: On the texts of Scripture that speak, as Hervey alleged, of righteousness *given*, Wesley wanted to affirm that they *included* a righteousness imparted subjectively to the believer, that is, an inherent righteousness in sanctification. 'The righteousness which is of God by faith', he wrote, 'is both imputed and inherent.'[1] On this interpretation 'justification' becomes an on-going process, not a permanent 'state'.

When the Minutes relating to justification of the 1770 Conference became known there was strong objection from Calvinistic evangelicals, some of whom appeared at Wesley's 1771 Conference. At this Conference Wesley authorized the following clarifying statement:

'Whereas the doctrinal points in the Minutes of a Conference held in London, 7 August 1770, have been understood to favour justification by works, now we, the Rev. John Wesley, and others assembled in Conference, do declare that we had no such meaning, and that we abhor the doctrine of justification by works as a most perilous and abominable doctrine . . . And though no one is a real Christian believer (and consequently cannot be

---

[1] *Works*, vol. 10, p. 331. Against this, Hervey quoted to Wesley one of the canons of the Council of Trent: 'If any shall affirm, that Righteousness received is not preserved, and increased likewise, by good Works; but that good Works are only the Fruits and Signs of Justification obtained, not the means of increasing it also, let him be accursed.' *Eleven Letters*, p. 74. Presumably it was on the basis of this quotation that Wesley was to allege that Hervey 'died cursing his spiritual father'. *Works*, vol. 10, p. 356.

saved) who doth not good works when there is time and opportunity, yet our works have no part in meriting or purchasing our justification, from first to last, either in whole or in part.'[1]

This statement satisfied the Calvinistic brethren, but only temporarily, for Wesley's close assistant, John Fletcher, who was not present at the 1771 Conference, had already been writing in defence of the 1770 Minutes. Wesley received his manuscript after the 1771 Conference but, instead of treating the matter as closed, he sent it to the printers. This opened six years of controversy, in which Fletcher's repeated publications in defence of the 1770 Minutes made clear that the teaching was indeed incompatible with the Protestant creeds on justification. Fletcher defended the idea that justification is a matter of 'degrees' – something that could be increased, or indeed lost altogether. Justification, he insisted, requires personal holiness – the image of God in us – and this, he asserted, was what Paul meant in speaking of 'the righteousness which is through the faith of Christ, the righteousness which is of God by faith'.[2] On this understanding, justification is a condition, in and out of which one can move, depending on conduct. So David, Fletcher said, was not justified when he sinned against Uriah, and Judas forfeited the justification he once had by his betrayal of Christ.[3] He will have none of the argument, in Richard Hill's *Review of All the Doctrines Taught by Rev. Mr Wesley*,

[1] Stevens, *Methodism*, vol. 2, p. 23. For other accounts of the controversy, see, Seymour, *Life and Times of the Countess of Huntingdon*, vol. 2, pp. 232–250; and Faith Cook, *Selina, Countess of Huntingdon* (Edinburgh: Banner of Truth, 2001), pp. 277–84.

[2] 'Fourth Check to Antinomianism,' in *Works of John Fletcher*, vol. 2 (London: Mason, 1836), p. 148.

[3] Ibid., pp. 64–5.

that works are the 'declarative evidences' and 'the witnessing effects' of justification; on the contrary, he denies
Hill's quotation from Bishop Cowper, 'In the act of
justification, good works have no place.'[1]

The main protagonists on the Calvinistic side in this
controversy were the brothers Richard and Rowland Hill,
and Augustus Toplady who died before it concluded.
There are aspects of Wesley's position in the controversy
on justification which are hard to understand. At times –
as in the 1765 sermon – it is hard to avoid the impression
that he was being devious. He could say, for instance, that
he did not speak of 'Christ's righteousness imputed'
because the words were 'ambiguous', yet he contributed
to making them ambiguous.[2] On his claim to stand where
Calvin stood on justification, made in his 1765 sermon
and elsewhere, he was either misled or misleading.[3] 'I
know him of old', a critic once said of the Methodist

---

[1] Ibid., p. 65. Fletcher could see that the question of general over against
particular redemption was closely tied to the nature of justification. Scriptures
(*Rom.* 5:15–19; *2 Cor.* 5:21) indicate that the extent of Christ's justifying
righteousness extends to all for whose sins he died, and therefore, rather
than believe in particular redemption, Fletcher held a 'general justification'
of all men, which was not, of itself, a saving justification at all. 'First Check
to Antinomianism,' *Works of Fletcher*, vol. 1, pp. 235, 250 etc.

[2] 'We rarely use that ambiguous expression of Christ's righteousness
imputed to us.' *Letters*, vol. 4, p. 144.

[3] 'I think on justification just as Mr Calvin does. In this respect I do not
differ from him an hair's breadth.' *Letters*, vol. 4, p. 298. But Calvin wrote of
justification, 'It consists in the remission of sins *and the imputation of Christ's
righteousness.*' *Institutes of the Christian Religion*, ed. John T. McNeill
(Philadelphia: Westminster Press, 1967), vol. 1, p. 727, my italics. In the pages
which follow the last quotation Calvin condemns the teaching which mixes
imputed and inherent righteousness (pp. 729–32). Wesley appears to have
had little acquaintance with the theology of the Reformation. Hearing a
commendation of 'Tindal on justification' in 1782, he replied, 'Who Mr
Tyndall is I know not.' (*Letters*, vol. 7, p. 106). Perhaps this was a slip of
memory in advanced years but his correspondent was surely referring to William
Tyndale (names had no standardized spelling in the eighteenth century).

leader. 'He is an eel; take him where you will, he will slip through your fingers.'[1]

Yet this criticism needs some qualification, for sometimes inconsistencies in Wesley's statements can, in part, be put down to the hurry in which he commonly wrote, a dangerous practice when it comes to controversial issues. The minute of the 1770 Conference – never intended for public consumption – which caused such controversy may well have been in that category. On another occasion, when a correspondent pointed out a mistake in something he had written, Wesley responded frankly, 'You and I the more easily bear with each other, because we are both of us *rapid* writers, and therefore more liable to mistake.'[2] This propensity would also go some way to explaining anomalies in the way he revised Puritan texts in his Christian Library. In re-issuing the *Westminster Shorter Catechism* he left untouched the answer to Question 33, What is Justification?

'Justification is an act of God's free grace, wherein he pardons all our sins, and accepts us as righteous in his sight, only for the righteousness of Christ imputed to us, and received by faith alone.'

Yet in his revision of *Pilgrim's Progress* he removed the fine treatment of that same truth expressed in connection with Bunyan's character 'Ignorance'. Richard Hill took Wesley up on such inconsistencies, but a part of the explanation is that he worked too fast and with too much indifference to strict consistency. Wesley was no leisured desk man or a litterateur. In addition, there was an element of impetuosity in his make-up which contributed to

---

[1] *Nichols's Anecdotes*, quoted in Southey, *Wesley* p. 474n.
[2] *Letters*, vol. 3, p. 167.

the confusion his statements could create. As 'John Smith' told him in 1746: 'Whatever side of the question is for the present uppermost in your mind, that you are apt to push with such impetuosity and excess as unavoidably occasions the appearance of great variety (not to say inconsistency) of sentiment.'[1]

Another explanation of Wesley's variations on justification warrants mention. Some of his words and deeds, when he got into controversy, give rise to the question whether he was as sure of his position as he professed to be. Writing to the Countess of Huntingdon, for instance, in 1771, he was to qualify the offending sentences in the 1770 Minutes with the words quoted earlier, 'There may be opinions maintained at the same time which are not exactly true; and who can be secure from these?'[2]

It may be that there was a measure of uncertainty in Wesley himself on justification. It must be significant that while he sometimes argued against imputed righteousness there appears to be no record that he ever *preached* against it. When his collected works were first brought together in 1771, at the head were his early sermons (from which we have quoted earlier) with their emphasis on grace and faith alone in justification. These sermons he never revised, nor did he modify his position in later sermons on the same subject, and it was his sermons, plus his *Notes on the New Testament*, which he appointed as the permanent doctrinal standard for his preachers. This has to be important. Without question, Wesley never had the slightest intention of promoting belief in salvation by

---

[1] *Works* (Abingdon), vol. 26, p. 210.
[2] *Letters*, vol. 5, p. 259.

works.[1] To suppose that would be to make nonsense of his ministry. Toplady was wrong in thinking that Wesley intended to be an opponent of grace.

Part of Wesley's problem was his obsessive concern with Antinomianism. In counteracting that danger, he would have been right if he had gone only as far as Thomas Scott in his words of warning, 'The doctrine of justification is not the whole of Christianity; nor being justified the whole of salvation.' But Wesley went further. He seemed doubtful how to answer the charge that, if justification makes salvation certain, then the incentive for holy living is taken away. To understand this we must remember that Antinomian writers had especially misused the doctrine of justification,[2] and that the teaching of the Epistle to the Romans, which makes the very decisiveness of justification the ground for Christian living, had almost died out in the years of Wesley's upbringing. Wesley was not listening when Hervey argued that the Christian's standing in the righteousness of Christ 'yields new and nobler motives to all holy living'.[3] That Wesley could not see this, is a mystery. The problem remains among

---

[1] This is also very clear in his *Notes on the New Testament, 1754* (reprint ed., *London:* Wesleyan Methodist Book Room, n.d.). While most of his notes treat justification as securing only forgiveness and acceptance, his constant emphasis is on 'the rich and free grace of God . . . The meritorious cause of all: not any works of righteousness of man, but the alone merits of our Lord Jesus Christ.' Contrary to his wavering in 1770, he treats sanctification as separate from justification. In justification: 'Justice is satisfied; the sin remitted, and pardon applied to the soul, by a divine faith wrought by the Holy Ghost, who then begins the works of inward sanctification. Thus God justifies the ungodly.' The graces in the soul 'are the fruits of justifying faith: where these are not, that faith is not.' See the notes on Romans, chapters 3– 5. This book was corrected by Wesley after its first publication and so cannot necessarily be taken only as his thought in the 1750s.

[2] For evidence, see John Flavel's reply to Antinomians in his *Works,* vol. 3 (London: Banner of Truth, 1968), pp. 551–91.

[3] Hervey, *Eleven Letters*, p. 277.

Christians today, and John Piper, in addressing it recently, makes the same point as Hervey did, when he writes:

'If the battle of sanctification is made part of our justification . . . a greater part of the foundation for triumphant warfare against sin is removed, and we are made to fight a battle that has already been fought for us and that we cannot win . . . What is distinctive about the Christian warfare is that we can only kill the sin that has already been killed when we were killed in Christ. Or, to put it positively, we can only achieve practical righteousness as a working out of imputed righteousness. The battle is to become what we are in Christ.'[1]

Had Wesley's occasional wavering on justification been built into his sermons the subsequent history of Methodism would have been very different. It is significant that Richard Watson, the leading Methodist theologian of the early nineteenth century, should say that Fletcher's writings, 'though greatly admired among the Wesleyans, are not admitted as standards of their doctrines'.[2] It is still more significant, perhaps, to find in the correspondence of Methodist leaders in 1840 the admission that it was the aberrant thinking of the Restoration divines that influenced Wesley with respect to the 1770 Minutes on justification. George Cobbitt, writing to Jabez Bunting on 6 January 1840, expressed his fear of the rise of a 'low Arminianism' in their midst and continued:

'Very naturally, the preachers have read the Arminian writers of the Restoration School; and the best of them,

---

[1] John Piper, *Counted Righteous in Christ: Should We Abandon the Imputation of Christ's Righteousness?* (Wheaton: Crossway Books, 2002), p. 50.

[2] Quoted by Sidney, *Life of Rowland Hill*, p. 436.

when not writing on the questions controverted between us and the Calvinists, *tend* – some of them do *more* than tend – to what may be termed Bishop Bull's school. It must have been the influence of such writings that led Mr Wesley to consent to the celebrated "Minutes", which, though *substantially* right, and even in *expression*, when properly connected and explained, less obscure than they would appear taken absolutely, and in their insulated form, are still both unguarded and capable of a very dangerous construction.'[1]

In other words, the Minutes had the potential to destroy clear teaching on justification by faith. That they did not have that outcome – as they would have done had Wesley been more consistent, and had Fletcher been taken as the standard interpreter – is happily apparent from Methodist history. As it was, in the nineteenth century, even a theologian as orthodox as R. L. Dabney could point to Wesley's sermons as guides to sound teaching on justification.[2]

The controversy of the 1770s unquestionably did harm. Language was used on both sides for which there was cause for repentance. A watching world rejoiced to see evangelicals divided. But it is arguable that good was also

---

[1] Ward, *Early Victorian Methodism*, pp. 237–8. George Bull (1634–1710) wrote his controversial book on Justification entitled *Apostolical Harmony* in 1669. Of this book it has been said that, 'under the cover of justification by faith, this is in reality justification by works'. See editorial comment in John Owen, *Works*, vol. 5, p. 3. The danger is crisply expressed in the words of a later writer: 'If justification is confused with regeneration or sanctification, then the door is opened for the perversion of the gospel at its centre.' John Murray, *Redemption – Accomplished and Applied* (London: Banner of Truth, 1961), p. 121.

[2] R. L. Dabney, 'The Moral Effects of a Free Justification', in *Discussions: Evangelical and Theological*, vol. 1 (reprinted London: Banner of Truth, 1967), pp. 81–3.

done. When the dust had settled, men on both sides of the divide re-assessed how much they had in common, and they were shocked at the element of personal hostility that had been allowed to enter the debate. This led to a determination that henceforth Calvinist and Arminian evangelicals, without minimizing their differences, should respect and aid one another wherever possible.[1] This led to a healthier position in the early nineteenth century, and is well illustrated by some remarks of a reviewer in the *Evangelical Magazine*. The review was of *Sermons on Various Subjects* by the Rev. John Hyatt. Hyatt, who inherited Whitefield's pulpits in London, was one of the most representative Nonconformist figures at the turn of the eighteenth century. His reviewer noted:

'John Hyatt embraced, as one of his earliest friends, a man from whose peculiar creed he saw reason to differ, for Mr Hyatt was himself a Calvinist, and his friend a follower of Wesley. Both held fast their opinions, and their mutual affection too. Now this is very delightful. The *odium theologicum* is a mighty despicable thing . . . How are we advanced since the day a Calvinist was applauded for throwing water into the face of an Arminian to try his principles.'[2]

Those who have commented on the 1770s controversy have rightly observed how much better it would have been if the antagonists had met rather than disputed in print. When, at length, some of them did meet, the

---

[1] An early instance of this change of mood is seen in the well-known exchange between Charles Simeon and Wesley in 1784.
[2] *Evangelical Magazine and Missionary Chronicle*, 1826, vol. 4 (London: Westley and Davis), p. 474.

fellowship was a happy one.[1] The fact is that Christians are not at their best in controversy, especially so when it is carried on at arm's length. What Abel Stevens said of Toplady is true of Wesley when it came to controversy, 'He presented one of those inexplicable combinations of great virtues and great defects, which at once excite our wonder and teach us a lesson of charity for the infirmities of our common humanity.'[2] Unlike most who shared in the controversy, the gentle James Hervey had learned that lesson. Not long before his death, after reading Richard Baxter's *Aphorisms on Justification* (which express views similar to Wesley's and contrary to his own) he wrote to a friend:

'Arminius, Calvin, Baxter, all excellent men in their own way, yet how divided in their notions! But Jesus, that eternal source of love, will, I would charitably hope, bless all who sincerely desire to magnify his holy name, notwithstanding their different apprehensions on these points.'

---

[1] Abel Stevens gives detail of the Hill brothers, Venn and Berridge, meeting with Fletcher. *Methodism*, vol. 2, pp. 30, 36. Toplady accidentally met Wesley's assistant, Thomas Oliver, with whom he had had an explosive exchange in print, and noted: 'To say the truth, I am glad I saw Mr Oliver: for he appears to be a person of stronger sense and better behaviour than I imagined . . . What pleased me most, was that appearance of honesty by which he is so greatly distinguished from that old fox, Mr Wesley.' *Complete Works of A. M. Toplady* (London: Cornish, 1861), p. 843. Unhappily there are no similar records of these men meeting Wesley.

[2] Stevens, *Methodism*, vol. 2, p. 29. Wesley was at his worst in his treatment of Toplady (see *Complete Works of Toplady*, p. 721) and his words on the mild and deceased Hervey merited the criticism of even so strong a Wesleyan as Luke Tyerman, *Wesley*, vol. 2, p. 529. Elsewhere Tyerman notes a similar unfairness in Wesley's words on opponents, Ibid., vol. 1, p. 320.

Chapter 10

Christian Perfection

'Christian perfection' was probably the most controversial topic in Wesley's teaching. Why that should be so, he said, was puzzling to him, for did not all Christians believe in the command, 'Be ye therefore perfect, even as your Father in heaven is perfect' (*Matt.* 5:48), and is it not the desire of all believers that they should be so? The theme warrants further comment.

First, what is not controversial should be underlined. The priority that Wesley gave to love in Christian experience is clearly justified in scripture. It is the subject of the first commandment. On this there should be no disagreement. It was a Welsh Calvinist who said, 'Love is the greatest thing in religion, and if that is forgotten nothing can take its place.'[1] Wesley's emphasis that progress in the Christian life is to be measured by love to God and man was right, and there is evidence enough in these pages of the immense good that came from it. Further, it should be noted that Wesley was careful not to emphasize love over against law, as though the two were antithetical. Just such an antithesis was found among the Moravians and was the major reason why Wesley separated from them. He knew that love does not replace

[1] William Williams, quoted by D. M. Lloyd-Jones, *The Puritans* (Edinburgh: Banner of Truth, 1987), p. 187.

law, it fulfils it, and the law it fulfils is the abiding moral law – set out in the Ten Commandments and expounded by Christ. So he writes:

'There is the closest connexion that can be conceived between the law and the gospel. On the one hand, the law continually makes way for, and points us to, the gospel; on the other, the gospel continually leads us to a more exact fulfilling of the law . . . "the righteousness of the law is fulfilled in us", through faith which is in Christ Jesus.'[1]

It can be further agreed that the word 'perfection' may not, of itself, be open to objection. Calvin used the word in French (*perfection*) and believed we are 'not to labour feebly or coldly in urging perfection', or in striving towards it.[2] Similar language is common among the Puritans. 'Labour to grow unto perfection', wrote John Downame.[3] 'Whereas there are', wrote John Owen, 'degrees in spiritual saving graces and their operations, we ought to press towards the most perfect of them.'[4] Wesley's own grandfather, Samuel Annesley, has a sermon bearing on the subject, entitled, 'How May We Attain to Love God with All Our Hearts, Souls, and Minds?'[5]

---

[1] Wesley, 'Sermon on the Mount,' Discourse V. 'The moral law stands on an entirely different foundation from the ceremonial or ritual law.' See also his two sermons on 'The Law Established through Faith.' 'Christ has adopted every point of the moral law, and grafted it into the law of love' (*Works*, vol. 11, p. 431). In his belief that the fulfilment of the law spoken of in Romans 8:4 refers to personal holiness, he has the support of such modern Reformed commentators as John Murray.

[2] See Index to his *Sermons on Galatians* (Edinburgh: Banner of Truth, 1997), and the chapter, 'Progress towards perfection', in R. S. Wallace, *Calvin's Doctrine of the Christian Life* (Edinburgh: Oliver and Boyd, 1959). But in the first of his *Sermons on Job* Calvin points out that the word 'perfect' is liable to be misconstrued.

[3] John Downame, *A Guide to Godliness* (London: Stephens, 1629), p. 474.

[4] Owen, *Exposition of Hebrews*, vol. 5, p. 201.

[5] *Puritan Sermons 1659–1689*, vol. 1, pp. 572–621.

The words 'Christian perfection' were not then, of themselves, the cause of the controversy. Indeed, Wesley could affirm in 1756 (though hardly later on): 'I have no particular fondness for the term. It seldom occurs either in my preaching or writings.'[1]

It was in the content that Wesley put into the words that he departed from the Protestant tradition. First, he used the term as describing the mature believer's obedience to the first commandment: 'By "perfection" I mean "perfect love," or the loving God with all the heart.'[2] 'Christian perfection, is neither more nor less than pure love – love expelling sin and governing both the heart and life of the child of God.'[3] It is the portrait of 'the happy mature Christian'. Had Wesley said no more there would have been little or no controversy. The love of God 'perfected in us' is a scriptural concept (*1 John* 4:12, 17). But it was in the deduction that Wesley drew that he went wrong. There is no biblical or logical connection between a maturity of love in the believer and the eradication of sin. But Wesley insisted that, where such love exists in the Christian, there is necessarily 'entire sanctification'. Love, he claimed, not only ends sins of outward conduct, it also expels indwelling sin. Hence the other phrase that he used for the same thing, 'full salvation', by which he meant 'salvation from inbred sin', being 'saved from inbred sin'.[4]

---

[1] *Letters*, vol. 3, p. 167.　　　　[2] Ibid., p. 10.

[3] Ibid., vol. 5, p. 223.

[4] Ibid., vol. 7, p. 129; vol. 8, p. 181. Similar references are innumerable. W. E. Sangster points out that, 'Normally, the people enjoying this high experience talked not of being cleansed from all sin but of being "filled with love".' The same author argues cogently that a profession of freedom from all sin 'is shaped in ignorance, for no man knows what is in him'. *The Path to Perfection: An Examination and Restatement of John Wesley's Doctrine of Christian Perfection* (London: Epworth, 1957), pp. 16, 163–5.

In the early 1740s Wesley spelt out this 'full salvation' as freedom from self-will, evil thoughts, and even from temptation itself. He later conceded that the claim was 'too strong', yet he continued to insist: 'Christian perfection implies deliverance from all sin.'[1] The person who has attained to this blessing 'experiences a total death to sin, and an entire renewal in the love and image of God.'[2]

To maintain this definition, however, required some adjustment in how sin is to be understood, for Wesley knew his Bible too well to teach an 'absolute perfection'. He thus argued that in speaking of the end of inbred sin he did not mean that a person was free from ignorance, mistake, infirmity, or 'a thousand nameless defects . . . From such infirmities none are perfectly freed till their spirits return to God.' But he did not believe that he was contradicting himself because, he argued, sin 'properly so called . . . is a voluntary transgression of a known law', whereas defects and mistakes that arise from our present bodily state, and lead to 'involuntary transgression', are improperly called sin.[3] Pressed on whether any believer can be described as 'sinless' he was ambivalent: 'It is not worth disputing about'; 'It is not worth while to contend for a term'; 'I do not contend for the term *sinless*, though I do not object against it.'[4]

But there was another ingredient in his teaching of Christian perfection which more sharply focused the issue. It was that such experience was to be expected and sought

---

[1] See *Christian Perfection*, in *Works*, vol. 11, pp. 379, 393.

[2] Ibid., p. 401.

[3] Ibid., pp. 394–6. This was his continued teaching: 'Every voluntary breach of the law of love is sin; and nothing else, if we speak properly' (*Letters*, vol. 5, p. 322).

[4] Ibid., pp. 418, 442, 446. Whether he was being consistent or not, Wesley was very definite that every Christian *always* needs the atoning work of Christ.

by all Christians now. 'The whole comes to one point –
Is there, or is there not, any instantaneous sanctification
between justification and death? I say, Yes.'[1] 'I believe this
perfection is always wrought in the soul by a simple act
of faith; consequently, in an instant.'[2]

Luke Tyerman, quoting one of the earliest biographers
of Wesley, questions whether this second strand of
perfection in 'an instant by faith' was present in Wesley's
teaching before about 1760 (the quotations in my previous paragraph are from after that date). It seems it was
not, and what brought the change in his thinking was
the testimonies he was now hearing from many of his
people: 'We thought it was to come gradually; we never
expected it to come in a moment, by simple faith, in the
very same manner as our justification'.[3]

Tyerman wrote: 'Now, for the first time, he found
people professing to experience and practise it.'[4] The
initial group were to be found in the society at Otley,
Yorkshire, in 1760; there were thirty in London in 1762
and, in August of the same year, Wesley recorded that in
his society at Liverpool: 'I spoke severally with those who

---

[1] *Letters*, vol. 5, p. 41.
[2] *Works*, vol. 11, p. 446.
[3] Tyerman, *Wesley*, vol. 2, p. 418. Here again the weight Wesley put on
alleged experience is striking. Back in 1741 his brother had warned him of
the danger: 'You spoke not from your own experience, and those on whose
experience you built your doctrine are but of yesterday' (*Works*, Abingdon,
vol. 26, p. 52). But Wesley persisted in determining doctrine by experience.
He resorted to it, for instance, with regard to the esoteric idea that Christians
may distinguish between the presence of Father, Son and Holy Spirit in their
communion with God: 'I have lately made diligent inquiry into the
experience of many that are perfected in love. And I found a very few of
them who have a clear revelation of the several Persons in the ever-blessed
Trinity. It therefore appears that this is by no means essential to Christian
perfection.' (Letter of June 11, 1777, *Letters*, vol. 6, p. 266).
[4] Tyerman, *Wesley*, vol. 2, pp. 417, 593–4.

believed they were sanctified. They were fifty-one in all.'[1]
The numbers professing this became still larger in London
and the south. When his brother Charles was wavering
on the subject in 1766 John wrote to him: '*That perfection*
which I believe, I can boldly preach; because, I think, I
see five hundred witnesses of it.'[2]

But if 'witnesses' brought Wesley this encouragement
they also brought him problems. First, if believers could
reach a condition in which sin had ceased it would seem
to mean that the Scriptures which urged progress in
holiness were no longer relevant for them. If it was
possible to arrive at 'perfect love' by one experience, what
need could there be for anything more? It was no wonder
some of his people spoke of 'sinless perfection', although
Wesley himself declined to use the phrase. To meet this
danger, Wesley responded that sanctification 'is both an
instantaneous and a gradual work', and that 'being perfected in love, filled with love, still admits of a thousand
degrees'.[3] In other words, there was the necessity of
stressing that Christian experience remains a process. It
is 'higher degrees' that are to be expected, and he cautioned against attaching 'magnificent, pompous words' to
one particular experience: 'You need give it no general
name, neither "perfection," "sanctification," "the second
blessing" nor "the having attained".'[4]

---

[1] *Journal*, vol. 4, p. 523.
[2] *Letters*, vol. 5, p. 20. 'I wonder,' he adds, 'you do not in this article fall
in with Mr Whitefield. For do you not, as well as he, ask, "Where are the
perfect ones"?'
[3] Ibid., vol. 5, p. 215. 'I believe a gradual work, both preceding and
following that instant.' *Works*, vol. 11, p. 446.
[4] These words, given in Outler, *Wesley*, p. 304, were written by Wesley in
the 1760s but not included in his final revision of his work on *Christian
Perfection*.

This was good advice, but his own teaching warranted the use of that very language. And instead of abandoning teaching the instantaneous, he continued to do so, while also speaking of the gradual. Inevitably people were confused.

A second and greater problem was that in very many instances the testimony of witnesses to their attainment was not lasting. Writing to a woman who professed 'deliverance from inbred sin', Wesley told her that he rejoiced 'the more because . . . so few, so exceeding few, retain it one year, hardly one in ten, nay one in thirty. Many hundreds in London were partakers of it within sixteen or eighteen months; but I doubt whether twenty of them are now as holy and happy as they were.'[1]

How was the experience of those lapsed from their high profession to be understood? Wesley was satisfied that it was to be put down to spiritual carelessness and a lack of watchfulness. But there are other explanations. The offer of an experience, to lift the individual at once to a high realm of sainthood, was bound to have a wrong attraction for certain individuals – the 'Diotrephes' type, for instance, 'who love to have the pre-eminence' (*2 John* 9). That some in Wesley's societies fell into this category there can be no doubt. John Newton, commenting on a Liverpool Methodist who 'pretended to sinless perfection', said he was 'one of the most disagreeable persons I ever met with among professors'.[2] Worse cases occurred elsewhere. In Ireland a preacher by the name of Samuel Mitchell, 'imbibed the unscriptural notion that there is a

---

[1] To Mrs Barton, March 15, 1770, *Letters*, vol. 5, p. 185. Two years earlier he wrote to Charles, 'I am at my wits' end with regard to two things – the Church and Christian Perfection' (Ibid., p. 88).
[2] Quoted in D. Bruce Hindmarsh, *John Newton*, p. 132.

state of grace attainable, in which it is impossible to make further progress, and from which there can be no declension'. But, after carrying with him two colleagues, and several others, the outcome was disaster: 'One of them left the work, and it is to be feared lost his religion; the other was expelled for immorality; while the author of the heresy became a shameless drunkard.'[1]

But if this explains the case of some of the lapsed witnesses, they were surely very much a minority. Most of those who disappointed Wesley remained sincere and conscientious Christians and it is too easy to explain so many 'failures' simply in terms of carelessness. It is far more probable that time had brought them to the discovery that 'entire sanctification' was not a true description of their on-going experience, and that, rather than being dishonest, they desisted from making their former profession. This is not to say the *experience* on which the profession was based had not been genuine. Promises of a larger experience and assurance of the love of God belong to the New Testament; they may be fulfilled suddenly; and when they are, the effect will ever be a stronger love in those who are the subjects of the blessing. This characteristic of many Methodists was no illusion.[2]

---

[1] Crookshank, *Methodism in Ireland*, vol. 2, pp. 164–5.

[2] That assurance may be given suddenly is a well-established belief; but danger arises when assurance is made to depend on one special experience. As noted earlier, Wesley wavered on the subject of full assurance; he could not identify it with being 'perfected in love' because, for one thing, he knew his friend William Grimshaw had the one but denied the other (*Letters*, vol. 6, p. 323). As Andrew Bonar has written, the Spirit may breathe through the heart of a Christian, imparting fresh life and unction to prayer, conversation, and preaching, but 'if any make this something by itself, instead of just the Spirit bringing in more of Christ, they are in danger of mysticism'. *Andrew A. Bonar: Diary and Life*, ed. Marjory Bonar (London: Banner of Truth, 1960), p. 343.

But Wesley's mistake was to identify such assuring experiences *with sanctification*, and the cessation of all sinning, as if the believer had entered a new state. In the warmth of fervent feeling it is possible for Christians – especially if they are so taught – to believe that they may never sin again and to speak accordingly. The value of such felt experience is not to be minimized, but feeling is not permanent; in Wesley's own words, 'this is seldom long at one stay'.[1] His treating an experience as evidence of 'full sanctification' was a serious mistake. Those whom he blamed for their spiritual carelessness were, after all, only resuming the type of Christian experience that he himself professed.

The extent to which Wesley's teaching on perfectionism caused confusion in the societies is impossible to determine. But there is one line of evidence to confirm that it was not sufficient to deflect Methodists from what is basic to the Christian. According to Christ, prayer for the forgiveness of sin, and for deliverance from it, belongs to all disciples (*Matt.* 6:12–13), and Methodist records are full of testimonies showing how such prayer marked the Methodists at the very gates of death. As they left this world their confidence was solely in the atoning work of Christ. We repeatedly read such words as these: 'The blood of Jesus is all.'[2] 'It is enough, Christ died for me. Victory through the blood of the Lamb!'[3] 'There is nothing on which I can depend, but the atonement.'[4] 'Precious atonement! the sinner's only hope.'[5] These are the typical testimonies.

What led Wesley to speak as he did of Christian perfection was unquestionably the desire to see believers

---

[1] *Letters*, vol. 7, p. 120.
[2] Smith, *Methodism*, vol. 2, p. 388.
[3] Ibid., p. 430.
[4] Ibid., vol. 3, p. 146.
[5] Ibid., p. 411.

reach the highest attainments possible in this life; he feared too many stop short, and that while they thought of what they were saved *from*, they considered too little what they were saved *to*. But he failed to see that what he desired could be achieved without holding out the prospect of an instant entire sanctification. To give that up, it seemed to him, would be to give up the great incentive.

Wesley was by no means original in stressing love as the key to the Christian life. It is present in the Puritan books which his parents had so deliberately put to one side before he was born. In that connection it is intriguing to ask whether Wesley ever read his grandfather's sermon on 'How We May Attain to Love God'. Annesley's sermon gave as high a place to love as Wesley ever conceived:

'Love is the enlargement of the heart towards God: when the "love of God is shed abroad in the heart", it is as the breaking of a ball of lightening, it sets all on a flame immediately . . . All manner of prayer is singularly useful to inflame the heart with love to God. Those that pray best, love God best . . . Did you know God better, you could not but love him more; and none can discover God to us, as he discovers himself, so spiritually, so powerfully. Take no denial; God will never be angry with your being importunate for hearts to love him. Seeing he is so earnest with thee for thy love, beg it *of* him *for* him; God is more willing to give every grace than thou canst be to receive it'.

But Annesley's sermon is undergirded by a doctrinal framework which Wesley was unable to receive. For his grandfather, sanctification was progressive from regeneration and not to be sought as a second experience: 'From the first infusion of grace, there is a graciously-natural antipathy against sin. Sin receives its death wound: it is too true, it may struggle for life, and seem to be upon recovery; but grace will wear it out, and will never leave the conflict till it has obtained the conquest.' The final conquest of grace, not the promise of *one* experience this side of heaven, was all Annesley needed for incentive and encouragement. God would save him, imperfect as was. Not that the Christian will rest in imperfection but his greatest comfort lies outside himself: 'While he is breathing after perfection in grace, he admiringly prefers God's wise love in saving him by Christ, before salvation by inherent grace: he utterly renounces the best of his graces, when pride would have them justle with Christ for the procuring of acceptance.'[1]

The question may be asked, if Wesley believed that Christian perfection was to be received by faith, why did he not receive it for himself? It was not part of his make up to comment on personal questions of that kind. Had he done so, his answer might have been that true faith is Spirit-given and that such faith had not been given to him.[2] In other words, notwithstanding all he said that might appear to point the other way, he did not believe that the experience he taught could be produced at will, nor could anyone be shown how to receive it. Certainly, his honesty as a Christian kept him from a profession of the experience he taught. What he had said in 1738 remained true, 'I cannot love our blessed Lord *as I ought.*' At a time of depression in June 1766 he even wrote to

---

[1] *Puritan Sermons 1659–1689*, vol. 1, p. 602.
[2] I admit this explanation does not fit with what Wesley says of others who failed to attain: 'We receive it by simple faith: But God does not, will not, give that faith, unless we seek it with all diligence' (*Works*, vol. 11, p. 403). The difficulty here is surely foundational to Wesley's whole teaching on the subject.

his brother, 'I do not love God. I never did.'[1] Other Christian leaders have had times when they felt the same.

Where Wesley's teaching ultimately did more serious damage was in the nineteenth century and later, when the 'second blessing' idea was picked up by many others. There arose a new sort of spiritual guide who had no hesitation in laying down the 'method' by which 'the blessing' was to be obtained. Thus Phoebe Palmer (whose father had been converted under Wesley before emigrating to the United States) launched a 'holiness movement' in the 1830s which taught 'entire sanctification' by three simple steps: (1) an act of consecration (2) faith that God keeps his promise to sanctify what is consecrated and (3) witnessing to the experience. Charles G. Finney, and others, promoted another form of Perfectionisn, while in 1874–5 Robert and Hannah Pearsall Smith did the same in England, teaching how 'the baptism of the Spirit' ensured a happy and victorious Christian life, and this was to be received in an instant 'by faith'. The Pearsall Smith teaching was to have enduring influence in England, and also in Germany where its leading exponents were Theodor Jellinghaus and 'Pastor' Paul. 'All Europe is at my feet', Smith was to claim on one occasion.[2]

As these movements had moved further from Scripture, it is not surprising that the casualties were more marked. Robert Pearsall Smith suddenly lost his reputation and his faith. His more-famous wife, Hannah – whose book,

---

[1] *Letters*, vol. 5, p. 16. He added: 'Yet I dare not preach otherwise than I do, either concerning faith, or love, or justification, or perfection.' And he exhorted Charles, 'Press the *instantaneous* blessing.'

[2] See B. B. Warfield on 'The "Higher Life" Movement,' *Perfectionism*, vol. 2 (New York: OUP, 1931). Warfield's two volumes remain the most definitive treatment of nineteenth and early-twentieth-century perfectionism.

The Christian's Secret of a Happy Life, sold in the millions – ceased to be an evangelical, and finally summarized her beliefs by saying that 'a *good* Creator can be got at through all sorts of religious beliefs and all sorts of religious ceremonies, and that it does not matter what they are'.[1] Unlike Mrs Pearsall Smith, Jellinghaus was to repudiate, 'with deep pain', the teaching he had long promoted: 'At one stroke he demolished the work of his life and declared himself to have been running on a wrong scent'.[2]

These developments were far removed from John Wesley, and yet it has to be admitted that it was he who first gave impetus to the idea of a two-staged Christian life. He had also, indirectly, given some encouragement to his greatest enemy, Antinomianism. For, as noted above, to claim that some had ceased to sin, he had to lower the biblical standard by which sin is defined, and to argue that sin 'is a voluntary transgression of a known law'. Out of that idea came the later teaching that 'sin is not sin unless we discern it and are conscious of it'. Whereas, as J. C. Ryle responded, sins of ignorance in the Old Testament brought guilt and uncleanness (*Lev.* 4:1–35; 5:14–19; *Num.* 15:25–29). 'A man may commit sin and yet be ignorant of it.'[3]

---

[1] *A Religious Rebel: The Letters of 'H. W. S'* (*Mrs Pearsall Smith*), edited by Logan P. Smith (London: Nisbet, 1949), p. 150. See also, Marie Henry, *The Secret Life of Hannah Whitall Smith* (Grand Rapids: Zondervan, 1984).

[2] Warfield, *Perfectionism*, vol. 1, p. 339.

[3] *Faithfulness and Holiness: The Witness of J. C. Ryle*, An Appreciation by J. I. Packer (Wheaton: Crossway, 2002), pp. 106–7. Ryle wrote: 'I decline to tell any converted man that he may some day or other pass by one enormous step into a state of entire consecration. I decline to teach it, because I cannot see any warrant for such teaching in the Scripture. I decline to teach it, because I think the tendency of the doctrine is thoroughly mischievous, depressing the humble-minded and meek, and puffing up the shallow, the ignorant, and the self-conceited, to a most dangerous extent' (p. 102).

But Wesley was not responsible for the idea of 'deliverance' from the law of God as a rule of conduct, held forth by 'Higher Life' teachers, who claimed a freedom from sin supposedly unknown to Christians not yet 'sanctified'. And he would have been profoundly shocked at the excesses and moral failures that marked some of the unbalanced leaders. On why the casualties occurred among them, W. E. Sangster makes the comment:

'They blunted their own consciences, believing that what they were doing was to the glory of God. When that inner monitor of the soul stirred in disapproval they flung "a promise" at it, and called the warning "unbelief". With passing time the conscience ceased to function with any accuracy or power and they are found proclaiming themselves free of sin while guilty of conduct which a worldling would know to be wrong.'[1]

It may be said that all perfectionist teaching grows out of an underestimation of what happens to the sinner when he receives new life in union with Christ at regeneration. Once it is assumed that nothing happens at the beginning of the Christian life to *ensure* its continuance and growth, the way is open for proposals which, however well-intentioned, are bound to distort the New Testament teaching.

In the end it is, of course, the text of the New Testament which must determine our understanding of this subject. In that connection it is noteworthy that in all the 500 or so publications credited to the Wesley brothers, not one item is a commentary on any part of Scripture. Wesley's *Notes on the New Testament* are far too brief to take a place in that category. Despite his linguistic

---

[1] Sangster, *Path to Perfection*, pp. 139–40.

ability, John Wesley was not a precise exegete. In this regard, as in others, he was a man of his times: full and detailed interpretation of the text of Scripture was not the province of the church in the eighteenth century. No Englishman of that century produced anything approximating to John Davenant's commentary on Colossians, or to John Owen's on the Epistle to the Hebrews. Not until the nineteenth century did commentators more generally adopt and advance the standard of those seventeenth-century expositors.

There is some justification for Albert Outler's accusation that Wesley was guilty of 'scattershot exegesis' in the way he sometimes quoted Scripture. When Hebrews 6:1 says, 'Let us go on unto perfection', it is a leap unwarranted by the verse or context to make it mean 'the sinless condition'; rather, the exhortation is surely to maturity of understanding. Or again, the 'perfect love' of 1 John 4 is not to be taken as identifying the 'sinless person'.

It is not given to anyone to be able in every sphere. Wesley was at his best as a popularizer of established truths; it was when he was more original that he ran into difficulties. Perhaps some of his own words in his work on *Christian Perfection* are a fitting conclusion to the differences we have considered in this chapter:

'There may be much love where there is little light. The heart has more heat than the eye; yet it cannot see.'[1]

---

[1] *Works*, vol. 11, p. 428.

Part Four

Methodism, with and without the Holy Spirit

God himself has condescended to teach me the way: For this very end he came from heaven. He hath written it down in a book. O give me that book! At any price, give me the book of God.

John Wesley, Preface to *Sermons*

We may multiply our guilds and bands; we may attract crowds by startling preaching, and give them the very best of music; we may do all this, and more, – and yet, if the Holy Spirit is not honoured, it will all amount to little more than 'a sounding brass or a clanging cymbal'.

William G. Taylor
The Life Story of an Australian Evangelist (1920)

Chapter 11

The Holy Spirit and Scripture

There is more than one way of reading the history of Methodism. In these pages we have followed the chronological order, starting with Wesley and proceeding to three representatives of later periods. Another approach, and a more startling one, would be to begin with Methodism at the height of its world-wide influence in the mid-nineteenth century. In 1861 the membership figure in Britain stood at 343,333, and 'with every individual under effective pastoral oversight'.[1] At that date the number hearing Methodist preaching (as distinct from members), instead of the estimated 300,000 in that category in 1800, had reached about one million.

Meanwhile the American branch of Methodism – the Methodist Episcopal Church – formally instituted by Wesley in 1784, had long passed these figures. As early as 1825 its membership stood at 348,195, to become 749,216 by 1839, an average gain of more than 28,644 per year. Part of that gain was among people with whom few others had made headway. 'In the slave States', wrote Dr Charles Colcock Jones of the Methodists in 1842, 'they have, next to the Baptists, the largest number of communicants. The Negroes are brought under the same church regulations as the whites, having class leaders, and

[1] Smith, *Methodism*, vol. 3, p. 521.

class-meetings and exhorters; and cases of church discipline are carefully reported and acted upon as the discipline
requires.'[1]

In the foreign fields there were between 400 and 500
men sent out as missionaries from the British Methodist
Conference. The West Indies had between 30 and 40,000
church members, and the West Coast of Africa, some
8,600. Advance was slower in India and China but some
of the church's finest men went to these countries. There
were others, such as J. Hudson Taylor (from Yorkshire
Methodism) who went independently but carried with
them the spirit of their background. Thus Taylor's key to
the locked doors of China was, 'Love first, then suffering,
then a deeper love – thus only can God's work be done.'[2]

By 1855 Australia had its own Conference. From the
outset, the establishment of churches in the Australian
colonies had been 'closely connected with the success of
the Gospel in the islands of the South Seas',[3] and such
was the outreach into those islands that by 1855 New
Zealand, Fiji, and Tonga were included in the Conference.
The region had 110 ministers (plus 40 on probation),
with many local preachers, the oversight of 33,964
members, with a further number of 7,657 'on trial'.
Tonga, and other islands in the Friendly Islands, had
initially been wholly resistant to the gospel and remained
so when Methodist missionaries first arrived there in the
1820s. The principal chief, 'King George', would only
listen to the preaching if his throne was placed con-

---

[1] C. C. Jones, *The Religious Instruction of the Negroes* (Savannah: Purse,
1842), p. 93.

[2] Howard Taylor, *Hudson Taylor in Early Years: the Growth of a Soul*
(London: CIM, 1962), p. 291.

[3] The words of John McKenny, who served in Cape Colony, Ceylon and
then New South Wales from 1836. Norman W. Taggart, *The Irish in World
Methodism*, p. 143.

spicuously opposite the pulpit. Then 'a most extraordinary outpouring of the Spirit' occurred, and we read:

'King George and Queen Charlotte were amongst the first to tremble before the new Power that was upon the people, and to rejoice in the pardoning love of God. Down came the royal throne opposite the pulpit of the church, never to be reared again! They released their slaves; they devoted themselves to study, and to the uplifting of their people. Both of them became useful Class-leaders; and the king qualified, by passing the proper examinations, for the Local Preacher's Plan.'[1]

No less remarkable was the way the gospel took hold in Fiji, amid much suffering and the darkest cannibalism. At length, by the 1850s, the murderous tyrant King Thakombau became as a little child and some 10,000 on the Fijian islands were in regular attendance at public worship.[2]

A number of the foremost pioneer missionaries to these Pacific islands also served in Australia. These were outstanding men. They had seen giants fall and were not to be disheartened by conditions in the penal colonies that had driven others to despair.

* * * * *

These facts, and so many more that could be given, would, as I have said, provide a startling introduction to

---

[1] G. G. Findlay and M. G. Findlay, *Wesley's World Parish: A Sketch of the Hundred Years of the Wesleyan Methodist Missionary Society* (New York/ London: Hodder and Stoughton, n.d.), p. 103.

[2] No easy admittance to baptism was granted to dignities such as Thakombau. He had publicly to acknowledge his sins. At his death, some years later, he said, 'Now, Jesus, is your time to help; no one else can . . . I am in the valley and the shadow of death; Jesus holds me fast!' Ibid., p. 109.

Methodism. At the height of its work and progress, with the dew of youth still upon it, it was a phenomenon. But whatever way we approach the subject, it is the same question that demands attention: what is the true explanation for such a movement?

One explanation must immediately fail. The growth cannot possibly be attributed to Wesley's personality, for we are talking of a period in which that personal influence had long-since ceased. If Wesley's leadership was the secret, then the success would have been greatest in his lifetime. The opposite was the case, Methodism spread further and faster after his death.

Perhaps, then, credit for the growth has to be given to the adaptability and effectiveness of the organization that had been put in place. It certainly contributed to it. George Smith, who knew Methodism at its meridian, summarized the organization in the words:

'Here there is work for every one, and every one is expected to work. Every degree of talent, every measure of intellect, every grade of power, and almost every peculiarity of disposition, may find suitable opportunities for doing good . . . They are not schooled in controversy; but in the art of teaching sinners the way to flee from sin and to find salvation in Christ, they are the best instructed people in the world.'[1]

But Smith is careful to say that the secret of success did *not* lie in the organization: 'Those who attribute this success to the mere ecclesiastical policy of our venerable Founder, and of those who have followed him in the continued application of his system, have done too much

---

[1] Smith, *Methodism*, vol. 3, pp. 497–8.

honour to the genius and sagacity of the Methodists.'[1] Abel Stevens, the American historian of Methodism, makes the same point and asserts that without something else the system would have been impossible: 'How can we conceive of a lifeless laity embodied in classes and meeting weekly to converse of Christian experience? Of love-feasts and prayer-meetings among dead formalists? Or of such a laity hearing and such a ministry preaching the distinctive doctrines of Methodism?'[2]

So what was the true explanation? I hope that the preceding pages have already made it clear. But a way to check that we have the right answer is to go forward a hundred years to Methodism in sharp decline in the mid-twentieth century, and to ask what was missing at the later date that had been prominent before. In the twentieth century Methodism was as weak as the religion it initially challenged. Speaking of the Free Churches in England – among which the Methodists were an integral part – J. C. Carlile said of the 1920s: 'There was less and less justification for optimism, and the Churches suffered a set-back that has shaken organised religion in England to its foundations. The Free Churches are a long way from having recovered: perhaps they never will recover.'[3] The Methodist leader, W. E. Sangster, who died in 1960, was more hopeful that the 'true emphasis and passion' of Methodism might be restored, but his biographer tells us that his labours were 'for a revival that never came'.[4]

In Australia in the twentieth century the scene among the once strong Methodist churches was largely the same. The old preachers who remembered earlier times spoke

---

[1] Ibid., pp. 185–6.
[2] Stevens, *Methodism*, vol. 3, p. 394.
[3] J. C. Carlile, *My Life's Little Day* (London: Blaikie, 1935), p. 241.
[4] Paul Sangster, *Doctor Sangster* (London: Epworth, 1962), pp. 230, 292.

of the Church having lost her true programme. John Watsford, born in 1820, wrote at the end of his long ministry:

'The desire to-day seems to be for less prayer and exposition of the word of God, and for more amusement . . .the growing worldliness of the Church is a great hindrance to success . . . The Churches need the Pentecostal baptism: then we shall have the Pentecost, holy living, simplicity, power, success, and perhaps, persecution.'[1]

Watsford was only repeating what had once been the universal conviction of Methodists. Forty years earlier, George Smith had written: 'The strength of Wesleyan Methodism will always be its sterling piety. Shorn of this, it will crumble into ruins, and be a thing of nought.'[2]

Whatever the word that is used to describe the inner principle of the older Methodism – whether 'piety', 'holiness', or 'fellowship with God' – the problem in the twentieth century was that it was this that had so largely gone. One has only to recall the characteristics of that former piety to see the proof. The first was faith: faith in the Word of God, faith in the redeeming love of God, faith in a divine Saviour and in the power of the Holy Spirit of God. Faith was the energizing, empowering principle both for personal living and for witness to others. What was said of local-preacher William Carvosso could have been said of thousands: 'Present, free and full salvation, by simple faith in the atonement, formed the theme on which he dwelt with delight, and almost

---

[1] John Watsford, *Glorious Gospel Triumphs* (London: Kelly, 1900), p. 321. I write more fully of the Australian scene in *Australian Christian Life from 1788* (Edinburgh: Banner of Truth, 1988).
[2] Smith, *Methodism*, vol. 3, p. 60.

without intermission.'[1] Faith is the master-principle that has ever been recognized when Christianity has overcome the world: 'The exercise of faith', wrote John Owen, 'is that whereon the flourishing of all other graces doth depend.'[2] Faith pleases God, 'According to your faith be it unto you', said our Lord; and we read in Luke 5:24: 'When he saw their faith, he said to the sick of the palsy, Son, thy sins are forgiven thee.'

To quote Watsford again at the end of his life:

'From first to last our ministers were believed to be sound in the faith. But is it so today? I fear not. The question we ask every year of every minister is, "Does he believe and preach our doctrines?" It is not enough that he preach them: he must believe them.'[3]

But piety is not made up of faith alone, and this was where Methodism showed its scriptural balance. Real faith – that is, response to Christ crucified – will ever have with it obedience, work, and self-denial. It will entail habits of prayer, and praise, and a disciplined life lived for God. The hard-working, sacrificial nature of the older Methodism was one of its most striking features. The men we have considered well understood what was written by a nineteenth-century Calvinist:

'Beyond a doubt, God could dispense with all the work and anguish which He lays upon the Church in the evangelization of the world. He could, in the flash of an instant, convert the whole human race and not leave a single rebel against His grace . . . But God has chosen to lay upon His Church this duty of proclaiming the Gospel

---

[1] *Memoir of Carvosso*, p. 8.
[2] Owen, *Works*, vol. 22, p. 233.
[3] *Gospel Triumphs*, p. 322.

by which the nations shall be saved. What sacrifices are imposed upon the heralds of the Cross, in the poverty and self-denial with which they proclaim "the glad tidings of great joy" to sinful men! It seems one of the deep mysteries of Divine Providence, that all this should be entailed upon those who are engaged in His work who could so easily relieve the pressure; until we recall the fact that the discipline which is laid upon the individual believer, is needful also to the collective Church.'[1]

In this same connection it should be noted that the old Methodist preachers never looked upon the possibility of an outpouring of the Holy Spirit as an alternative to present toil and labour. Where 'faith' is separated from discipline, as sometimes happens, then waiting for God to work, and believing that God only works by the extraordinary, can be made a substitute for present duty. That was not Methodist belief or practice. They prayed for the Holy Spirit but they knew that in whatever measure that prayer was answered it would be sufficient for present duty, and their belief in revival in no way lessened evangelistic passion in times and places where there was no evidence of the extraordinary. On that point George Smith has these wise words after describing an awakening at Sheffield:

'We must, however, guard our readers against supposing that these extraordinary visitations are regarded by the Wesleyan Methodists as the chief means of extending and maintaining the work of God. The constant ordinary ministration of the Gospel is, in their judgment, the grand means of true evangelization. But, when the preaching

---

[1] B. M. Palmer, *Sermons* (1875,1876; reprint ed., two volumes in one, Harrisonburg, VA: Sprinkle, 2002), vol. 2, pp. 351–52.

of the word is clothed with extraordinary power, and crowned with deep and widespread success, such seasons are hailed as Pentecostal visitations, and gratefully acknowledged as special interpositions of mercy.'[1]

When faith and discipline are seen as the essential ingredients of Methodist piety, there is no mystery about the collapse in the twentieth century. If faith cannot rest on the Word of God it has nothing to rest on, and it was the Word of God which, in the name of 'scholarship', was now taken away. Instead of being ready, as Wesley was, to be called a 'Bible bigot', men now fled from the term, and the Methodist Colleges honoured such teachers as A. S. Peake. Peake's *Commentary on the Bible* (1919) undermined the authority of Scripture, yet it became a text book for probationers for the ministry. In Australia a disciple of Peake's successfully pleaded for the adoption of his teacher's *Commentary* despite the protest of Dr W. H. Fitchett of Melbourne that the decision would mean 'a tattered Bible and a mutilated Christ'.

Leaders regarded the words of Fitchett as causing needless alarm but time was to prove that faith was indeed being destroyed. The Bible as the Word of God was being put aside. In J. Ernest Rattenbury's 300 pages on *Wesley's Legacy to the World* (London: Epworth, 1928) nothing is said on the way the Bible became the light of nations. Within fifty years there would be presidents of the Methodist Conference in Britain speaking in open opposition to Scripture. One of them, Donald Soper, held that the Scriptures 'represent an incubus', and proposed that there should be a ban on Bible reading for the year 1965; Leslie Weatherhead, one of the best-known of all

[1] Smith, *Methodism*, vol. 2, p. 246.

Methodist authors, argued that 'William Temple was just as inspired as Paul, and T. S. Eliot more inspired than the author of the Song of Solomon'.[1] One could believe or disbelieve whatever one liked, and the deity of Christ and the atonement were among Weatherhead's dislikes. On the text, 'Without shedding of blood is no remission of sin', Weatherhead declared, 'In our modern view this simply is not true.' His biographer, recording this, smiled at the simplicity of an old-fashioned Methodist who wrote to ask, 'Was John Wesley deceived? Have our hymn-writers been deceived in their immortal songs? Was Saul of Tarsus deceived? Have we all been deceived?'[2]

The truth was that men were now leading Methodism who would not have been received as probationers a hundred years earlier. Among questions put to candidates for the ministry in the old Methodism were these: 'In what light do you regard the death of Christ? How do you define the nature of that atonement or propitiation which Jesus Christ made?'[3] At Plymouth in 1965 an amendment was moved at the Methodist Conference to restore such questions by recalling the Church to her own articles of faith, and to faith in the atonement, in particular. It was defeated by a vote of 601 to 14! It was no wonder that at the same period an article in the *Methodist Recorder*, entitled, 'The Old Methodism Gone Forever', argued that all the doctrines of justification, of saving faith, of assurance, and of holiness, 'belong to an intellectual and theological world which is no longer ours. They

---

[1] Kingsley Weatherhead, *Leslie Weatherhead, a Personal Portrait* (London: Hodder and Stoughton, 1975), p. 214.

[2] Ibid., p. 61. Even Albert Outler, normally respectful to Wesley, allows himself to say that 'his theory of the atonement strikes me as blinkered'. *Methodist History*, News Bulletin, July 1974, p. 65.

[3] Smith, *Methodism*, vol. 2, p. 708.

describe experiences which are no longer normative for Methodist people'.[1]

Others acknowledged the change that had taken place but were at a loss to explain it. W. J. Palamountain, after speaking of the evangelistic power of the older Methodism in Australia, commented in 1933: 'It was a type of evangelism that seemed to run its course and cease to be.'[2]

* * * * *

What was involved here, in addition to the truth of Scripture, was the whole interpretation of Methodist history. Was it just a colourful episode in history, about men whose beliefs were only their own? Or were they men taught and convicted by the Spirit of God? And was it *His* work or theirs that accounts for what happened? Scripture makes a sharp distinction between speaking 'words of man's wisdom', and preaching 'in demonstration of the Spirit and of power'. The latter is essential in order that 'faith should not stand in the wisdom of men, but in the power of God' (*1 Cor.* 2:4–5). Wesley and Whitefield learned what that meant at a time when those words were no longer believed in the national Church; and because they acted on them, as J. C. Ryle has said, they faced 'slander, ridicule and persecution from nine-tenths of professing Christians in our land'.[3] They persisted because their faith was not in 'the words which man's wisdom teaches but which the Holy Ghost teaches' – that is, in inspired words, 'the sword of the Spirit is the word of God' (*Eph.* 6:17).

---

[1] John C. Vincent, *Methodist Recorder*, Sept, 7, 1961.
[2] W. J. Palamountain, *A. R. Edgar: A Methodist Greatheart* (Melbourne: Spectator, 1933), p. 107.
[3] J. C. Ryle, *Holiness* (London: Clarke, 1952), p. 60.

The power in the old Methodist preaching is not a fairy story, and it was bound up with the conviction that honouring Scripture and honouring the Holy Spirit cannot be separated. The preachers carried a message that was not their own and it put an awe upon them. They knew the command, 'If any man speak, let him speak as the oracles of God' (*1 Pet.* 4:11). What was said of Richard Roberts might have been said of them all: 'He never took liberties with eternal realities. He *trembled* at the word of God.'[1] The results of such preaching belonged to the One by whose anointing they spoke. 'It stands in the very fore-front of our history', said William Arthur, 'that no authority under heaven, that no training, that no ordination could qualify men to propagate the Gospel, without the baptism of the Holy Ghost.'[2]

The power of Scripture to enlighten minds and remake lives is the power of God. And the great effect of the Evangelical Revival upon national life is exactly what Scripture would lead us to expect; the Bible came to stand supreme over mind and conscience. No Methodist doubted that 'the Bible and the strength and godliness of England have gone hand in hand'.[3] The fact was clear for all to see. 'The Methodist people are taught to make the Bible, and the Bible alone, the ground of their faith', wrote George Smith, and such was the fruit of their testimony, combined with that of others, that he could also say:

---

[1] Dinsdale T. Young, *Richard Roberts, A Memoir* (London: Kelly, n.d. [*c*.1911]), p. 64,
[2] William Arthur, *The Tongue of Fire*, 24th edition (London: Mullan, 1877), p. 307.
[3] William Arthur, quoted in Norman W. Taggart, *William Arthur: First Among Methodists* (London: Epworth, 1993), p. 50. Arthur, biographer of Ouseley, had served in India before ill-health forced him home. He died in 1900.

'It has been acknowledged from the throne, by successive monarchs, and is the deep inwrought conviction of the wisest and best among all classes in the country, that Great Britain holds her present position among the nations of the earth, mainly through the influence of the Bible on the people.'[1]

Denying the divine inspiration of Scripture, twentieth-century Methodism denied its own history. The real meaning of that history was lost. The truth was that the denomination's leaders had adopted the very kind of thinking that had marked the chief opponents of the eighteenth-century awakening. Spiritual power and piety could not survive in such a situation. Yet to explain the evident decline and weakness of Methodism, all manner of explanations were offered, from the rise of science to the availability of popular entertainment – as though the fault lay not in the church but in the world.

There was a small rearguard of the old Methodism who did understand what was happening in the early twentieth century. William G. Taylor, whom I have quoted above, was one of them. After a ministry of widespread usefulness, he died in Sydney in 1934. As a young man Taylor had been present at the Australian Methodist Conference of 1884 that met shortly after an evangelistic enterprise along 'modern' lines had signally failed. On that occasion, George Hurst, the 'Nestor of the Conference', recognised a temptation to discouragement among the brethren, and Taylor never forgot the hush that fell upon them as the old man pleaded, 'Is Methodism bankrupt? Have we quite lost our historic evangelistic fervour? Have we no men

---

[1] Smith, *Methodism*, vol. 3, p. 490.

among us of the old school?'[1] At that date there were still such men in the denomination, but at the age of seventy-one Taylor wrote of the painful change he had lived to see. He saw it first in England on visits in 1893 and 1911, and says how Thomas Cook, 'that greatest of Methodist evangelists', attributed the different atmosphere in the their churches to 'the increased worldliness of the members, the lack of discipline, and the altered tone of preaching in many of our pulpits'.[2] Taylor's own conclusion is repeated in varied forms throughout his autobiography: 'It would pay us a magnificent dividend to cease for one twelve months all our aggressive evangelistic agencies, and to give ourselves to the one task of bringing back the Church herself to apostolic lines. No wonder that failure has so often to be written across our evangelistic efforts! We lack the foundation elements of successful evangelism.'[3]

Apostasy is not the end of the story. Once-honoured names and organizations may change, churches may lose their candlesticks, but the great lesson of Wesley and the Evangelical Revival is that sin and unbelief are not in control of history. Millions now in heaven attest that truth. 'God is sovereign', said Wesley. More: he, and all the men we have considered in these pages, would remind us that God's love for the world remains the same. Jesus is the Saviour 'high over all' who lives to give repentance and forgiveness. Not on the basis of what the church deserves, but on account of what Christ has done, the Spirit is sent to convict of sin, of righteousness, and of judgement. And whenever and wherever that work of

---

[1] W. G. Taylor, *The Life-story of an Australian Evangelist*, also published with the title *Taylor from Down Under* (London: Epworth, 1921), p. 131.
[2] Ibid., p. 307.   [3] Ibid., p. 108.

grace is found, men and women will cry, 'O give me that book! At any price, give me the book of God.' Or, in the words of the first disciples, 'To whom shall we go? thou hast the words of eternal life.'

> 'For all flesh is as grass, and all the glory of man
> as the flower of grass. The grass withereth,
> and the flower thereof falleth away:
> but the word of the Lord
> endureth for ever'
> (*1 Pet.* 2:24–25).

Author Index

General Index